Ready for CAE

teacher's book

Peter Sunderland
Amanda French
Claire Morris

Suitable for the updated CAE exam

Macmillan Education
Between Towns Road, Oxford OX4 3PP
A division of Macmillan Publishers Limited
Companies and representatives throughout the world

ISBN 978-0-230-02890-6

First published 2008

Designed by eMC Design Ltd
Illustrated by Peter Campbell
Cover design by Barbara Mercer

Authors' acknowledgements
The authors would like to thank Roy Norris, Lucy Torres, Amanda Anderson and Sarah Curtis.

The publishers would like to thank all those who participated in the development of the book, with special thanks to José Vicente Acín Barea, Coral Berriochoa Hausmann, Javier Buendía, Sue Bushell, Jacek Czabánski, Debra Emmett, Elena García, Loukas Geronikolaou, Emilio Jiménez Aparicio, Roula Kyriakidou, Juan Carlos López Gil, Arturo Mendoza Fernández, Jackie Newman, Carolyn Parsons, Javier Redondo, Lena Reppa, James Richardson, Yannis Tsihlas, Malcolm Wren and Mayte Zamora Díaz.

The authors and publishers are grateful for permission to include the following copyright material.
Extracts from 'Alex Gray's top tips' by Gillian Thornton copyright © Gillian Thornton 2003, first published in *Writing* Magazine Feb/March 2003, reprinted by permission of the publisher.
Adapted extracts from 'McGregor the Brave' by Nigel Farndale copyright © The Telegraph 2003, first published in *Sunday Telegraph* Magazine 07.09.03, reprinted by permission of the publisher.
Extract from article about John Lennon's House by Gaynor Aaltonen, copyright © National Trust Magazine 2003, first published in *National Trust* Magazine Summer 2003, reprinted by permission of the publisher.
Extracts from 'Medicine and Mortality: the dark world of medical history' by Jeremy Laurance copyright © Independent Newspapers 2007, first published in *The Independent* 21.06.07, reprinted by permission of the publisher.
Extract from *www.computer.toshiba.co.uk*.
Extracts from 'NZ Trust for Conservation Volunteers Inc' July 2005 taken from *www.conservationvolunteers.org.nz*, reprinted by permission of the publisher.
Extracts from 'Fresh from the Farm' by Phillipa Jamieson from *Sunday Star Times* (Escape Supplement) 09.09.07.
Extract from 'The X-pert Files' by Duane Harland copyright © The New Zealand Herald 2006, first published in *The New Zealand Herald* 06.01.06, reprinted by permission of APN Editorial Syndication & Photosales.
Extracts from 'Bright and Breezy' by Louise Elliott copyright © National Magazine Company Limited 2004, first published in *Country Living* April 2004, reprinted by permission of the publisher.
Extracts from 'How Colman Cut the Mustard' by Simon Hendry copyright © The New Zealand Herald 2007, first published in *The New Zealand Herald* 28.05.07, reprinted by permission of APN Editorial Syndication & Photosales.
Extract from *Sweets: A History of Temptation* by Tim Richardson copyright © Tim Richardson 2003 (Bantam Press, 2003), reprinted by permission of The Random House Group Ltd.
Extracts from 'I Remember Now' by Noel O'Hare, first published in *The New Zealand Listener* 02.07.05.
Extracts from 'Hive Aid' by Ben de Pear copyright © Ben de Pear 2004, first published in *Waitrose* Magazine March 2004, reprinted by permission of the publisher.
Extracts from 'Mind Reading' by Anne Murphy Paul taken from *Psychology Today* Magazine September/October 2007.
Extracts from information taken from interviews which appeared in *Writing* Magazine April 2003, reprinted by permission of the publisher.
Extracts from 'Replica Viking Warship set sail for Irish Homecoming' by David Keys copyright © Independent Newspapers 2007, first published in *The Independent* 02.07.07, reprinted by permission of the publisher.
Adapted extracts from 'Japan Eyes Robots Support Elderly' by Masayuki Kitano copyright © Solo Syndication 2007, first published in *Daily Mail* 12.09.07, reprinted by permission of the publisher.

The authors and publishers would like to thank the following for permission to reproduce their photographs:
Alamy pp213(t), 214 (t); Corbis pp213 (m), 214 (m); Getty pp213 (b). 214 (b)

Printed and bound in the UK by Martins the Printers.

2012 2011 2010 2009 2008
10 9 8 7 6 5 4 3 2

Contents

Contents Map of the Coursebook

Introduction

Ready for CAE consists of the following components:
- Coursebook (with and without key)
- Teacher's Book
- Three CDs
- Workbook (with and without key)

Coursebook

Each of the 14 units in the Coursebook contains 10 pages, providing a balance and variety of activity types aimed at improving students' general English level as well as developing the language and skills they will need to pass the Certificate in Advanced English (CAE) examination. At the end of every unit there is a two-page Review section, containing revision activities and exam-style tasks, which enable students to practise the new language they have encountered in the unit and, as the course progresses, in previous units.

The book also contains five supplementary 'Ready for ... ' Units, which provide students with information, advice and practice on each of the five papers in the CAE examination. These are situated after Units 3, 6, 9, 12 and 14 and may be used in the order in which they appear in the book. However, they are intended very much as a flexible resource which may be exploited at such time during the course as the teacher feels appropriate.

At the end of the Coursebook you will find a Wordlist and Grammar reference, each closely linked to the 14 units in the book, as well as the Listening scripts for each of the listening tasks. There is also an Additional material section, to which students are referred in certain units. The Coursebook is available with or without the answer key.

The following boxes, which appear throughout the Coursebook, provide help and advice to students when they perform the different tasks:
- **What to expect in the exam:** these contain useful information on what students should be prepared to see, hear or do in a particular task in the examination.
- **How to go about it:** these give advice and guidelines on how to deal with different examination task types and specific questions in the unit.
- **Don't forget!:** these provide a reminder of important points to bear in mind when answering a particular question.
- **Self help:** these contain supplementary activities and study tips, many of which are aimed at helping students increase their vocabulary store.

Teacher's Book

The Teacher's Book contains detailed teaching notes for each activity in the Coursebook. A typical unit of the Teacher's Book provides you with:
- a summary of examination task types contained in the Coursebook unit
- assistance with exam strategies for new tasks
- guidelines and ideas for exploiting the Coursebook material, including:
  - further suggestions for lead-in and follow-on activities
  - further ways to extend vocabulary and maximize speaking
  - additional extra activities
- answers to exercises
- scripts for the listening activities
- sample answers for a selection of the writing exercises, together with the examiner's notes and the mark awarded.

At the end of the Teacher's Book you will also find the following:

• Photocopiable exercises

These are optional exercises which can be used to exploit the vocabulary in reading and listening texts. They are intended as **post-reading** and **post-listening** activities and there is one set of exercises per unit. The exercises are designed to stand on their own as far as possible, but students should feel free to look back in the text if they need further help to complete the exercises. Rubrics will tell you when students **need** to look back at the text in order to do the tasks, for example those which require them to 'Find words in the text which mean the following' (Units 7, 8, 10, 13).

• Five photocopiable Progress tests

These are intended for use after Units 3, 6, 9, 12 and 14 and provide teachers with the opportunity to assess their students' progress on the course at regular intervals. They contain useful practice in examination task types as well as revision of the language that has been presented in the previous three or more units. Each test follows the same format:

One CAE-style Reading exercise
Two or three Use of English exercises
One vocabulary exercise
One CAE-style listening exercise
A CAE writing task

In each case the exam task types in the test will already have been encountered by students in the Coursebook.

• **One photocopiable Final test**
This is a full CAE-style examination, including all five papers. It is intended for use towards the end of the course, as a final practice before students take the CAE examination. Paper 5 should not be photocopied.

Workbook

The 14 units of the Workbook follow the same order and general topic areas as the Coursebook. They have been designed to provide students with further practice, revision and extension of the language presented in class, as well as examination practice and skills work. Each unit follows the same format:

• **Reading**
To ensure variety, the reading task type in most units of the Workbook is different from that in the corresponding unit of the Coursebook. Students will, however, already be familiar with the reading task type they encounter in the Workbook and are thus provided with an opportunity for revision. In some units there is an exercise exploiting the vocabulary which occurs in the reading text.

• **Vocabulary**
These exercises revise and develop the vocabulary which appears in the Coursebook. Some exercises extend this vocabulary by drawing on items from the Wordlist at the end of the Coursebook. As in the Coursebook, there is a strong emphasis on collocation throughout the Workbook.

• **Language focus**
This section contains further controlled practice of the grammar presented in class.

• **Use of English**
In most units there are at least two Use of English practice exercises. Some of the language tested in these exercises will already have been encountered by students in the corresponding unit, or previous units, of the Coursebook.

• **Writing**
The Workbook contains a complete writing syllabus to complement that in the Coursebook and to ensure that students are fully prepared for Paper 2 of the CAE examination. Extensive help is given in the form of useful language, model answers and/or planning guidelines. A feature of the Workbook's writing syllabus is that whilst the writing task in each unit is relevant to the topic area of the corresponding unit in the Coursebook, the task type is the same, in most cases, as that of the previous unit of the Coursebook. This enables revision to take place and ensures that students are given the opportunity to practise the same task type with different topic areas.

• At the end of the Workbook there is a **Word formation list**.
This reference list contains all the words which are taught and tested in the Word formation sections of the Coursebook and Workbook, together with further examples. The words are arranged according to their word class and the affix used to form them.

The Workbook is available with or without the answer key.

Using the course to prepare students for the CAE examination

Whilst *Ready for CAE* can be used as a general course for students at an advanced level of English, one of its main aims is to prepare students for the Cambridge Certificate in Advanced English examination. An overview of the examination can be found on pages 4 and 5 of the Coursebook. A range of support is available in the various components of the course to help you prepare your students for the different aspects of the CAE exam.

Vocabulary

In every unit of the Coursebook there is at least one section devoted to vocabulary which is relevant to the theme or themes covered in the unit. Throughout the book there is a strong emphasis on collocations, words which are commonly used together. The vocabulary from the units is reproduced in the Wordlist at the end of the book, where it is grouped according to the unit in which it appears, together with further relevant words and collocations. Vocabulary activities in the Workbook both revise the topic vocabulary presented in the units, and provide practice of the additional items from the Wordlist. This enables students to build a substantial vocabulary store in preparation for the CAE examination.

In addition, students are frequently provided with relevant vocabulary to help them perform specific speaking and writing tasks using a wide range of language. In some cases this vocabulary appears in Useful language sections accompanying the tasks; in others, students are referred to the Wordlist at the end of the book. Students are also encouraged to notice vocabulary, especially collocations, in the texts they read and to record this language systematically in their notebooks. Many of the Self help boxes are aimed at helping students increase their vocabulary store in this way.

Grammar

Each unit of the Coursebook contains one or more Language focus sections, which generally use contextualized examples from a reading or listening text to introduce a particular grammar point. Where relevant, basic features are revised before the grammatical area in question is developed and students are exposed to more advanced structures of the type they are expected to be able to understand and use in the CAE examination. Frequent use of the Grammar reference is made for the checking of answers and ideas, and each Language focus section concludes with a written and/or spoken practice activity. Further practice is provided in the Review sections at the end of each unit, as well as in the relevant unit of the Workbook. This practice often takes the form of Use of English exercises.

Some Language focus sections move from a grammatical to a more lexical focus; students are presented with words, collocations and phrases which express similar concepts to those conveyed by the grammatical structures which have been taught. This provides students with a number of different alternatives to communicate their ideas, enabling them to demonstrate the range and variety of language required at CAE level.

Reading

Authentic texts from a variety of sources (magazines, newspapers, brochures etc) are used to develop students' reading skills and prepare them for Paper 1 of the CAE examination. Students are provided with useful strategies to adopt when performing each of the different tasks: multiple matching, gapped text and multiple choice. By using appropriate techniques for each reading text, students learn to read efficiently and stand a greater chance of completing the tasks in the examination in the time allowed. Throughout the Coursebook there are 'What to expect' and 'How to go about it' boxes, containing information and advice on how to approach each of the task types, with further advice on appropriate reading strategies contained in the Ready for Reading unit on pages 42 to 47.

Texts are usually preceded by a short speaking activity to introduce the topic, and followed by a 'Reacting to the text' section, which provides students with the opportunity to discuss the content of the passage and express their own opinions on the issues involved. Further reading practice is provided in each unit of the Workbook.

Writing

All of the main CAE writing tasks are covered, both in the Coursebook and the Workbook. The writing sections in both books prepare students thoroughly for each new task and may focus on one or more of the following features: planning answers; help with ideas; paragraph organization; useful language; appropriate register or tone. Model answers appear throughout the course and always when students encounter a particular task type for the first time.

In addition, the Teacher's Book contains authentic examples of students' answers to some of the writing tasks in the Coursebook, particularly for the earlier units. These are accompanied by comments from the examiner and a mark of between 1 and 5, where 3, 4 and 5 are considered to be of pass standard, 5 being the maximum mark attainable. An important feature of the writing syllabus in *Ready for CAE* is the Ready for Writing unit on pages 192 to 205 of the Coursebook. This serves both as a reference, with examples of all the main writing types, and as a bank of writing tasks for students to answer. For each writing type, there is:

- a task
- a model answer with the main features highlighted
- a further task for students to answer
- a 'Useful language' section which students can refer to when doing this and other similar tasks in the Coursebook and Workbook.

The Ready for Writing unit also contains an indication of the criteria used by examiners when marking answers to writing tasks, as well as a procedure for students to follow when planning and checking their answers.

Use of English

The Vocabulary and Language focus sections, together with the Wordlist and Grammar reference, contain the types of individual words, collocations, phrases and structures which appear in the CAE Use of English paper. No coursebook, however, can hope to expose students to *all* the language they are likely to encounter in this part of the CAE examination. Consequently, throughout *Ready for CAE*, students are encouraged, and shown how, to notice and record language when reading texts, both in and out of the classroom.

In order to prepare students for Part 3, the Word Formation task, a systematic approach to word building is adopted, with a number of units each focusing on a different aspect of affixation. In addition, the Workbook contains a Word formation list, a reference containing all the words which are taught and tested in the Word formation sections of the Coursebook and Workbook, together with further examples. The Coursebook syllabus is as follows:

Unit 1 **Nouns**
Unit 3 **Adjectives & Adverbs**
Unit 7 **Verbs**
Unit 9 **Alternatives from the same prompt word**
Unit 11 **Nouns formed with *in, out, up, down* and *back***

In addition, students are provided with plenty of opportunity to practise all five task types of the Use of English paper, both in the Coursebook and the Workbook. Care has been taken to ensure that at least some of the items tested in a particular exercise have been taught either in the same unit in which the exercise appears or in an earlier part of the course. This helps build students' confidence and shows the link between the language they are learning and its possible application in the examination. The Ready for Use of English unit on pages 84 to 87 offers further useful information.

Listening

Each unit of the Coursebook has either one or two listening activities of the type students will encounter in the CAE Listening Paper 4. A wide range of sources has been used for the listening texts and the recordings contain a variety of different accents. Again, information on listening in the CAE exam and guidance on how to tackle the tasks are given in the 'What to expect' and 'How to go about it' boxes, particularly in the earlier stages of the course, when students require most support. The Ready for Listening unit on pages 124 to 127 contains an example of each of the four parts of the listening paper, together with further help and advice. Here, and throughout the Teacher's Book, suggestions are given for classroom exploitation of the Listening scripts, which appear at the end of the Coursebook. These can be particularly useful for checking answers, raising students' awareness of distractors or focusing on useful words and expressions used by the speakers.

Speaking

Guidance is given throughout the Coursebook on how to approach the four parts of the Speaking Paper. There are regular 'How to go about it' and 'Useful Language' boxes, particularly for parts 2 and 3, where students need most help with procedure and technique. The Ready for Speaking unit on pages 164 to 167 contains further useful practice and advice, and includes a recorded interview of two students performing the different tasks in Paper 5.

Clearly, the more speaking practice students have in class, the faster their oral skills will improve and the better prepared they will be for the Speaking Paper of the CAE examination. *Ready for CAE* provides regular opportunities for students to speak in pairs, in pre- and post- listening and reading activities, as well as in Vocabulary and Language Focus sections. These are indicated by the special speaking icon, most usually found in the left-hand margin.

1 Aiming high

Content Overview

Themes

This unit is concerned with challenge, ambition and motivation.

Exam-related activities

Paper 1 Part 3	**Reading** Multiple choice (long)
Paper 2 Part 2	**Writing** Competition entries
Paper 3 Part 4	**Use of English** Word formation (review)
Paper 4 Part 1	**Listening** Multiple choice (short)
Paper 5 Part 2	**Speaking** Long turn

Other

Vocabulary	Collocations
Word formation	Nouns
Language focus 1	Modal verbs 1: *might, could, may, can*
Language focus 2	Spelling
Extension	Further ways of expressing future possibility

Speaking: CAE Part 2 Long turn Page 6

Lead-in
Brainstorm big challenges which people face in their lives (if no ideas are forthcoming, suggest leaving home, starting a new job, going to live abroad, getting married etc). Next ask students to work individually and write down three challenges they have faced personally in their lives to date. They then rank their choices in order of importance. Finally, students pair up and speak about their three choices, saying why they have chosen this order of importance.

Now introduce students to the exam task. Go through the task and the advice together. Explain the following points:

- at this stage students should not worry about timings, but just concentrate on speaking fluently and fulfilling the task.
- student B should not interrupt while A is talking, but must listen carefully in order to reply appropriately when A has finished.

Useful language
Students complete this section in pairs. Check your students' answers before asking them to attempt the exam task. Encourage students to use the useful language during their spoken long turn.

Answers

very happy	delighted elated thrilled overjoyed
sad or *wanting to cry*	tearful miserable close to tears weepy
nervous or *worried*	anxious apprehensive tense on edge

Exam note: In Part 2 of the Speaking Test candidate A speaks for one minute about a set of pictures. The candidate is expected to go beyond basic description, and should therefore pay careful attention to the details required by the question. Candidate B comments briefly (no more than 30 seconds), prompted by a 'follow-up' question which involves some kind of reaction to what candidate A has said. Then the roles are reversed and the process is repeated with different pictures. In the exam the number of pictures will be slightly different – this is dealt with in Unit 9 of the Teacher's Book.

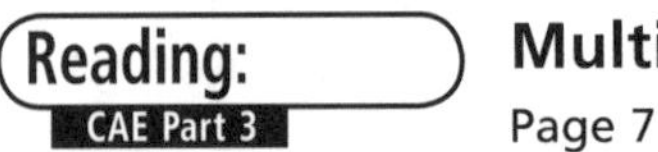

Multiple choice
Page 7

Photocopiable vocabulary exercise on page 149.

Note: Derbyshire is a county in central England, many miles from the nearest coast.

1 Students answer the speaking questions in pairs or small groups.

2 The 'How to go about it' section takes students through the process of tackling a multiple-choice reading step by step, with things to do at each stage, so teachers need to control this strictly in the classroom.

- Read out the first bullet point in the box, explaining that it is essential to have an overview, or 'big picture' of the whole text first. The smaller details in the questions will be much easier to answer if students have already seen the main ideas of the text. To ensure that this initial skim read does not become a detailed read, ask students not to touch their dictionaries yet and to give themselves no more than three minutes.

To give a focus to this skim read, read out the italicized words in the first bullet.

Note: The introduction is separate, so the numbering of paragraphs refers to the text after the introduction.

Answers

1 – the type of person who would take up such a challenge
The last paragraph talks about 'the simple Derbyshire girl' and mentions a change to 'a heroine and an inspiration to others of her generation'.
– their reasons for doing so
The beginning of paragraph 3 talks about how her passion for sailing started.
– the preparation required
In paragraph 3 we read about the 2,000 letters she wrote to get sponsorship and the 60,000 miles she sailed in preparation.
– their feelings during and after the event
During: From her comments at the end of paragraph 6 we understand that she was very determined, but we learn little, if anything about her feelings
After: In paragraph 5 we are told that 'she looked remarkably composed and seemed to take the change from solitude to public adulation very much in her stride'. We also read about her disappointment at not winning.
– the conditions they experience at sea
The harsh conditions are mentioned in paragraph 4.

- Now look at the second bullet point, and ask students to look at the meanings in context of the words in bold, as instructed.

Answers

'fêted': admired, honoured and entertained
'runners-up': a person or team that does not finish first in a competition or race, but that wins a prize
'landlocked': surrounded by land
'tenuous': weak, easily proved false
'spark off': cause something to start, especially suddenly

- Go through the third bullet point. Students mark in pencil in the margin beside the text. Note that each of the seven paragraphs after the introduction contains an answer to one of the seven questions. This will often be the case in the multiple-choice readings in the exam.
- The fourth bullet point is where students do a more detailed read individually, around the parts of the text they have marked in the margin. They should now underline the phrase or sentence which gave them the answer. Point out that with some questions (typically the last question which may be a global question referring to the whole text) the answer may be the idea of a whole paragraph or even a larger section of text.

Answers

1C Lines 11–14 the winner ... were reversed
2B Lines 35–41 Auntie Thea ... lifelong passion.
3D Lines 61–62 She wrote ... sponsorship + lines 66–74 And in terms ... 60,000 miles.
4C Lines 83–86 She endured ... windless Doldrums.
5C Lines 112–117 Her thoughts ... or five years.
6B Lines 123–134 But despite ... into victory.
7A Lines 150–end she is a heroine ... .

- The final stage of the process can give students excellent fluency practice, since they must 'negotiate' why answers are correct or wrong in English.

Reacting to the text
Students follow instructions.

Further practice
Copy this box and sentences onto the board. The words in the box are useful time expressions from the text. Students should put them into the appropriate sentence.

for weeks at a time from that moment on for the previous four or five years in the eight months leading up to the race

1 ____________________ there was no keeping her away from the water
2 ____________________ she sailed no fewer than 60,000 miles
3 a survival suit that stayed on ____________________
4 the ambition that had dominated her life ____________________

Students should get into the good habit of doing such a search for useful collocations or fixed phrases from each text they read. See the photocopiable materials on page 149 for more examples of this.

Exam note: In the multiple-choice task, questions will focus on important details, as well as attitude and opinions expressed.

The final question may be 'global', such as the writer's purpose in the text as a whole.

Language focus 1: Modal verbs 1

Page 10

Might, could, may, can

1 Students follow instructions. Students may need help with the meaning of 'concession'. You could illustrate this by an example stem such as 'I accept that x, but/although ... '.

Answers

1 Annoyance
2 Past possibility which did not happen
3 Past possibility
4 Future possibility
5 Present possibility
6 Lack of enthusiasm – point out that 'might/ may as well' is a fixed phrase.
7 Concession

2 Take a lot of answers from various students by way of whole-class feedback, as the repetition of the grammatical idea will be a useful way for them to remember it.

Answers

Possible answers
1 I'm so angry with him. I do think he might have phoned to say he couldn't come.
2 We've missed the beginning, so we may as well go home and watch a video.
3 It was rather dangerous. Someone could have fallen over it and broken their leg.
4 I can't find it anywhere. I think I may have left it on the bus on my way home.
5 She might have a university degree, but she has no idea how to talk to the public.
6 Cheer up! It might stop raining later and then we can go out.
('*Cheer up! It might never happen' is often said to someone who looks sad*.)

3 Now test students' knowledge of different uses of 'can'. Point out that 'can' is very common, but that it has a great many different functions. If students need help with 'deduction', use the following example: 'Who's that ringing the doorbell at this time? It can't be Dad because he's got his key, it must be the postman!'

Answers

1 theoretical possibility
2 criticism
3 request
4 inability
5 deduction
6 prohibition

4 In whole-class feedback, collect different contexts, in order to give students the chance to use 'could be' and 'might be'.

Answers

Suggested/possible answers if none are forthcoming

2 This could be a girl telling off her boyfriend. It could be that he played a practical joke on her, but she didn't see the funny side of it.
3 This might be a magician, asking someone in the audience for help.
4 This could be a younger brother. He could be trying to retrieve a football from a tree.
5 This might be a parent trying to dissuade a teenager from eating a bar of chocolate.
6 This could be a parent refusing to allow their young child to stay up beyond their bedtime to watch something on TV.

Further practice

In pairs, students choose one of the sentences containing a modal verb in exercises 1 and 2, and write a mini-dialogue of six lines, ending with the sentence they have chosen. They then read their dialogue to other pairs in the room, stopping at the last line, so that the others have to guess how the dialogue ends. They could write a total of three such dialogues if time and interest permits.

Refer students to page 216 of their books, and give them time to read the relevant part of the Grammar reference.

Extension

1 Make the important point that in English you also convey possibility through phrases.

Answers

a 'faint' suggests that it is not very possible. The other adjectives express the opposite.
b 'fair' express a reasonable degree of possibility. The others suggest it is not very possible. Note that *could*, *might* and *will* can all be used with these two sentences, *may* is less frequent.
c 'good' is not correct. ('a good' would be correct)
d 'Predictably' is not possible here. It is an attitude marker meaning 'as is to be expected', often found at the beginning of a sentence and usually with past reference: *Predictably, house sales rose as a result of the cut in the interest rate.*
He was predictably turned down for the job because of his poor health.
It is also often used to qualify adjectives.
He is predictably upset at what happened.
e 'highly likely' means 'very probable'
f 'hardly likely' means 'not very probable'

2 Give students a few minutes to complete these in writing, before taking extensive feedback.

Answers

Possible sentences

1 I think I stand a good chance of passing the CAE exam.
2 To improve my chances of doing so, I need to read a lot outside of the class.
3 In the world today we face the very real possibility that computers will one day replace books in schools.
4 There's an outside chance that I could be going to the States on holiday next year.
5 It seems highly unlikely that I will get a decent pay rise this year.

Vocabulary: Collocations Page 11

Lead-in

If you need a link for this activity, and/or need to introduce the concept of collocation, write down the following sentence from the Ellen MacArthur text: 'The public will now be hoping to see a suitable encore, some new **feat of endurance** to justify her **celebrity status**.'

Point out that the words in bold are examples of collocation, that is, the way in which words naturally co-occur with other words. The words 'celebrity' and 'status' commonly go together, forming a strong partnership.

It can be useful to learn collocations that relate to each other in terms of topic, and there are many useful collocations to do with the theme of 'challenge'.

1–5 Students follow the instructions.

Answers

1 **a** success **b** ambition **c** motivation **d** failure **e** challenge
Note that 'an overnight success' means it is sudden and unexpected.

4 fulfil <u>*an ambition*</u> / realize — end in <u>*failure*</u> / result in

achieve <u>*success*</u> / enjoy — improve <u>*motivation*</u> / lack

take up <u>*a challenge*</u> / rise to

5 **a** challenge **b** ambition **c** failure **d** success **e** motivation

6 This activity could be done, or repeated, as a revision exercise at the beginning of the next class.

Listening: CAE Part 1 — Multiple choice

Page 12

1 Take these as whole-class speaking points. If the class needs prompting, mention TV, film and music industry awards.

2 Tell students not to look at their books. Go straight into the first listening, which picks up on the speaking points in exercise 1. Stay in whole-class mode for this. After the first play ask the class what they can remember. Elicit the key point that Steve turned down his prize at the music awards ceremony.

Now ask students to look at Extract One. Read the questions together. Do the second play of the CD. Stay in whole-class mode and give feedback on the answers (1A, 2B).

Explain to students that they have just heard a CAE Part 1 extract. Direct them to the 'What to expect' box, and read together. Point out that Part 1 is the 'short' multiple-choice task – in Part 3 they will encounter the 'long' multiple-choice task. Also point out that although the three extracts here all relate to the topic of Unit 1, in the exam itself the extracts are not thematically related in Part 1.

Now play extracts 2 and 3. Students answer the questions in their books.

Answers

1 A 2 B 3 C 4 A 5 C 6 B

Students can see the listening script in their books on page 226, should you wish to feed back in detail on the answers, or use the script to look for useful expressions.

Listening script 1.1–1.3

(I = Interviewer, S = Steve, R = Richard, L = Lily)

Extract One

I: Thanks for being here, Steve, especially when you've got the pressure of a European tour. Now you know what I'm going to ask. You won Best New Artist yesterday, and you didn't turn up to collect the award. *Why?*

S: You know, when we heard we'd been nominated – and we knew who the other nominees were – well, just for a brief moment I guess we got a bit of a kick out of it – I mean the other bands are guys we really respect – but we've always used our music to attack capitalism – it would be incredibly hypocritical to accept an award from the corporate world.

I: OK – I get that, but even if you have no respect for the music industry, it was your fans that voted for you.

S: I don't know if that's true. Look, we've been together for four years now, and the people who liked our music from the start, the ones who keep coming to the gigs, they know what we're about, our politics, our principles. And they wouldn't go in for that kind of thing. But, you know, you get your first number one single and the mainstream music listeners think you're a new band and *they* go out and vote for you. For a moment in time you're on everyone's iPod – and then – then you're deleted.

Extract two

I: Twenty years in the game, Richard, and no-one has yet come close to breaking the records you set. What do you put your success down to?

R: Well, I've had a lot of experience after all that time – endless hours of practice. But for me it's more to do with the psychological approach: maintaining discipline and focus – setting an aim and not getting distracted, no matter whether the game is going well or against us. I reckon for some sports it's about a physical advantage you're born with – but with cricket – it's applying your mind in the right way.

I: Is there any advice you'd give to up-and-coming young players?

R: Not advice as such. Whether a match has been a resounding success or it's ended in failure, we each have to analyse our strengths and weaknesses, and use that to get the best out of our next team performance. Something I find to be a negative development, though, I'm afraid, is the rather aggressive manner in which certain young players celebrate their performance – I mean the way they now punch the air – and those other gestures of victory. Cricket is supposed to be a dignified game – there's no place for showing off.

Extract three

I: Lily – for listeners who have maybe never heard of *40-hour Famine* – can you tell us a little bit about it?

L: Yeah, sure. Well, it's about young people – students mainly – *not* eating food for 40 hours – although *water* is allowed. The idea is to promote a bit more awareness of what it's like for poor people who are starving because of famine. Many students are too young to volunteer to go overseas and help out directly – and they haven't got the cash to make monthly donations to charity – but taking part in 40-hour Famine is something they *can* do – to show they care. And of course, the sponsorship they get does go to excellent charities.

I: And this is the second year you've taken part?

L: Yes – last year I only made it to 35. I felt really dizzy and had to give up. But no-one made me feel like I'd let them down – they were simply concerned with my health. I thought "Oh well, I'll just have to have another go. I've got a year to prepare and next time round nothing will stop me." And look ... in another four hours – I will have fulfilled that promise to myself.

3 Students react to the first extract in pairs.

Word formation: Nouns Page 13

In exam terms this is building towards Part 3 of the Use of English paper.

1 If you need a link as a lead-in to this exercise, put the following on the board:

a Sailing single-handedly round the world was Ellen MacArthur's greatest _________.

b The desire to win was Ellen's greatest __________.

c The greatest sports people do not consider the possibility of __________.

Answers

1 **a** achieve-ment **b** motiv-ation **c** fail-ure

2 Add to the instructions the fact that here the new word will involve one or two grammatical changes. Show this on the board:

succeed → success = 1 change
succeed → successful = 2 changes

In the exam itself it may sometimes be necessary to make three changes:
succeed → unsuccessful

Also draw students' attention to the bold print in the questions. The bold print highlights collocations with the target word or shows fixed phrases containing the target word.

Answers

1	refreshments	**7**	secrecy
2	disapproval	**8**	membership
3	eagerness	**9**	breakage(s)
4	procedures	**10**	likelihood
5	insignificance	**11**	independence
6	simplicity	**12**	anxiety

Students record useful collocations and fixed phrases in their notebooks.

3 The quiz element in this exercise could be exploited ('see how quickly you can find the ending which connects the three words for each of the 12 sets').

Answers

1	pleasure	exposure	closure
2	appearance	annoyance	reliance
3	storage	shortage	package
4	rehearsal	renewal	proposal
5	efficiency	intimacy	vacancy
6	enjoyment	requirement	commitment
7	prosperity	originality	familiarity
8	leadership	companionship	partnership
9	neighbourhood	fatherhood	adulthood
10	absence	persistence	evidence
11	selfishness	tiredness	carelessness
12	explanation	interpretation	application

Further practice
Put students in groups of three. Student A calls out any word from the three columns, student B calls out the noun formed from the word and student C has to think immediately of a short sentence to illustrate how the noun is used.

eg *father – fatherhood – Jack gave every impression of adapting well to fatherhood.*

This activity also makes a nice 'warmer' as revision at the start of a future lesson.

4 Students follow instructions.

Answers

2 endurance, reluctance
4 survival
6 disappointment
8 sponsorship
11 thoroughness
12 imagination, information, preparation, realization, inspiration
Also: heroine, spectator, winner, competitor, desalinator, success, thoughts, runners, achievers, savings, favourites, heat, solitude, conference
The following have typical noun endings but are not formed from a commonly used verb, adjective or noun: emotion, conditions, adulation, ambition, celebrity

Language focus 2: Spelling Page 14

Point out that spelling is an important issue in the Use of English paper. This section could be done as a pairwork activity or given for homework.

1 Verbs ending in consonant + vowel + consonant double the final consonant if the final syllable is stressed or if there is only one syllable. Note the difference in the position of the stress between *oc'cur* and *be'gin* on the one hand, and *'happen* and *'open* on the other.

2

Answers

referring limiting setting upsetting targeting (*targetting* is also used. This is true also of *focusing/focussing* and *benefiting/benefitting*) forbidding writing waiting travelling (*traveling* in American English) panicking

3

Answers

1 pleasent – pleasant
Note the differences between the noun *appearance* (see example 0) and the adjective *apparent*.
2 neccesary – necessary
3 publically – publicly
4 definate – definite
5 irresponsable – irresponsible
6 leafs – leaves
Other examples with this spelling change are *calf – calves*; *half – halves*; *life – lives*; *loaf – loaves*; *self – selves*; *shelf – shelves*; *wife – wives*
7 preceeding – preceding (from the verb *precede*)
Note the spelling difference between *exceed/proceed/succeed* and *precede/recede/concede*.
8 bussiness – business
9 dissappointed – disappointed
disappear is also commonly misspelt by students.
10 recieve – receive
Seize and *weird* are correct, exposing the often quoted spelling 'rule' of 'i before e, except after c'. This only seems to be true (and worth learning) for words such as *believe*, *relieve*, *achieve* and *conceive*, *receive*, *deceive*.
11 influencial – influential
12 factery – factory

4 In this further practice stage, some of the dictated words are from exercise 3, others are new. Students should not look at each other's words until they have completed the activity. Make sure they cannot see each other's words.

Writing: CAE Part 2 — Competition entries Page 14

1 Stress that it is very important in CAE writing of all types to fulfil the task completely. Each question will have a number of key content elements, and they must all appear in a candidate's answer. Marks are lost immediately when content elements are missed out.

Encourage students to underline the key content points in the question. This can also be done when sitting the exam itself. Elicit the three content points:

- the secret ambition and why it is important to you
- what it would take to achieve it (requirements)
- why you think you should be chosen (qualities/reasons)

Then students read the model answer to check for these points. They will find that the answer does indeed address all parts of the task and would have a positive effect on the judges.

2 Ensure students are aware that A and B are two different but equally acceptable paragraph plans. The writer follows paragraph plan B.

Reinforce the message here – clear planning is very important, reflected in clear paragraphs. It is worth leaving a gap between paragraphs (rather than just indenting a new line) to emphasize this visually to the examiner/marker. Clear paragraphing not only makes the piece much easier to read, it also shows evidence of clear planning. 10–15 minutes spent reading the question, thinking about content points and planning may seem like lost writing time, but in the long run it is time well spent, as it will enable the writing to be done more quickly, relevantly and efficiently.

3 Examples of sophisticated language

Answers

the likelihood that I will ever fulfil my ambition ... doesn't seem very high
my lifelong passion
achieving fame and fortune
be put off by dull statistics
research their genre thoroughly
My bookshelves ... are stacked with the novels ...
despite knowing all the time 'whodunnit'
I've turned out dozens of short crime stories
possess enormous self discipline
devote the necessary time and effort to producing
that has meant burning the midnight oil
in anywhere near publishable form
no easy task
who could possibly fail to

The writer uses a variety of language to talk about the requirements and potential problems:

Requirements

Answers

Reading is important
all writers need to research their genre thoroughly
being a writer requires imagination
You have to develop your own personal style
successful writers possess enormous self-discipline

4 Register

Answers

Elements of informal language
Contractions: I'll, doesn't, I've, We've
Linkers: And, But, So (at the beginning of the sentence), Last but not least
Punctuation: dash: 'important – all writers need to' and 'magazine – some have been published'
Phrasal verbs: put off by dull statistics, turned out dozens of short stories
Use of 'get': only one gets published, we've all got a novel inside us, getting it out
Use of *you/your*: eg 'You have to develop your own personal style'

5 Engaging the reader

It is important for students to write in a style which is appropriate for the piece, whether it is a report, article or, as here, a competition entry. The type of piece provides the basic shape and framework for their writing.

Answers

The title and opening paragraph are crucial in this respect. The title should grab the reader's attention and the opening paragraph should make him or her want to carry on reading. The writer here uses a statistic in the form of a question to interest and involve the reader from the very first sentence.

The choice of idiomatic language adds colour to the piece and also suggests informality: ('put off by dull statistics', 'stacked with', 'burning the midnight oil').

The final paragraph rounds off with a summarizing and thought-provoking statement, 'We've all got a novel inside us' and a question to make people think: this could apply to anyone and their secret ambition. The writer begins and ends with a rhetorical question – it is a nice stylistic device if the end can mirror the beginning in some way, so that there is a sense of 'full circle' or completion.

6 Students follow the instructions.

Exam note:
Assessment
We have focused attention on content, organization, range of language and register/format. These are all features that examiners will look for. The other important aspect is cohesion (linking of ideas). We will look at this in later units.

Each piece is given a mark out of five.

In keeping with the importance of fulfilling the task, it is essential to realize that irrelevance is penalized, no matter how well written!

At this stage there may be too much going on to expect students to think about the length of their answer. However, in the exam, writing to the 220–260 words specified is also part of fulfilling the task.

Sample answer

A professional golden boot?

My secret ambition has always been to become a professional football player. That's what I'd really like to do in my life, just playing football every day so I can delight all the items relationed with the job, as money, cars, fame ... Time is getting on and I am not getting younger, so now is the time to act.

First of course you need be good at football. In my local amateur league I was principal goal scorer last season and I think I have every chance of winning the 'golden boot' trophy again this season. Friends say I have the necessary skills, but you also need have a stroke of luck and perhaps can be seen by a scout from a big team. 'Masterclass' could be the opportunity I am waiting for.

Then of course to improve your chances of becoming a professional, you need train a lot and be fit. There is no one day when I do not kick a ball, or I am in a gym doing exercise. For me it is like drug: I am addicted to training and I think I am in good condition for being professional.

Finally, however, you also need be a bit special if you want that other people consider you as good player. By this I don't mean you cause problems for trainers or other players, but you need have a creative character, if you want to be star player. My teammates call me 'crazy horse' which I think is a compliment.

So, I think I have the ingredients to be a professional player. Now all I need is a stroke of luck and if I have an appearance on your programme.

Examiner's comment
Content: The content of the task is covered.

Organization and cohesion: Clearly organized and paragraphed. The penultimate paragraph is a little confused and there are problems with coherence in some sentences, eg *'so I can delight all the items relationed with the job, as money, cars, fame …'.*

Accuracy: Reasonably accurate, though there are some errors in the use of articles, *need* is consistently used with the bare infinitive and some grammar is rather awkward, eg *'you also need be a bit special if you want that other people consider you as good player'.*
Range: There is evidence of a good range of structures and vocabulary eg *'I have every chance of winning the 'golden boot' trophy', 'a stroke of luck'* and *'to improve your chances of becoming a professional'.*

Register: The register is consistently neutral and appropriate.

Target Reader: The target reader would be reasonably informed, though might be slightly confused by the penultimate paragraph.

Mark: Band 3

Review 1 Pages 16 and 17

Modal verbs
1 can, have **2** may/might **3** to, well
4 unlikely/improbable, may/might/could
5 at, no **6** in, to

Spelling

1 important	**6** themselves	**11** were
2 generally	**7** of	**12** interest
3 objective	**8** to	**13** their
4 identifies	**9** confident	**14** improvement
5 successful	**10** factors	**15** perceive

Use of English: Word formation
CAE Part 3

Review sections will normally only contain answers in the Teacher's Book. However, Word formation appears for the first time in *Ready for*

CAE in this review section, so we include some notes on how to help students with this task type.

- First ask students to read the article, ignoring the gaps. Ask for a one-sentence summary of what it is about (= Should parents offer cash rewards to their children to encourage good exam results).

While students are reading put the following on the board:

pay
The **monthly payments** on my house went up by 1% last week.
In my job I have the option of taking **unpaid leave**.
The amount you have borrowed is **repayable** in twelve monthly instalments or ...
My company has 250 employees on the **payroll**.
The amount of tax deducted is shown on your **monthly payslip**.

These sentences exemplify ways in which the base word 'pay' (gap 2) could be made into other words. (The bold words show useful collocations.) Discuss the meaning of any of these that are unknown to your class.

Ask the following:
In which one is 'pay' made into a negative adjective? (= unpaid)
In which one is 'pay' made into another adjective with a prefix? (= repayable)
In which ones is 'pay' made into a compound noun? (= payroll; payslip)
In which one is 'pay' made into a plural noun? (= payments)

Explain that these are typical changes to the base word which can be made in this exam task.

Then read out the first two sentences of the text. Ask 'Which of the words we have formed from 'pay' goes into the second gap?' (= payments).

Elicit from students what they have to do for this task. (= for each gap they must form a new word from the base word in capitals on the right.)

Now ask students to complete the rest of the text. The word they form must fit both grammatically and contextually (in other words it must make sense in the context).

Answers

1 expectations
2 payment(s)
3 performance(s)
4 recognition
5 ability
6 academically
7 difficulties
8 financial
9 failure
10 judgement/judgment

Exam note:

- Many answers involve adding prefixes or suffixes, but candidates can also be required to make internal changes to a word (LONG → LENGTH).

As with all parts of the Use of English paper candidates need to read the text carefully. It is particularly easy to miss negatives and plurals if this is not done.

Note: The types of change made to the base word are explained on page 84 of the Ready for Use of English section.

Review answers

Word combinations

1 strong
2 slightest
3 every
4 stand
5 tears
6 delighted
7 enjoyed
8 rose
9 lifelong
10 light

2 Times change

Content overview

Themes

This unit is concerned with history, the past, changes in your life.

Exam-related activities

Paper 1	**Reading**
Part 4	Multiple matching
Paper 2	**Writing**
Part 1	Formal letter
Paper 3	**Use of English**
Part 2	Open cloze
Part 1	Multiple-choice cloze (review)
Paper 4	**Listening**
Part 2	Sentence completion
Part 4	Multiple matching
Paper 5	**Speaking**
Part 3	Collaborative task

Other

Vocabulary	Changes
Language focus 1	Talking about the past
Language focus 2	Nouns in formal English

Listening 1: CAE Part 2 — Sentence completion

Page 18

1 Encourage students to take their time and discuss in pairs or threes.

- Such fluency activities are often better opportunities than actual exam practice tasks for monitoring students' oral performance. In fluency tasks students should be encouraged to relax and say as much as possible. As you circulate among the class, try to listen out for English which could be improved from a lexical point of view. Make a note and feed back briefly to the whole class after five minutes or so. You might say things like: 'Joe, when describing the woman you said x, but you might have said … ', 'Maria, you were translating from your own language when you said x, but the expression in English is … '. (You may prefer not to name students directly.) Concentrate on whole phrases if possible.
- It is important that students should make the most of all opportunities to try out their English. In the exam aspects such as communicative fluency and range of expression are important – more so than occasional minor grammatical slips.

2 Do the second speaking point with the whole class.

3 Read the first bullet point together from the 'What to expect in the exam' section. Make the point that the sentences containing the questions focus on important details in the listening. As such, the sentences provide summary information of the whole listening. So students can help themselves a great deal during the pause before the listening begins.

Then go through the other bullet points.

4 Give them a minute or so to read the eight questions and to predict what kind of information will come in the gaps.

Answers

Possible answers

2 probably a time expression (for ages? for x years? etc)
3 probably something which people making time capsules sometimes forget to do
4 two nouns which are things related to TV programmes
5 a place/room
6 something the doctor was researching
7 a room/part of the grounds
8 something valuable/worth stealing

Then play the CD and do the exam task.

Answers

1 buried (underground)
2 more than/over a century
3 keep (proper) records
4 costumes and props
5 (film studio) car park
6 ancient civilizations
7 basement
8 (real) (items of) jewellery

It can be very useful for students to look at the listening script (page 226) after the answers have been given out.

- It is a good way of checking answers to play the recording again while students follow the listening script.
- It enables the class to pull out useful phrases and other vocabulary from the listening script.
- It means you can draw students' attention to some aspect of the task.

Refer students back to the third bullet point in the 'What to expect in the exam' box. Students need to be clear on this. What they write in the gap is normally the actual words used on the recording. But the wording of the question will be different from the wording they hear on the recording. Show this on the board with the first two questions.

For reasons of security, time capsules are usually **buried underground** = question 1
... and in most cases **buried underground** for safekeeping. = recording

People have been putting things in time capsules for **over a century**. = question 2
... the idea of storing objects for posterity in this way goes back **over a century** ... = recording

Listening script 1.4

Hello, good evening. Well, as you know I'm here to talk about my great passion in life – time capsules. Now if you're not sure, a time capsule is a container filled with typical objects from a particular time and in most cases buried underground for safekeeping. The idea behind this, of course, is that future generations will be able to learn about life in the past when they open up the capsule and study the objects.

So, when did all this burying business begin? Well, the idea of storing objects for posterity in this way goes back over a century to the nineteen hundreds. The problem was, and indeed still is to some extent, that most of these have been lost to history. 'Why is this?' you might ask. Well, it's either because of thieves and the fact that the capsules weren't sufficiently well protected, or – and this is the most usual explanation – because no one bothered to keep proper records and we don't know for sure where the capsules are.

To give you just one example, they buried seventeen of them back in the Thirties in California in a place called Corona – and not one of them has ever been found. Amazing, isn't it? And do you remember the popular television programme M*A*S*H? Well, in 1983, some of the cast put costumes and props from the show in a capsule and buried it in a secret ceremony, refusing to tell anyone not connected with the show where exactly they'd put it. All they'd say was that it was somewhere in the 20th Century Film Studios car park in Hollywood. Now, of course, they've built a huge hotel on the site and no one knows where on earth to look for it.

But the, er, the modern-day passion for time capsules really began in the late nineteen thirties, when a man called Dr Thornwell Jacobs, the President of Oglethorpe University in Atlanta, was doing some research into ancient civilizations. Well, he was so frustrated by the lack of accurate information that he came up with a plan to ensure that the same thing wouldn't happen to future generations. He built the 'Crypt of Civilization' – that's what he called his time capsule – in an area the size of a swimming pool, in the basement of one of the university buildings, Hearst Hall. You can still see it today, in fact. But you can't see any of the contents – the crypt won't be opened for another 6,000 years!

It's got all sorts of things – newsreels, important radio speeches, er, scientific instruments and – wait for it – over 640,000 pages of material on microfilm, including the Bible, the Koran, the Iliad and Dante's Inferno. But it's not all serious stuff. There's also a Donald Duck doll, and literally thousands of everyday objects like cooking utensils, ornaments and tools. Very sensibly, Dr Jacobs didn't put in any real items of jewellery, because he thought that might attract robbers. But he did include models of necklaces and earrings, as well as papier maché fruit and vegetables and even a small capsule of beer.

Since then, of course, all sorts of people have put all sorts of objects into time capsules. Now, if you're interested in burying your own time capsule, I can ...

Speaking: CAE Part 3 — Collaborative task

Page 19

- Read the instructions together, then refer students to the first bullet point in the 'How to go about it' section. Explaining why you make your various choices is an important part of the task. Provide a few more examples of your own to give students some ideas: eg 'I would definitely want to include a remote control in the capsule. I think this is a powerful symbol of society today. TV is all-important in most people's lives and the remote control has really changed the way we now watch TV and the way we demand short bursts of entertainment in our lives.'
- Allow the discussions in pairs (or threes) to go on beyond the three minutes allocated in the exam if students are entering into the topic with enthusiasm. But do interrupt to remind them when you wish them to start considering the

second aspect of the task: which two objects would be of most interest to future generations. At this point they should begin to round up their discussion.

- As a whole-class activity, briefly ask each pair what their final conclusion was.

Exam note:

- This stage of the speaking test lasts about four minutes with students speaking for three minutes of this time. It involves students in a problem-solving task.
- Each pair or three receive the same set of photographs or pictures. (These are different pictures from the ones used in Part 2 Long Turn.)
- The task involves negotiating and collaborating towards a final conclusion. If partners are unable to reach agreement, that is ok.
- Negotiating towards the conclusion is an important part of the task. Candidates should show that they are turning their discussion towards a final conclusion.
- As with all interactive parts in the Speaking test, candidates should not dominate a discussion. Negotiating involves asking your partner what (s)he has to say, and responding appropriately to what (s)he has said.

Useful language

- Warn students that when doing a task such as collaborating on a set of pictures, it is easy to keep on using one phrase that you are keen on (eg I think we should, I think people will).
- Remind them of the second bullet point in the 'How to go about it' section. It is important to use a good variety of expressions. We now consider some of these.
- Students complete the six gaps individually and then compare what they have written.

Answers

1 would not be complete without
2 is a part of everyday life
3 be intrigued to see
4 would demonstrate very clearly
5 might conceivably be obsolete
6 are unlikely to be using

Optional extra activity

Write the following questions on the board. Students discuss in pairs, developing their ideas as fully as possible.

- Would you include any further items from other aspects of life today?
- How useful will time capsules be for future generations when studying the past?
- Do museums still have a role to play in the fast-moving, hi-tech 21st century? Why/why not?
- Which people have had the greatest impact on your country's history? How have they affected it?
- 'We learn nothing from history except that we learn nothing from history.' What is meant by this? Can you give examples?

From an exam point of view, this looks ahead to Part 4 of the speaking test, which is introduced in the Coursebook in Unit 5.

Use of English: CAE Part 2 — Open cloze

Page 20

1
- For all Use of English tasks students should get into the habit of doing a quick skim read of the text before attempting to answer any questions. Once they have understood the surrounding context, the gaps will be much easier to complete.
- The doll is Barbie – the clue is in the girl's name, Barbara.
- Remind students of the type of word they are typically looking for: can, as, have, be, on, a etc.

2 Students follow the instructions in their books.

Optional: If you feel your class will have difficulty with this task, ask them to close their books and put their pens down. Read the complete text to them, including the gapped words. When they then do the task, it is unlikely they will be able to remember any individual items – the point of the exercise is rather to give them 'the whole picture'.

Answers

1 since	**6** At	**11** did
2 by	**7** down	**12** such
3 as	**8** however/though	**13** whose
4 that	**9** into	**14** not
5 with	**10** as	**15** an

3 Ask students to cover their books and get a volunteer to say in their own words what point was made by critics of Barbie at the end of the text.

There are various other questions you could ask, depending on the interest of this topic to your particular students. These might include:
Did you ever possess a Barbie as a girl?
What did you like about her?
At what age would most girls grow out of (= be too old for) Barbie?
Would you buy a Barbie doll for a niece/daughter?

Language focus 1: Talking about the past Page 20

If you are doing this in class time, the most interesting way may be to take a diagnostic approach:

- Students go into pairs and try to agree on the correct answer.
- They read the Grammar reference section on pages 216–217 of the Coursebook.
- They look again at their answers to see if they would change anything.
- The answers are checked.

Answers

A 1 (had) never kissed/met
The past perfect of 'kiss' is optional since the sequence of events is made clear by 'until'.
2 have had
3 has been crying
4 was always losing (*indicating irritation*)
5 ate (*first she ate the chocolate, then she started to feel sick*)/was eating (*she started to feel sick while she was eating it*)/had eaten (*focus on the completed action: she had finished eating it before she started to feel sick*)/had been eating (*focus on the activity rather than the completed action*)
6 Marjorie left when Paul arrived: *She left after Paul arrived, possibly as a consequence of his arrival.*
Marjorie had left when Paul arrived: *She left before Paul arrived.*
Marjorie was leaving when Paul arrived/was arriving: *Both events occurred simultaneously.*
7 told/were telling (*no difference in meaning*)
bought/have bought *The speaker may be situating in his/her mind the action of buying at some specific past time (eg last week), hence the possible use of past simple. The present perfect can be used to indicate a recent past event with a present result (the book he/she is holding now).*
8 didn't do/hadn't done did (do)/had done *The past tenses in both these sentences are used to refer to past time. The past simple indicates a regular action. The past perfect can be used to emphasize the sequence of events.*

B 1 used to know/knew. *would* cannot be used with a verb which is used statively.
2 I've ridden/I rode
3 All three are possible.
4 I'd seen
5 hadn't made
6 going to work/to have worked (*thinking of/about working*)
7 After he'd done/Having done *For more work on participle clauses see Unit 10.*
8 All three are possible.

2 This fun activity might be ideal for the beginning of a class. During the comparing with your partner stage, the partner should pick up on something that has been said and initiate an appropriate conversation around each one.

Formal letter
Page 21

Teachers may prefer to do the Reading text and Language focus on nouns (pages 24/25) before the writing. The principle of using nouns will be useful for the writing task.

Lead-in
Write the following words on the board:
medieval, knight, joust, jousting tournaments, Medieval Society, Medieval Fair.
Give students one minute only to skim read the whole Part 1 question (as far as the sample answer). Then ask them to go into pairs and define the words on the board. When they have finished ask different pairs for a suitable definition.

Answers

Suggested answers to Lead-in

Medieval – means 'from the Middle Ages' (AD1100–1400)

Knight – a man of noble rank whose duty was to fight for the King. In stories knights are typically shown on horseback with a sword or lance, slaying dragons and rescuing maidens in distress.

Joust – to fight with another knight on horseback using a lance

Jousting tournaments – fighting competitions between knights

Medieval Society – a club for people interested in all things medieval

Medieval Fair – a special event organized by club members, where everyone dresses up in medieval costume, eats medieval food, holds imitation fights etc.

1 Ask a few students to give their personal reactions to the advertisement and pictures. If they have only negative thoughts about it, ask what the appeal might be to those who take part in such events. Ask the class if anyone knows of similar events in their country.

2 Elicit from students what is fundamentally wrong with the sample answer. The tone is rude and threatening and the editor would be unlikely to print a new article. So it would be unlikely to achieve its purpose to the target reader. Point out that this is the most important point in assessment of pieces of writing.

3 Students read the letter again and answer the questions.

Answer

Content: Has the writer answered the questions fully?

No, she has failed to mention the fact that there was not enough room for all the demonstrations.

Has she expanded on any of the points in the input material?

No, she has limited herself to writing the bare minimum, adding no relevant information of her own.

Organization: Is the letter organized into suitable paragraphs?

Yes, each point is dealt with in a separate paragraph.

Vocabulary/Structures:

The language in the letter is mostly accurate but there is no evidence of a wide range of language; what the writer has not copied from the input material is expressed in very simple, conversational language.

Register: Is the register consistently appropriate?

No, it is mostly informal – contractions, informal punctuation, phrasal verb (turn up), linking and other informal language. The opening paragraph is too blunt and aggressive and the closing paragraph too threatening. The last paragraph is an example of inconsistent register.

4 Explain that a feature of a good formal letter is the use of formal nouns and noun phrases. Students try this exercise in pairs.

Answers

Possible Answers

1 There was a (complete/total) lack of parking facilities/space.

2 It was a huge/resounding/great/real success.

3 You suggested that attendance was poor/low.

4 Many commented on the high standard of (the) dancing.

In 1 & 3 above the verb 'was' might not be necessary. Consider the following:

'In your article you draw attention to the low attendance at the fair ... ' where the adjective 'low' is used as a modifier before the noun.

5 The writing task should be given as homework. Draw students' attention to the Useful Language section in the Coursebook (see page 195).

Exam note:

- The Part 1 writing task is compulsory.
- Candidates have to read and process different pieces of input, such as extracts from letters, emails and advertisements.
- Typically one of these texts is annotated with handwritten comments.
- Candidates have to pull together information from the instructions, texts and handwritten comments.

- It is important to fulfil all elements of the task.
- In Part 1 candidates must write 180–220 words (in Part 2 they write 220–260 words).

Sample answer

Dear Editor,

I am writing on the part of the Black Knight Medieval Society to express our dissatisfaction with the report published on November the sixth about Brampton's fifth annual Fair. Our performance has been missinterpreted and we feel that we deserve at least, public excuses.

To begin with the entertainment value, we must expose that the consideration of dull event according to the low attendance might be easily explained if the lack of parking facilities are taken into account. Our sources testify severe difficulties in arriving to the venue with their own vehicle. In the same time, our demonstrations were unfortunately limited to the availability of the space.

As for the criticism of our show, we can assure that our high standards of dancing, music, superb cookery and overall costume ambience have been always praised.

The captivating archery is one of the children's favourite activities, as well as a pleasure for everyone with feeling for this skillfully sport decorated for the occasion with medieval attire.

To sum up, our jugement of the event results very positive and without doubt it has been a resounding success. Consequently, we request a professional report based on analysis rather than superficial impressions as a signal of respect for the readers and the quality of the newspaper.

We are looking forward to reading a decent article.

Yours sincerely
Cécile Dupont

Examiner's comment

Content: The writing attempts to cover the highlighted points indicated in the task. However, successful communication is not always fully achieved. *'The captivating archery is one of the children's favourite activities, as well as a pleasure for everyone with feeling for this skillfully sport …'*

Organization and cohesion: The introductory paragraph introduces the purpose of the letter well and subsequent paragraphs are reasonably well organized. There are problems with coherence at sentence level eg *'To sum up, our jugement of the event results very positive …'*.

Accuracy: The grammar is sometimes awkward. In addition, there are a number of spelling errors (*'missinterpreted', 'skillfully sport'*) and cases of inappropriate word choice (*'public excuses', 'costume ambience'*).

Range: The writer attempts to display a range of vocabulary and tenses but this results in frequent error and evidence of translation from L1.

Register: The register is generally appropriately formal.

Target Reader: The target reader would be informed in the main but confused in patches. The tone of the writing is also somewhat aggressive and might have a negative effect on the reader. The criticism of the newspaper is rather too strong given that the task is to persuade them to publish a correction.

Mark: Band 2

Reading: Multiple matching

CAE Part 4

Page 23

1 This could be done in small groups initially, then as a brainstorming activity involving the whole class.

Answers

From left to right:
The Berlin Wall, York City Wall,
Hadrian's Wall, The Great Wall of China.

2 Go through the 'How to go about it' box with your students. This combination of skimming (reading text very quickly for general gist) and scanning (searching a text for specific information) is the basic approach we recommend throughout *Ready for CAE* for multiple matching.

With this approach the starting point is the sections of text, and students look back at the questions to see which of them apply to a particular section.

However, please be aware of the alternative approach, as follows, which you might choose to adopt with your class.

> Alternative approach
> - Skim through all four texts quickly to get an idea of their content and where information is located in them.
> - Underline key words in questions and find parts of text where these ideas are discussed.
> - Read in more detail the sections of text where the answer is likely to be found.
>
> With this approach the starting point is the items, and students scan the texts for answers to the items.

To give students some initial help, read through Section A together, and match the underlinings with four of the questions.

Answers

On the east side of the wall, tank traps and ditches were built Q3
A number of successful escape attempts Q14
lost its relevance in 1989, when Hungary allowed East Germans to pass through Q11
Now very little of it remains Q6

Either
Then students read section B. Holding the information in B in their heads they read the remaining questions and put B against those questions which refer to this section of the text.

They repeat the procedure for sections C and D. For any questions that remain unanswered, they skim read the text to search for the answers.

Or
If you wish to reduce the reading load at the beginning of the course, divide the class into three groups. Group 1 read only Section B, Group 2 read Section C, and Group 3 read Section D. Each group searches the items for information which relates to their section. Establish that each group has its answers correct. Then redivide the groups, to form new groups, each one comprising one person from each of the three old groups. In their new groups they feed back to the rest of the group and tell them where the answers are located in their section.

Answers

1 B visible from outer space
2 C vulnerable to erosion and visitors are discouraged from walking on it
3 A on the east side of the wall, tank traps and ditches were built
4 D caused disease by preventing the free circulation of air
5 B the wall soon began to crumble
6 A Now very little of it remains
7 B joined the three separate walls
8 D Non-residents and those who were not members of a guild were charged a toll
9 B using ... intellectuals who had been sentenced to forced labour
10 C ranks alongside some of the more famous architectural treasures in the world
11 A lost its relevance in 1989, when Hungary allowed East Germans to pass through
12 D York Corporation began dismantling sections of the wall
13 B evolved from a mere defence system ... into a safe haven where trade could flourish
14 A a number of successful escape attempts
15 C providing a fascinating glimpse into the lives of the Roman soldiers

Reacting to the text
Students follow instructions.

Language focus 2: Nouns in formal English Page 25

In exam terms this relates most directly to formal task types in the Writing paper (eg formal letter, report).

1 Go through the instructions together.

Answer

The main difference is the greater number of nouns in the second sentences from the text and the higher frequency of verbs in the first, alternative sentences. For instance, in **3**, there are five verbs and one noun in the first sentence, compared with one verb and three nouns in the second.

Point out to students that the use of nouns like this helps to express ideas:

- more concisely. Note the shorter length of the second sentences in the second and third examples.
- in a more impersonal way. Note the absence of personal pronouns in the second sentences.

2 Students write answers individually and then compare with a partner. For students who are having difficulties, simplify the process for them by telling them where the gapped information comes from in the first sentence:

1 He was clearly a bit disappointed ⟶ He was unable to hide his ________
when he heard they'd turned him down ⟶ at their rejection of his ________

Answers

1 disappointment; application
2 disapproval; suggestion/proposal/request; reduction
3 dissatisfaction; delay(s); claim/assertion/ guarantee/assurances
4 failure/inability; importance; result/ consequence; awareness/knowledge; education/teaching

3 Students who have done the FCE exam should be familiar with some of the differences between formal and informal style through their acquaintance with the Writing paper.

Answers

The following features appear in **a** and are more characteristic of an informal style.

- contractions
- phrasal verbs *turned down*
- informal language such as *get* (3a), *a bit* (1a), *just* (2a)

Note also there are more words in **a** than in **b**, eg (2a) 33 words (2b) 17 words.

Multiple matching

Page 26

Photocopiable vocabulary exercise on page 149.

Optional lead-in
Ask students to look only at the five cartoons at the bottom of the page. Play the recording once and ask them to match each of the five speakers with one of the cartoons.

Answers

Answers to optional activity in Teacher's Book.
Speaker 1 – the fifth picture
Speaker 2 – the fourth picture
Speaker 3 – the second picture
Speaker 4 – the third picture
Speaker 5 – the first picture

Note:
Although we introduce this task here in Unit 2, we will look in more detail at strategies for dealing with it in Unit 4. There is a lot of new information for students to take in over the first two units, so we do not want to overload them.

Go through the 'What to expect' box together. Students will hear the script in a different way from Part 1. Here they will hear the whole script, all the way through – the script is not repeated after each speaker.

Tell students it is not a good idea to focus solely on task one during the first play, and solely on task two during the second. That would mean students were listening only once to each piece. Instead, tell them to try to look at both tasks for each speaker. So when they hear Speaker 1, they should try to complete question 1 and also question 6. For Speaker 2 it is questions 2 and 7, and so on. Of course, it is hard to do these two things at once, so the best thing is for students to *concentrate* on task one for the first play, but also attempt task two, and for them to concentrate on task two for the second play, but also check on their answers for task one.

Answers

1 C **2** E **3** F **4** D **5** A **6** B **7** F **8** E
9 A **10** C

Listening script 1.5–1.9

Female

I'd given up just about everything – the job, the house, the car – and gone to Spain to be with my husband. Then six months later it was all over. Both of us believed we'd rushed into marriage too soon and there was little that made us compatible as spouses. At the same time, we felt the friendship that had drawn us together in the first place was just too valuable to throw away and the only way to save it was by splitting up. The thing is, I remember hugging Alfonso at the airport, boarding the flight to Manchester and waiting to feel some kind of relief. It didn't come. By the time we landed, I had this awful sense that we'd rushed just as fast into a divorce. A year has passed and I still can't help wishing we'd put a bit more effort into staying together.

Male

I was a no-hoper at school, see. No one had heard of dyslexia in those days, so my teachers just classed me as an 'idiot'. I might have behaved myself later if I'd been given a bit more attention then but I was told time and time again that I was going to be a failure. It surprised no one, including myself, that I ended up in prison, but all that time on my hands gave me the chance to think. I realized I'd turned out just how they said and I wanted to be prove it could be different. I did a law degree while I was inside, and it was tough, I tell you, but since I got out, I've never looked back. I'm about to become a partner in a law firm and that's an achievement that gives me immense satisfaction.

Female

I'd always wanted to do voluntary work, ever since I qualified as a nurse. Marriage and children always got in the way of my plans, though, but now that the kids were older, there didn't seem any reason to put it off, even though I was coming up to my 50th birthday. And once I'd got their backing, there was no stopping me, really. Of course, I missed them all when I was there, but I just threw myself into my work. I had to really.

It was a very isolated rural area – there was no running water, no medicines and so much poverty. But I can't tell you how much I appreciate the fact that I was given the chance to go – it was a real eye-opener and I learnt so much about their culture and about myself – for that I'll always be thankful.

Male

I'd worked my way up to supervisor and got just about as far as I could go in the company. It was a responsible position and gave us a certain amount of security and I suppose that's why I stuck it for so long. Inevitably though, it got to the point where the routine just got too much. I wasn't developing professionally and nothing about the job pushed me to better myself. So when Sue suggested taking over a café franchise, I jumped at the chance. Neither of us had a background in catering but we refused to be daunted. We had to learn all aspects of the business in a very short time but I found it all very thrilling, and still do. Even now I wake up every day really looking forward to going in to work – being in a new environment and dealing with the fast pace.

Female

I'd been biting my nails since I was a three-year-old, apparently. It had never really bothered me before, despite my parents' constant moaning. They made me put this liquid on them called 'No-bite'. Tasted horrible, it did – until I got used to it, that was. When I started work, though, I began noticing the looks of mild horror on the customers' faces. Every time I was wrapping up a present or was just resting my hands on the counter, I could sense them staring and it made me incredibly self-conscious. So I had these plastic tips put on and that gave my nails the chance to grow. No one notices them anymore so the problem is essentially solved but it has nothing to do with my will power. It's actually humiliating for a 23-year-old to be wearing plastic tips. It's a secret I would hate my boyfriend to find out.

Note:

Speaker 4 mentions a franchise. One could paraphrase this with the word 'business'. Literally, a franchise is a right to sell a company's products in a particular area using the company's name. Franchises are often found in large department stores.

3 Give an example of something from your own life (it doesn't have to be true!), and supply suggestions; a new school, moving house, some news you received, or something like one of the speakers in the recording.

Vocabulary: Changes Page 27

A This task combines useful vocabulary input with fluency, given that most of the items should be known to students. They should give spontaneous definitions of those they know (as in the example) and ask another pair/group or use a dictionary for those they are unsure of.

Answers

Possible answers

your name	you don't like it/you become a performer/you get married (some women in some countries)
your mind	someone persuades you or you realize you're wrong/your opinion simply changes
your tune	(= to express a different opinion or behave differently) when your situation changes and it no longer interests you to express a certain opinion

gear	(on a bike or in a car) you want to increase or decrease your speed/you go up or down a hill
the subject	(= to start talking about a different thing) what you are talking about is embarrassing or causing people to get upset or angry
sides	you no longer share the opinions of the people or group (eg political party) you have previously supported
places	to see a film, play etc better/you want to sit next to someone else/you want to move to a non-smoking section
a tyre	when you have a puncture or when the tyre is bald (= worn down)
your ways	(= behave much better) after a period of time in prison or bad behaviour at school.

B/C These should be done as class writing activities, still in pairs.

Answers

B 1	**1** c	**2** d	**3** a	**4** b	
C 1 D	**2** C	**3** C	**4** A	**5** B	

Optional activity

Each student chooses a verb from C which was not one of the correct answers.

They write two sentences to show how the verb is used.

They leave gaps where the verb should be and give the sentences to their partner to complete.

Extra speaking task

Write the following on the board:

- something you try to vary in your life
- how easily you adapt to change
- a time when you have had to modify your views, behaviour or language
- the problems someone might encounter when converting to a different religion
- something which has changed significantly in your town or city in recent years
- any changes you would like to make to your lifestyle

While students are speaking, either use the monitoring technique suggested for fluency activities on page 20 of the Teacher's Book or make a note of some spoken errors that students have made. These can be examined after the activity or at the beginning of a new lesson.

Review 2 answers Pages 28 and 29

Language focus: Talking about the past

1 had been/gone/travelled/worked ...
2 Having achieved/fulfilled/realized
3 has worn
4 have played
5 was taken
6 would read/tell
7 been given/granted
8 did let

Vocabulary: Changes

1

1 Same: both mean 'to get used to a new situation by changing your behaviour and/or the way you think'.

2 Different: if you adjust a piece of clothing, you move it slightly and correct its position so that it is in the right place or more comfortable. eg *He looked in the mirror and adjusted his tie*. If you alter a piece of clothing, you make changes to it so that it fits better. eg *The jeans I bought are a bit too long, so I've asked my mum to alter them slightly.*

3 More or less the same: both mean to change a building in order to use it for a different purpose. ('Transform' perhaps emphasizes the fact that there has been a complete change.)

4 More or less the same: both express the idea of changing the negative aspects of your behaviour in order to make it more acceptable. 'Modify' usually suggests that these changes have been small.

5 Different: if you change your tune, you behave differently or express different opinions when your situation changes. eg *He always used to be criticizing management, but he soon changed his tune when he got promotion.* (See **4** for 'change your ways'.)

6 Different: if a restaurant varies the menu, it changes it regularly. If a restaurant adapts the menu, it makes changes to it to suit a particular situation or group of people eg vegetarians, children, a wedding party.

7 Same: both can have the meaning of no longer sharing the opinions of the people or group you previously supported.

8 Different: if a country switches to the euro, the euro is adopted as the official currency of that country, replacing the previous one. If someone converts money into euros, they change a certain amount of the money of their own country, in order to use it, for example, on holiday or on a business trip.

2

2 convert **3** adjust **4** switch **5** modify

Use of English: CAE Part 1 Multiple-choice cloze

1 In the second paragraph, the writer is negative. In the final paragraph, the writer is positive.

2

1 B	**3** D	**5** C	**7** A	**9** C	**11** C
2 A	**4** C	**6** D	**8** A	**10** B	**12** A

3 Gathering information

Content overview

Themes

This unit is concerned with the media and advertising, language and communication.

Exam-related activities

Paper 1	**Reading**
Part 1	Multiple choice
Part 2	Gapped text
Paper 2	**Writing**
Part 2	Reports
Paper 3	**Use of English**
Part 2	Open cloze (review)
Part 3	Word formation (review)
Part 5	Key word transformations (review)
Paper 4	**Listening**
Part 3	Multiple choice
Paper 5	**Speaking**
Part 3	Collaborative task

Other

Word formation	Adjectives and adverbs
Vocabulary	Smell
Language focus 1	Hypothetical past situations
Language focus 2	Present and future conditionals

Collaborative task

Page 30

Lead-in

- Students get into pairs and choose one of the pictures. They have three minutes to make notes on the advantages and disadvantages of each method.
- Ask a few pairs to feed back to the rest of the class, and allow others to comment on what has been said.
- Be ready to input ideas to keep the discussion flowing; eg political bias in newspapers, the 'dumbing down' of TV, the convenience of mobile phones, the poor standard of much information on the internet and the difficulties in finding what you want etc.
- Once enough good ideas have been raised by the class, turn to the Useful language section.

Useful language

Write the following on the board: 'I think the telephone is good because ... ', 'It's good for getting information.'

Tell students these phrases are grammatically ok, but are not really at CAE level. CAE requires a richer, more ambitious use of English, with plenty of variety.

- Check the meaning of some of the adjectives, by asking questions such as:
  Which adjective means you don't always get what you want? (= unreliable)
  Which adjective means giving the best advantage for the lowest price? (= cost effective)
  Which adjective could mean that a newspaper favours a particular political party? (= biased)
  Which adjective suggests the information given is wide-ranging? (= comprehensive)
  Which adjective suggests the information given is not enough? (= limited)
- Then students put P or N against each adjective, as instructed.

Answers

1 Positive: efficient/convenient/cost-effective
Negative: costly/unreliable/frustrating
2 Positive: accurate/up to date/comprehensive/reliable
Negative: biased/misleading/useless/limited

Now turn to the exam task. Ask students to form new pairs. They must close their note books, so they are speaking spontaneously.

- Remind them that the exam task involves a second element – they must decide which is most effective and which is least effective in providing information.
- Set a five-minute time limit on this.
- As you circulate, try to collect some examples from your students of rather bland or repetitive English. When the activity is finished, put them on the board and ask how they could be improved.

Reading 1: Multiple choice

CAE Part 1

Page 31

Read the rubric together and the first bullet point in the 'What to expect' box. Ask students to skim read the three texts, concentrating especially on the titles and opening sentences. Explain that you are going to give only a minute for this, as you do not want them to read in detail at this stage. Ask them in what way each text relates to the connecting theme (ie gathering information). You may need to give more help/input with the third text.

Answers

Suggested answers to activity in Teacher's Book
Text 1 is about some new sports shoes. A sensor in them gathers information about how much exercise the wearer has done.
Text 2 is about a man who receives a telephone call from a market research company doing a survey about insurance.
Text 3 is about junk mail. Market research companies gather information about people's lives, tastes and spending habits. They then sell this information to companies who wish to sell direct to the public at home. Alternatively, one could say that the recipient of junk mail is gathering information, assuming they actually read it!

Students will get a chance to discuss issues relating to these in the later 'Reacting to the texts' section, but it would be useful here to personalize the material in order to generate interest in the topic. Ask students questions such as: Have you come across any other examples of 'smart technology'? (eg in certain clothes shops now a smart machine bleeps if the top chosen by a member of the public does not match the trousers/skirt). Have you ever taken a call from a market research company? What was it about? Was it difficult to end the conversation? What kinds of junk mail do you or your parents receive? (Many are financial eg inviting people to take out a loan, others concern people's houses eg offering new windows, others are advertising a new product.)

Now read the second bullet point together from the 'What to expect' box. Draw students' attention to Questions 5 and 6. Point out that question 5 is about a small bit of text, whereas question 6 is about the whole text. The first sentence will give information ('In the first paragraph', 'throughout the extract') which helps students know where to look for the answer.

Put students into pairs for the reading task. Ask them to read the first text and look at questions 1 and 2 together, discussing which option is correct and why. When they are satisfied that they have the right answers, they move on to Text 2, and so on. Feed back with answers to the whole class only when everyone has finished the activity.

As a learner training activity, spend some time analysing where the answers come from in each text.

Answers

1 B 'The design was inspired ... British teenagers', and 'We looked at ... with my design.'
2 D the whole of the last paragraph, particularly 'But her shoe ... deceive.'
3 A 'I suppose I was ... other insurance claimants,'
4 C 'This' refers both backwards and forwards in the text. By reading on we know that 'this' is a process, which means that only C can be the answer.
5 D Lines one and four of the first paragraph.
6 B The cumulative evidence from the text is that the writer is being ironic and satirical. It is clear that he considers it to be a wasteful use of resources and harmful to the environment: 'the truly awesome consumption of natural resources' and 'The animals and insects that were wiped out when billions of acres of forest and moorland were turned over to single crop, factory, fir tree farming'.

Reacting to the texts
Students discuss these issues in pairs. It is useful to have other questions in reserve, such as: 'What is the computer equivalent of junk mail? Do you know of any ways of stopping junk mail, invasive phone calls and spam? Do you think companies should be allowed to target individuals in the privacy of their own home?

Language focus 1: Hypothetical past situations Page 33

A1 • Establish that, in the clause 'If only she had seen them,' Chrissy didn't see them. So if we then talk about her seeing them, the situation is unreal or, in other words, hypothetical.

Answers

1 a Yes
b The speaker is very unhappy about this.

Optional extra activity
Expand by writing the following on the board:

If only I was young again.
I wish I had been born a princess.
I'd rather you didn't smoke in here.
I'd rather you hadn't told him.

Ask students to say what time is being referred to for each sentence, and what the tense is.

Answers

Answers to extra activity in Teacher's Book

If only I was young again.	Time = present	Tense = past
I wish I had been born a princess.	Time = past	Tense = past perfect
I'd rather you didn't smoke in here.	Time = present	Tense = past
I'd rather you hadn't told him.	Time = past	Tense = past perfect

Elicit from them that with unreal/hypothetical situations time and tense are different. The tense is one stage further into the past than the time.

A2 Some students may not understand what is meant by 'the subject is the same'. Explain this with reference to the first example. 'I'd rather (subject = I) have seen it (subject = I)'. Compare 'I'd rather (subject = I) we went to the theatre (subject = we)'.

Answer

2 The sentences will refer to the present or future if the present infinitive is used.

Practice

1 have gone to France (instead)
2 you'd/you had phoned earlier
3 you hadn't done that
4 you'd/you had gone to university
5 have mentioned it before
6 to have stayed longer

B 1–3

- Point out the link between past conditionals and the previous exercises. Both refer to an unreal situation. Write the following sentence on the board:
  'If only I'd told him about the letter before he left for work that day. **If I'd told** him about the letter, our lives could have been so different.'
- Exercise 2 (matching) is an individual activity but exercise 3 can be done as a whole-class activity.

Answers

2

1 c **2** f **3** a **4** e **5** b **6** d

3

1 Sentences 1, 2, 3
2 Sentences 4, 5
3 Sentence 6

Draw attention to the mixed conditionals in this exercise. Point out that mixed conditionals like these are common. They are used (as in sentence 5) when we want to say 'If something had been different in the past, the consequence now would/could be this.'
Or they are used (as in sentence 4) to say 'If the situation were different now, this would/could have happened in the past.'

Optional extra activity
Write the following on the board, and ask students to finish the sentences, using mixed conditionals, in a suitable way:

If only I'd paid more attention at school ....
(consequence now)
If I hadn't gone to the disco that night ....
(consequence now)
If I wasn't married to Jack ....
(x would have happened)
If I was a bit more dynamic ....
(x would have happened)

Answers

Suggested answers to optional extra activity in Teacher's Book

I wouldn't be stuck in this miserable job now.
I wouldn't be married with three children now.
I'd have left this area a long time ago.
I would have applied for that surfing course.

Practice
1–3 Follow the instructions in the Coursebook.

Answers

1 Possible answers

1 He wishes he'd revised for his exams.
2 If I'd taken a few books with me on holiday, I might not have got bored.
3 If it hadn't been for Steve, we couldn't have got the car started.
4 I'd rather my parents had bought me a DVD player (than a video recorder).
5 I'd really like to have seen the film on telly last night.
6 I might have got the job if my French wasn't so bad/was better.
7 I'd rather have watched the football than looked at all their holiday snaps.

Word formation: Adjectives and adverbs Page 34

- Write the following on the board:
  I was beginning to feel distinctly uncomfortable.
  Perkins was comfortably the best player on the pitch.
- Put a circle round the 'un' and the 'y'. Ask students what the technical name is for the bits you have circled (= prefix and suffix).

- Ask if anyone knows in which part of the exam prefixes and suffixes are particularly tested. (clue Use of English – answer = Word formation task). Explain that we will now look at some prefixes and suffixes, and then relate this to Word formation.

1 Students follow the instructions in the Coursebook.

Answer

1 countless/heartless/pointless
Note that the suffix *-ful* cannot be added to these three nouns.

2 Go through the example with students, pointing out that although they all end in -ic, other changes need to be made to the base word.

Answers

1	approachable	applicable	believable
2	argumentative	administrative	provocative
3	introductory	contradictory	preparatory
4	chatty	muddy	rocky
5	luxurious	mysterious	monstrous
6	endless	priceless	sleepless
7	persistent	apparent	obedient
8	managerial	secretarial	territorial

Select any words that you think your class may not be sure of, and ask quick oral questions, such as:

Which word might describe a person who is easy to talk to if you have a problem? (= approachable)
Which word describes something you do that is intended to annoy someone? (= provocative).
Which word describes something you say which goes against what you said before? (= contradictory)
Which word means extremely valuable? (= priceless)

Extra activity
Write the following further common adjectival endings on the board:
-ful successful, careful, hopeful
-ary literary, precautionary, complimentary
-ible responsible, accessible, horrible
-ant defiant, resistant, tolerant
-ly daily, fatherly, cowardly
-ed amazed, delighted, pleased
-ish foolish, childish, shortish
-al alphabetical, global, seasonal

Ask students orally to put a few of them in phrases or sentences (eg in alphabetical order, seasonal work in the hotel industry, a literary agent, complimentary medicine). Then give them five minutes to supply three more adjectives in each category.

3 Students will need to make one or two changes to the words in bold.

Answers

1 imagin**ative**	5 knowledge**able**
2 **un**satisfact**ory**	6 hope**lessly**
3 increas**ingly**	7 substant**ial**
4 **dis**courte**ous**	8 strateg**ically**

After the answers have been given out, draw students' attention to number 8. The adjective suffix is '-ic'. The '-ally' adverb suffix is common in these cases. Consider for example, *scientifically*, *specifically*, *dramatically*, *stylistically*, *optimistically* but *publicly* (where *-ic* is not an adjectival suffix).

Writing: Reports Page 34
CAE Part 2

Optional lead-in

- Students will find it easier to engage with ideas about advertising in the report if they have discussed the topic in other ways.
- Bring some advertisements from magazines to the class, or make a recording of some advertising sequences from TV. Invite students to react to each one. Put the following on the board:

  What is the product?
  Who is the advert targeted at?
  What is the point of the advert?
  What techniques does it use to interest the reader/viewer?
  How effective is it?

- Then put the following on the board for students to discuss:

  Do you have advertising on all your TV channels?
  Are there any kinds of adverts that are not allowed?
  Describe a favourite advert to your partner.
  Is there anything which disturbs you about TV advertising?
  Is it acceptable for adverts to persuade people to buy products?

1 Students read the question and the two versions.

Answers

1 A is the better answer. The register is appropriately formal and shows a wider range of language (see **2** below).

2 • For a more detailed analysis, students should get into pairs. A confident class may be able to comment on the features spontaneously; a less confident class may need five minutes of individual preparation before an oral pairwork stage. Either way, encourage them to take their time and analyse in detail.
• 'Linking devices' means expressions such as 'on the other hand', but also includes other ways of linking ideas.

Note: The feedback for this activity is very comprehensive, for the benefit of the teacher. It is not necessary or desirable to read it all out! Let the students do most of the work, and use this reference guide to input additional information which they have missed.

2

linking devices

A More formal:

The aim of this report is to	*Equally distracting*
Moreover,	*Furthermore*
Unfortunately, however,	*On the other hand*
In addition	*Additionally*

A also links ideas by means of relative clauses
rural areas, where they appear unsightly
light aircraft, which fly for extended periods

and reference words
These add a touch of colour
This is largely due to

B Use of linking devices is rare and restricted to basic, more informal words such as:
And, But, also.

number of nouns

As a more formal piece of writing (see Unit 2) A has a far greater number of nouns, particularly abstract nouns such as *effectiveness, pithiness, concentration, irritation, location, consumption, originality.*

B relies more on verbs.

types of adjective

A More sophisticated and often as part of a collocation with a noun or adverb
eg *drab landscapes, memorable, unsightly, relatively common cause, equally distracting, extended periods, built-up areas, popular coastal resorts, harmful, mainstream alternatives*

Note also verb + (adj) + noun collocations
attract the attention of passers–by
lose their concentration
enjoying great success
reduce the risk of accidents

B More basic and often after the verb 'to be'
eg *funny, good, sad, grey, big, interesting, ugly, noisy, bad*

<u>Other differences</u>

organization of ideas

• The paragraphs are organized in the same way, namely:

1 Introduction
2 Positive aspects of Hoardings & Effectiveness
3 Negative aspects of Hoardings
4 Negative aspects of Aeroplane Advertising
5 Positive aspects of Aeroplane Advertising & Effectiveness
6 Recommendations

A, however, has given headings to four of the sections whereas B has not.
B has copied the content of the question almost word for word to write the introductory paragraph.

• The register of B is inappropriately informal throughout and contains numerous contractions eg *I'm going to describe* and *And they're very big too.*

• B relies heavily on repetition, showing a poorer vocabulary resource

<u>Specific references in A to writer's own country</u>
in my country (though students should mention their own country by name)
our otherwise drab urban landscapes
our built–up areas and popular coastal resorts
currently enjoying great success here

3 Students write their own report for homework.

Answers

How else could you structure your report?
Students could reverse the order of paragraphs 4 and 5. They might also have two recommendations paragraphs – one for each advertising medium.

Exam note:

- Writing a report in essay or letter format would be misunderstanding the task. Therefore, while candidates are not expected to write in perfect report format, they will impress if they can use underlinings/headings/bullets, for example.
- Reports also tend to have a clear beginning, stating the purpose of the report, who commissioned it, what its scope is etc and a clear conclusion at the end.

Sample answer

Introduction
The aim of this report is to describe the situation of two of the most important ways of advertising in Spain: TV and the sponsorship of sports.

TV
Undoubtedly, TV is the most important mass media. An advertisement broadcasted at prime time can grab the people's attention in a way absolutely unthinkable for any other form of publicity.

Nevertheless, the high price of this kind of advertising is an inconvenience that prevents companies from offering their products through TV. Moreover, the interruption of the programs with the best audience rating by an advertisement usually annoyes the viewers who, frequently, switch channel until the end of the break.

Sport
Nowadays, sport is one of the preferred pastimes of people. Consequently, the sponsorship of sports events or even the existence of teams with commercial names, like it happens in cycling, is a very profitable way of advertising.

However, something to take into account is the great rivality and hatred around the world of sport; the presence of a brand's name in a football team shirt may be free advertising for the competitors among the rival team supporters.

Recommendations
Since the high cost of a TV commercial is a considerable problem, a good solution could be the making of shorter adverts. The saving would be significant without affecting the effectiveness. In fact, the most resounding successes in the last years have been achieved by marketing campaigns whose adverts lasted few seconds.

As far as the sporting world is concerned, the key point is probably the carefulness at the time of choosing the event or team to sponsor. This decision can led either to a huge success or to a total failure.

By José Vicente Acín Barea

Examiner's comment

Content: The task has been completed reasonably well. It is informative and deals with each of the bulleted items. The introduction could be rather longer. More references could be made to the situation in Spain – this is, after all, the point of the report. In a few places the report reads a little like a discursive composition.

Organization and coherence: Report features are included and the writing is appropriately paragraphed. However, sentences are sometimes too long and slightly difficult to follow eg *'Moreover, the interruption of the programs with the best audience rating by an advertisement usually annoyes the viewers who, frequently, switch channel until the end of the break.'* It is not clear what is meant by the references to advertising for competitors.

Accuracy: The writing is generally accurate despite a few errors of word choice and spelling eg *'annoyes'*, *'rivality'*.

Range: There is evidence of a range of vocabulary and tenses in use, with some good collocations in the final section.

Register: The register is appropriately formal

Target reader: Would be fairly well informed (but see comments in *Content* section).

Mark: Band 3

Listening: CAE Part 3 — Multiple choice
Page 36

Lead-in

- Remind students that this unit has focused on the theme of communication. Now we move to a different aspect of this – language. Ask students what a 'minority language' is.
- Then explain that you will first look at some other key words on this topic, most of which are in the listening.
- Put the following on the board:
  decline status die out mother tongue
  native speaker

Ask students for some phrases or short sentences that show how the words are used – they should hopefully come up with ideas such as:

The decline of (Gaelic) has been very noticeable in recent years.
Attempts have been made by the government to give (Gaelic) higher status.
(Gaelic) is in danger of dying out unless ...
My mother tongue is ...
I am a native speaker of ...

1 The first four languages and their locations are mentioned in the listening.

Answers

Sami	northern Norway, Finland, Sweden and part of Russia
Breton	Brittany, north-west France
Ladin	South Tyrol, northern Italy
Provençal	Provence, south of France
Frisian	coastal area – northern Netherlands, north-west Germany, west of Denmark
Galego	Galicia, north-west Spain

2 Suggest students try the following listening strategy to cope with multiple choice.

- Elicit/explain the following possible difficulties with this task:
  (1) It is difficult to listen and read four options at the same time.
  (2) There is also a danger that if you spend too long reading the options and thinking about the answer, you will miss the answer to the next question.
  (3) This can mean you are unable to find your place again and miss all the other answers as well.
- It is important therefore to use the preparation time to get familiar with the questions. Students should underline the keywords in the questions. These then serve as 'markers' so that students know when to listen out for each question.
- Elicit possible underlinings as follows:
  Q1 Helena's journey
  Q2 problem of living in the mobile home
  Q3 the people she met
  Q4 punished for speaking Provençal
  Q5 local people in a tourist area
  Q6 language
- As they listen students should focus only on the question, not the options. They should answer it in their own mind. Then they should look very quickly at the four options to see which one is nearest to their answer.
- Play the recording. Students try out this technique. They can feed back on whether it helped them.

Answers

1 D **2** A **3** B **4** C **5** D **6** B

For variety give the answers by playing the CD again. Students follow in their books (page 227). Pause the recording at the underlined points, which are where the answers are located, in the script below, and explain why each answer is correct.

Listening script 1.10

(P = Presenter; H = Helena)

P: With me today on *Infospeak* is journalist and writer, Helena Drysdale. Hello, Helena, and welcome to the programme.

H: Thank you. Good morning.

P: Helena, you spent the last two years travelling round Europe doing research for a forthcoming book. What were you trying to find out?

H: Yes, we went in search of Europe's minority languages to determine exactly what state they're all in, particularly given today's climate of mass culture and so on. We travelled right up to northern Scandinavia and the Arctic circle, where the Sami reindeer herders live, and we got down as far as Corsica and Sardinia in the sunny Mediterranean. Then there were the mountains of northern Italy where Ladin is spoken, and we had a rather wet and rainy time in Brittany in the west of France with its Celtic Breton. Thirteen countries and fifteen minor languages in all.

P: By 'us' and 'we', you're referring to your family, of course.

H: Yes, my husband Richard, and our two young children, Tallulah and Xanthe – not forgetting the Mob, of course, our trusty mobile home.

P: What was that like? Two years together in a mobile home can't have been easy.

H: It got a little cramped at times, particularly when the weather kept us in. The kids couldn't run around, they'd start playing up, tempers would overheat, and everyone fell out. But apart from that, fine.

P: Yes, I can see. And how did you go about gathering your information? What were your sources?

H: I did some research in the library and on the Internet after we came back, but the only real way to get the kind of information I was looking for was by actually talking to people. We met writers, teachers and artists, who generally gave a more intellectual analysis of the situation, and we were able to balance that with the more down–to–earth, personalized accounts of people in the rural areas. That's where many of these languages are most frequently spoken and also where people, particularly the older generation, seemed less reluctant to open up and give us their honest opinion.

P: And I imagine they had some very interesting stories to tell about the past.

H: Yes, indeed. For example, we often heard stories of punishments that people received for speaking their own language at school. One old lady in the south of France told us how she used to have to wear a stone or a stick round her neck if she was caught speaking Provençal. She had to keep it on until someone else committed the same offence and then they'd have to wear it. And whoever had it at the end of the day was made to pay a fine, or sometimes even beaten.

P: Hard to believe, really.

H: Mm. She's able to laugh about it now, but at the time it was considered deeply shaming to have to wear le symbole, as she called it. Sometimes it could be a wooden shoe or a pottery cow, which represented the country bumpkin, someone to be despised.

P: And were these punishments effective? Did they contribute to the decline of some of these languages?

H: Yes, they lowered the status of a language. But sometimes they helped to keep a language going – at least in the short term, anyway. They caused resentment and made people more defiant towards the authorities. You know, it can be a bit like pruning a tree – if you cut it back, it grows much stronger. But there were and still are other more powerful forces which represent a much bigger threat to the survival of Europe's minority languages.

P: By that you mean globalization, I presume.

H: That's right. And tourism. Now although tourism can give a language status by attracting outside interest in it, it can also have a negative effect on local cultures. You know, in one place we visited, the natives moan about the influx of outsiders and how they buy up land at giveaway prices to build holiday cottages and how it's destroying their culture and so on. But then the very same people are selling up their farms so they can run hotels or open souvenir shops. Understandable, perhaps, but they're encouraging the very thing they're complaining about.

P: Are languages like Sami and Provençal endangered species, then?

H: Well, I think it's true to say that if no positive action is taken, they'll simply die out. The problem is that some people are indifferent, and even hostile to their own language. They think it's of no use in the modern world, which they so desperately want to be part of. Fortunately, though, there are enough people around who realize that to lose your mother tongue is like losing a part of yourself. Your language makes you who you are. And if you spoke a different language, you'd be a different person. But people on their own can only do so much. It really is up to the European Union to legislate to ensure the survival of minority languages.

P: And how exactly do you legislate to save a language?

H: Well, I think there are several things you can do. Firstly, of course, the EU would have to bring in ...

3 Speaking

Students answer the questions in pairs. You could extend the discussion to talk about different accents or dialects, and whether it is seen as acceptable for these to be used in schools/by presenters on TV etc.

Language focus 2: Present and future conditionals

Page 37

1 Present the three conditional types to the whole class, and ask them to match with the explanations.

Answers

Zero conditional: c
First conditional: b
Second conditional: a

2 Students read through the different ways of expressing first and second conditionals.

Answers

B The first sentence refers to the present.
The second one refers to the past.

3 Students correct the sentences.

Answers

1 broken	**3** would	**5** have
2 happen	**4** if	**6** to

If + will/would/going to

1 These are exceptions, where 'will' or 'would' etc can be used in the 'if' clause.

Answers

1 Insistence (stress 'will' very strongly when saying this)
2 Refusal
3 Result
4 Intention
5 Willingness

2 This exercise should involve a written and spoken element. This is a more creative stage, so students can think of examples relevant to their own lives or even introduce some humour into their examples. Take answers orally from various people in the class. This will help reinforce the grammatical form.

Reading 2: CAE Part 2 Gapped text Page 38

Photocopiable vocabulary exercise on page 150.

1 Give an example of your own favourite smell and why it is particularly evocative for you in order to get the ball rolling. Students might do this activity in pairs, but be sure to get whole class feedback on the last question about precautions, as this leads into the text students are going to read. If no answers are forthcoming on this, prompt students with 'what about food? And danger in the house?'

2 Read out the first bullet point in the 'How to go about it' section. The 'base text' (ie the text from which the gaps have been removed) is designed to contain most of the important information – candidates should be able to read the base text and get a fair idea of what the text is about. So encourage them to get into the habit of reading the base text first without looking at any of the gapped sections.

Answers

Smell is part of the body's reaction system to danger. (paragraph after gap 2).
If we have no sense of smell we may not be able fully to appreciate food (paragraph after gap 3).
Smells are often the trigger that give us 'flashbacks' of memory. These things can be very powerful and make our lives richer. (paragraph after gap 4).

Then look at the second bullet point.

- Do gap 1 as a whole class to show how the linking of ideas works. Explain that most of the gapped sections will link both backwards to the paragraph before them and forwards to the paragraph after them.
- The first paragraph in the base text tells us that the writer was born without a sense of smell. Gapped paragraph E picks up on this idea – there are clues both in the reference to her age and in the word 'this'.
- E speaks of a particular occasion which convinced the writer's mother that her daughter could not smell. The words 'That experience' in the main text refer directly to that occasion.

Point out that students should underline the words in the gapped paragraphs A–G which link back-wards or forwards to something in the main text.

Answers

1 E **2** A **3** G **4** B **5** F **6** C
D is the extra paragraph

B 'About 17% ... going out.'
C 'Steroid-based drug treatments can help further', 'treated medically' and 'less can be done to rectify causes one is born with'.
E The first sentence connects backwards and the whole of the second tells an anecdote which connects forwards.
F 'taking you back in time' and 'pass on two sets of immunity advantages to your offspring.'
G The first sentence connects backwards and the last sentence connects forwards.

Exam note:

- Students should look out for clues such as pronouns (he, her, this) in a gapped paragraph, which indicate that a person has probably been named in the previous paragraph.
- However, in many cases there are no such linguistic clues. The gaps can only be placed by looking at the logical flow of ideas through the text (coherence).

Vocabulary: Smell Page 39

Students follow the instructions for exercises 1–4 in their books. Vary the interaction focus between whole class treatment and pairwork, writing and speaking. 1b could be done as a fun spoken activity.

Exercises 2 and 3 would best be done in pairwork, as dictionary use may be needed.

Answers

1a

1 smoke, bodies
2 coffee, bacon
3 rubber, fumes
4 milk, date
5 spices, fruit

1b Possible answers

2 a kitchen or a café
3 an airport runway or a car racing track
4 a fridge in an abandoned house **5** a market

2–3

Positive	**Negative**	**Neutral**
mouth-watering	stale	pungent (often negative)
fresh	acrid	strong (often negative)
sweet	rancid	unmistakable
	sickly	faint
	musty	
	overpowering	

4 Possible answers

your classroom	an unmistakable odour
a rose garden	a pungent aroma
disinfectant	an overpowering smell
old books	a musty smell
freshly baked bread	a mouth-watering aroma
your favourite cheese	a strong smell
decaying rubbish	a sickly odour

Review 3 answers Page 40 and 41

Use of English: CAE Part 3 Word formation

1 global
2 suspicion
3 factual
4 editorial/editing
5 objective
6 reliable
7 inaccuracy/inaccuracies
8 controversial
9 expertise
10 trustworthy

Use of English: CAE Part 2 Open cloze

1 was
2 more
3 by
4 which
5 then/and
6 more/longer
7 in/with
8 A
9 had
10 not/hardly/barely
11 way
12 off
13 to
14 can/may
15 its

Use of English: CAE Part 5 Key word transformations

This is the first time students have met this type of task. In Unit 4 we give more detailed information and strategies for dealing with this task.

Tell students that this task is testing their ability to 'paraphrase', in other words to say things in another way. This is very important in the exam as a whole.

Look at the example sentence together. Write the following on the board:
The words you write must
- use the given word
- connect with what follows the gap.

Thus, in the example,
- 'refuses to' in the first sentence becomes 'turns down'
- 'ask your parents' becomes 'our request'
- the preposition 'for' must be put in to fit the grammar of the second sentence.

Do item 1 in whole-class mode, in the same way. Elicit the following from the class:
- In the first sentence the speaker is expressing a regret. When we use 'I wish …' for a past regret, we need the past perfect, ie 'I wish I had …'. In the text 'I wish we had …' is used as the speaker is talking about a holiday they went on with somebody else.
- The verb which fits with 'on holiday' is 'go'. If we are using past perfect, this must be the past participle of 'go' ie 'gone'.
- This only leaves the given word, which goes in the middle, ie 'had never gone'.
  Students try the rest of the task in pairs.

Answers

1 we had never gone
2 you had kept my news secret
3 would prefer to have given/would have preferred to give
4 not for his strange sense of
5 should/if you happen to come, if you should happen to come
6 he does/will keep (on) turning/showing
7 would probably not have/probably would not have come/jumped
8 have given Tom a second chance/opportunity

Ready for Reading

CAE Paper 1

Reading

Part 1 Multiple choice (short)
Part 2 Gapped text
Part 3 Multiple choice (long)
Part 4 Multiple matching

This is the first of five 'Ready for … ' units which focus on the five different skills areas tested in the CAE exam: Reading, Writing, Use of English, Listening and Speaking. In each of these 'Ready for … ' units there is a clear explanation of the different kinds of exercise types students can expect to find in the exam. This serves to give the students a useful overview and summary of each paper. Students are also provided with and reminded of useful strategies that they should use in the exam to help improve their performance.

Although the material is designed for classroom use it is suitable for individual study and the Reading, Writing and Use of English units can also be set for homework.

The material in these units can be worked through step by step, as indicated in the Coursebook, or you may decide to select from the suggested guidance exercises depending on your particular class and the time available.

Whatever approach you decide to use, encourage students to justify their answers.

Introduction

Good time management is essential in the Reading paper, where there is a heavy load of long texts. It is very important for students to appreciate the importance of not reading and understanding every word of the text.

Parts 1 and 3: Multiple choice Page 42

1 In addition to opinions, attitudes and the author's purpose, questions might also focus on gist, inference and features of text organization.

2 The writer certainly feels the record is worth buying. He says the music is powerful and full of conviction, all the more so for Rea's brush with death, and much better than Rea's previous 'middle-of-the road hits.' He also praises the instrumentals, especially the guitar solo.

3 Refer students to the second bullet point in the 'What to expect' box, then ask them to do the task. You may also wish to refer them to the 'How to go about it' box in Unit 1 (page 7).

Answers

1 C *that would make the world reappraise their idea of Chris Rea.*
2 A *I began to wonder if my throwaway comment had proved to be the final straw in the mind of some EastWest executive that a double was out of the question.*
3 D *A man who … saw a career for himself along the lines of guitarist Ry Cooder found himself instead bracketed for his vocals alongside Dire Straits and Phil Collins.*
4 D *he blames himself for being too compliant.* (and following quote)
5 C *I don't know how many copies the new album will sell.*
6 C *This is real pain he's talking about.* (and following quote)
7 A *is surprisingly radio-friendly … catchy tunes*

Now refer students to the third bullet point in the 'What to expect' box. We focus here on distraction in an awareness raising activity. The three wrong options are definitely wrong, but there may be something in them to tempt you if you have not understood the ideas in the text, or if you have not read carefully enough. This is distraction.

Explain this with reference to the example (1). If you don't read the text carefully enough, you might think that *(1) I added that it might benefit from being a little shorter* sounds very similar to option *A He preferred its length to that of his other work*. In fact, if you read carefully, you see that option A is actually the opposite of what the text is saying at this point.

Put students in pairs to complete the task.

Answers

These are the distractors which refer to the remaining highlighted sections of the text.

2 B **3** B **4** A **5** A **6** B **7** D

Part 2: Gapped text Page 44

Photocopiable vocabulary exercise on page 151.

Note: In the exam paper, the base text comes before the paragraph options.

1 The main text will contain most of the key information. A skim read of it should give students a fair idea of what the text is basically about.

2–3 There are no correct answers here, but the base text mentions the following:

Answers

making a pizza: shape balls of dough into a perfect circle using your hands only. This involves covering it with flour, pressing out the dough at the edges, slapping it with the palm of the hand and twirling it to shake off the flour. Then it is covered in tomato sauce and mozzarella cheese and put into a hot oven.

going wrong: He had problems shaping the dough to make a circle. The wet dough got stuck to his fingers. Then he overdid the stretching and pressing with the result that his pizza was all thick edges and had a hole in the thin centre.

4–5 Exercises 4 and 5 could be done simultaneously. Or, students complete exercise 4 first and then use the information they have found to help them complete the gaps correctly.

Answers

4 Possible answers

1 He might feel depressed or it might make him more determined to get it right the next time. We know from our reading of the base text that he makes two further attempts.
He might have cooked and eaten it, or thrown it away. (See 5 below)

2 *it* is probably the dough, and *he* is Francesco. Francesco is most certainly not struggling; some mention of this contrast with the author may be made in the missing paragraph.

3 He probably hasn't finished; as yet he only has a small round circle, but not a full-sized pizza base. The 'Now it was my turn' that follows suggests that the missing paragraph will continue to focus on Francesco's pizza making.

4 He will probably become nervous and make mistakes. Note the 'to my horror' of the preceding paragraph. Note also the 'Then the worst thing of all happened' of the following paragraph, which suggests that something bad might have happened previous to this.

5 He clearly progresses well, as the content of the following paragraph tells us.
We are told that 'my second pizza went where the first one had gone: on the fire'.

6 Some mention will probably be made of 'the best place for (the pizza) in the oven'.
The pronouns refer to the pizzas of the author and Francesco. These will be mentioned in the missing paragraph.

Answers

5

1 F 2 A 3 D 4 G 5 C 6 B

Part 4: Multiple matching Page 46

1 Draw students' attention to the sentence 'It is not necessary to read every word in the text to complete the task.' Point out that it is also not necessary to understand every word. This is especially true of this text, which contains a lot of 'ski' words which non-skiers may not be familiar with. Demonstrate this through the following activity.

Activity

Put the following extracts from the text on the board:

1 What I love about this run is that it's got the lot: cornices, wind lips, powder fields and trees. (section C)

2 so you'll need to beware of the extra hazards that this throws up, such as crevasses lurking unseen. (section D)

3 generous reds and challenging moguls (section E)

Point out that in 1, we do not need to know the exact meaning of cornices, wind lips and powder fields. It is enough to know that they are all aspects of this run which the writer enjoys. They are obviously technical terms known by expert skiers. In 2, it is enough to know that crevasses are unseen hazards (dangers). Again this information can be found by reading the text around the difficult word. In 3, the word 'mogul' may not be known, but we know from 'runs' (two lines previously) that a mogul must be a type of run.

Note to teachers
Note also that most of the technical ski vocabulary is not tested in the questions. An exception is 'grooming' which is part of the targeted text for Question 9. This question is an example of students being expected to use context to understand meaning. Students can get to the likely meaning of grooming by appreciating that in this paragraph it is piste preparation that is being talked about.

2 It is important to interact with the text first, to form an opinion of what you are reading. This means reading for the 'big ideas' in the text, rather than the detail. Naturally, a class of skiers could also be asked which of the five slopes they would choose to ski down.

Possible answer

They are clearly enthusiasts with a lot of technical knowledge.

3 This simply means, for example, that questions 12 and 13 could be written A/B or B/A.

Look at the 'How to go about it' box and follow the instructions with the class. These instructions follow the procedure recommended in the early units of the Coursebook. For more details see the Teacher's Book notes for the Multiple matching task in Unit 2 (page 25 of Teacher's Book) which also gives an alternative strategy for this task type. Answers for text A are included in the key below.

Answers

1 C Normally, trees can be tricky for snowboarders, but these are just right.
2 A It's important to pick a run that isn't too tough.
3 E It's not the kind of place you start admiring the view – which is a shame
4 B you can follow it for 8km down to the resort, or branch off towards Valtournenche and go even further
5 D you'll need to beware of the extra hazards that this throws up, such as crevasses lurking unseen
6 E a sheer drop on the other, screened with safety nets
7 A Once they've mastered the basic skills, the big hurdle for skiers is the run that gives them their first serious mountain experience.
8 C is tucked away across the valley from Verbier and you'll get a good idea of how busy it is over there compared to your side of the valley.
9 B they are fanatical about their piste-grooming.
10 E a dramatic close-up of the imposing Eiger, Monch and Jungfrau, which rise up on the other side of the valley
11 A Ski it once, and you'll feel you've finally made it into the ranks of the grown-ups.
12 C/D in any order a guide is a must the first time you attempt it
13 D/C you must have a guide to show you the way.
14 B the quality of the snow, especially along the upper reaches, is superb.
15 A they could end up scaring themselves silly, and it could take them years to learn how to enjoy themselves on skis again.

4 Work time

Content overview

Themes

This unit is concerned with work and jobs.

Exam-related activities

Paper 1	**Reading**
Part 4	Multiple matching
Paper 2	**Writing**
Part 2	Formal letters: application
Part 2	Character reference
Paper 3	**Use of English**
Part 4	Gapped sentences
Part 5	Key word transformations
Paper 4	**Listening**
Part 2	Sentence completion
Part 4	Multiple matching

Other

Vocabulary	Time
Language focus 1	Punctuation
Language focus 2	Gerunds and infinitives

Optional lead-in

1 Brainstorm jobs with the whole class.

2 Select a few students and ask them each for three jobs they would be interested in doing. Then ask a few other students for their career plans over the next five years or so. Students will no doubt have considered this in their first languages, but not necessarily expressed their wishes in English.

Language focus 1: Punctuation Page 48

Note: Tell students to ignore the mistakes in each quotation – they will be dealt with later.

1 It can be difficult to work with 'raw' quotations like this, so spend some time going through each quote, and elicit from students what is the main idea/discussion point in each quote.

1. Life is all about enjoying yourself/work is just to pay the bills.
2. No point in working too hard/work is not the most important thing in life.
3. self-explanatory
4. I pretend to like work but actually I never do any.
5. What is more valuable – a university degree or attending 'the university of life'?
6. Quality versus quantity. People who work long hours don't necessarily achieve good results.
7. It is through their work that a person is defined (an idea traditionally expressed about men).

Allow five minutes or so for students to discuss.

2 Before students try this activity, put the following on the board and run through the English terminology for them:

,	comma
.	full stop
'xxxxxx' or "xxxxxx"	speech/quotation marks
-	dash/hyphen
it's	apostrophe (pronounced /ə'pɒstrəfi/)

Answers

1 avoided."	**4** me. I	**6** It's
2 chance?"	**5** don't	**7** offers
3 People who		

3 Students work individually to punctuate the article, putting what they have learnt from the Grammar reference section into practice. Tell them it may help if they 'say' the text to themselves in their heads (ie they imagine themselves reading it out aloud).

4 Direct students to the Additional material section in the coursebook.

Draw attention to selected points, such as:

- There is normally no comma after the penultimate items in a list.
- Words like 'moreover' and 'however' need a comma after them if they come at the beginning of the sentence, and need commas around them if they come in the middle of the sentence.

5 Background information – With many people now having home computers, and with the cost of time wasted in travelling to work, many companies are now taking a practical attitude towards home-working. Typically this might be one day spent at home per week, or allowing home-working in particular tasks that do not need to be done in the workplace. Some companies are now using the prospect of some 'home-working' as a way of attracting newly-qualified graduates.

If students have difficulty coming up with ideas, here are some that you might introduce:
Pros: It enables greater flexibility in juggling your home and work life, such as being able to visit the dentist, being at home to collect children from school etc.
Cons: It is easy to be distracted, so you have to be very self-disciplined. Your working life invades your home life, which can cause stress and arguments with other members of your family.

Writing 1: CAE Part 2 Formal letters: application Page 49

1 Background note: Personal Assistants, or PAs, are attached to managers, and perform a range of secretarial and other duties. Their importance tends to mean they are on a higher level than secretarial/administrative staff.

Answers

Suggested answers
possess good communication skills, be well-organized, have relevant experience, an eye for detail, an ability to work well under pressure, an ability to work to deadlines, an ability to use your initiative, be dynamic, of smart appearance, versatile etc.

Put the answers on the board, as they are likely to produce some useful, current expressions, such as the above.

2 See if students can spot which exam task this is practising (Use of English, Part 1, Multiple-choice cloze).

Before students attempt the task, put the following on the board and ask for an explanation of what they are:

a character reference/a referee (= a letter from someone who knows you well in support of your application/the person who writes the letter)
give two months' notice (= tell your employer that you intend to leave your job. Most jobs have a specified period of notice. In this case, you must tell your employer two months before you intend to leave.)

Students try the exercise individually and then compare answers with a partner.

Answers

The following are incorrect:

1 apply
2 must
3 enveloped
4 destined
5 place
6 number
7 chores
8 conduct
9 sorting
10 learned
11 rise for
12 own
13 complete
14 welcome
15 actual

As students give their answers, write on the board those answers which have fixed phrase/collocation status:

in reply/response to your advertisement
the/my enclosed/attached CV/letter etc
the post/position of
the day-to-day management/running of the office/department etc
making/organizing travel arrangements
acquire/gain experience
respond to/take up the challenge (also: rise to)
deal with/meet the demands of the job

Encourage students to record these in phrase form.

Background notes:

- While students will not lose marks for not knowing such conventions, the correct convention in formal letter writing is:

Dear Sir or Madam (when you don't know the name of the addressee) → Yours faithfully
Dear Mr Smith (when you know the name of the addressee) → Yours sincerely

- Dear Sir is correct, but going out of usage. Dear Sir/Madam is more politically correct.
- While bigger companies tend to have their own application forms for job vacancies, many smaller companies still use the more personal and traditional CV + covering letter.

3 This task could be set for homework. Students should use the letter from Lara Goodrich as a model. Run through the advice in the 'How to go about it' box beforehand.

Answers

Answers to How to go about it

Paragraph organization in Lara Goodrich's letter
1 Reasons for writing
2 Relevant experience

3 Reasons for applying. Suitability for job.
4 Availability
5 Closing comment

Listening 1: Multiple matching
CAE Part 4

Page 50

1 Use this brainstorming session to build vocabulary on the board. Aim to get a board full of useful language such as:

keep a cool head
don't get flustered
arrive in good time
check out any company literature on display (eg brochures) before your interview
maintain eye contact – look people in the eye when you speak
keep a good body posture – don't slouch
be confident and relaxed – try to smile
have a few questions about the company 'up your sleeve'
keep/stick to the point when you answer questions
don't ramble/stray from the point when you answer questions
be yourself – don't try to show off or invent details

2 Go through the 'How to go about it' box with students. In particular, draw their attention to:

First bullet point – It is very important for students to follow the wording of the two tasks. This will usually be different from the focus in the main rubric (ie in this task 'talking about interviews they attended').

Third bullet point – You hear all five speakers on the first play. Then you hear them all again on the second play. Students who use the first play to listen for task one and the second play to listen to task two are taking a risk. They are limiting their listening to a 'once only' task.

Also note – Each of the five extracts is a different speaker. Extract 1 contains the answer to questions 1 and 6. In this part of the test, the answer for task two may come before the answer for task one in each extract.

Possible approach (see alternative approach below)
Begin the task. As the procedure is complicated, go through the first question together.

- Play the first extract only. Ask students to look at both tasks, but concentrate more on the first task.
- Then play the extract again – but do point out that this will not happen in the exam. Tell students to complete questions 1 and 6.
- Feed back with the answers. 1D – 'I was told the best way to prepare for an interview is by going to the company's website and finding out everything you can about them.' 6B 'The trouble was that they hadn't done theirs – the webpage hadn't been updated for over a year.'

Then do the rest of the task, questions 2–10 without further pauses to the recording.

Alternative approach
If you feel your students need more help with the task, play each extract with books closed and get students to recall the information.

- Play the first extract and get students in pairs to recall as much as they can.
- Then repeat the extract and get students to recall any information they missed first time round.
- Then allow students to open their books and look at the questions 1–10. They answer in pairs.
- Then play the extract a third time for them to check their answers.
- Repeat this procedure for each of the five extracts.

Answers

1 D	3 H	5 G	7 D	9 C
2 F	4 A	6 B	8 F	10 G

Play the recording one more time, allowing students to read the script at the same time, to check their answers.

Listening script 1.11–1.15

Speaker 1
I was told the best way to prepare for an interview is by going to the company's website and finding out everything you can about them. The idea, of course, is that it creates a good impression and proves that you are keen on working for them because they can see you've done your homework. The trouble was that they hadn't done theirs – the webpage hadn't been updated for over a year, so I asked all these questions about products they didn't produce and subsidiaries that no longer existed. They must have thought I wasn't very well prepared. It wasn't my fault, though, and I kind of lost enthusiasm for the job once I found out what had happened. I mean, it's a bit slack, isn't it?

Speaker 2

So there I was the night before, in the living room talking to the dog. A bit strange, you might think, and you'd probably be right. But I was getting ready for the next day, you see. The dog was the interviewer, and I was trying out all my questions and answers on him. I'm not sure that's what the writer of the article had in mind when she said, 'Rehearse the situation with a friend', but it seemed like a good idea to me. Anyway, it was all a bit of a waste of time really. I overslept the next morning and by the time I got there they'd already taken somebody on.

Speaker 3

'Now you're not to get all uptight and on edge, like you normally do,' was what my mum said. And that's more or less what the careers teacher told us at school: 'Projecting self-confidence at an interview is vital for success'. Those were his exact words. So I put on my best suit to give me that confidence, cleaned my shoes and off I went. Well, my hands were shaking so much, you wouldn't believe it. I nearly spilt my coffee down my trousers. I think I managed to hide it, though. Course, what I couldn't hide was the fact that I'd failed my maths GCSE. They wouldn't take me on without it. Shame, really – the money wasn't too bad.

Speaker 4

'Don't lean back in your chair', he says. 'If you do that, it might look as though you're trying just a bit too hard to cover up your nerves. Either that or you're not interested in the job.' So according to this Dr Benson, it's advisable to lean forward, keep your legs uncrossed and smile confidently. Well, I did all that. In fact, I smiled so much my face began to ache. But they somehow seemed to realize that I don't normally walk around with a permanent grin from ear to ear – they said they were looking for lively, bubbly people for their sales team, and they weren't convinced that I fitted the bill.

Speaker 5

I saw this video in the university careers office where they recommended imagining the interviewer in the bath, playing with a plastic duck, of all things. The idea is that they're only human, so there's nothing to be frightened of. So, anyway, I thought about the type of questions they might ask me and I got to the interview about half an hour early so I could go over the answers I was going to give. But, bath or no bath, the interviewer turned out to be not so human after all. It was like an interrogation, and the things he asked were really tricky – nothing like what I'd prepared for. I just didn't know what to say. I felt pretty sick about the whole thing afterwards, I can tell you.

3 Students answer in pairs.

Language focus 2: Gerunds and infinitives Page 51

A–B Note: If this grammar point is likely to be revision for your class, treat A and B as revision, and let students speak and write the answers in pairs. When they have finished they can read the Grammar reference section on page 219. Then they go back and check their answers.

If this grammar point needs teaching to your class, look first at the Grammar reference section before doing A and B.

A The meaning of item 3 may prove difficult for students. 'You're not to' means 'You must not'. 'Uptight' and 'on edge' both mean nervous/agitated.

Answers

A Review

2 Modal verbs (*can, should, must* etc) are followed by the infinitive without 'to'

3 Here, the verb 'to be' + infinitive is used to give a kind of order.

4 If the verb is the subject of the sentence, the gerund is usually used.

5 The infinitive of purpose (to = in order to), giving the reason why he put on his best suit.

6 'manage' is followed by the infinitive of the verb.

7 'to be' + adjective + infinitive

8 'recommend' is followed by the gerund (or object + infinitive – see 7 in section B Common problems)

B Common problems

1 a *let me leave/allow me to leave*
'let' is followed by an object and the infinitive without 'to'. 'Allow' is also followed by an object, but is used with the full infinitive.

2 b *get used to sharing*
'to' is a preposition in both sentences and is therefore followed by the gerund

3 a *It's not worth making*
'It's not worth' and 'There's no point' (and 'It's no use') are all followed by the gerund

4 b *would like you to be*
'would like' (+object) + infinitive. The use of the possessive adjective 'your' before a gerund (appreciate your agreeing) is typical of more formal English. The object pronoun 'you' would also be possible.

5 b *stop ringing*
'stop + gerund'; 'stop' can be used with the infinitive of purpose, meaning 'you stop doing one thing *in order to* do another' eg 'He stopped eating (in order) to have another cigarette'. This is not the case here in sentence b). ('Start' can be used with the infinitive or the gerund, with no difference in meaning.)

6 a *mind going*
'mind' + gerund

7 b *recommended him to have/recommended having/recommended (that) he (should) have*
the infinitive is only used with 'recommend' if 'recommend' is followed by an object.

8 b *breaking/having broken* 'admit to doing something'. In this case, 'breaking' would be a more elegant answer, avoiding the repetition of 'have' and 'having'.

B2 Don't let this activity go on too long. The point is simply to get students using the target structures in a personalized way.

C When going through the answers, make the important point that the language practised in this exercise is typical of formal written English. Put the following on the board to reinforce this point:

She tends to → She has a tendency to
He has tried very hard to → He has made a great effort to
He is unable to → He lacks the ability to

Answers

C

1 determination, effort
2 tendency, attempts
3 opportunity, refusal
4 capacity, decision
5 willingness, ability

Reading: CAE Part 4 — Multiple matching

Page 52

Photocopiable vocabulary exercise on page 151 of the Teacher's Book.

1 Allow students to read the introduction below the title in order to answer this question. As with many newspaper articles, the title is a clever play on words. A young businessperson who shows great talent may be earmarked by their boss for a senior managerial role within the company in the future. They are put on the 'fast track' for promotion. In other words, they can expect to be promoted more rapidly than is normally the case. 'Burnout' occurs when people work too hard and feel they cannot go on. The normal phrase in business circles is 'The Fast Track to Management', so the title of this article is making the point that a lot of young 'high-fliers' are being pushed too hard by their employers.

2 Ask students if they can remember the procedure for dealing with Multiple Matching. Then refer them back to the 'How to go about it' box on page 24 of Unit 2 to check.

Students complete the task.

Answers

Possible answers for underlinings of items

5 showing off the things she could afford
6 accepted the job, benefits that were additional to the salary
7 young age, unable to cope, stressful situation
8 find a way to leave, before
9 people she worked with, could not relate to
10 lack of money in her childhood, high salary more desirable
11 other people could have done her job
12 does not have any negative feelings
13 feelings, quickly changed
14 One of her qualities, disadvantaged
15 wanted more freedom, still young

Answers

1 C 2 A 3 D 4 B

5 A I got sucked in too at first – you'd make sure other people knew what designer labels you were wearing, that they could see your cell phone was top of the range

6 C She accepted the one that was offering perks such as free tickets to major sporting events and a flash company car.

7 B The whole experience was quite traumatizing and I was too emotionally immature to deal with it.

8 C But, exceptionally, in her case, she had already been looking for an escape route

9 D 'My colleagues seemed utterly mystified and tried to talk me out of it.'

10 A 'We weren't poor but I don't think my parents ever bought anything that wasn't secondhand. That definitely played a role in my motivation.'

11 C '... but there were plenty of workmates perfectly able to step into my shoes,' she admits

12 A Tanya Burrows bears no grudge towards the corporation that rewarded her with five promotions within the same number of years. 'At twenty-seven, I was able to buy my own luxury apartment,' she says. 'For that reason I'll always be grateful to them.'

13 B after receiving news of the promotion she was elated. 'I rang round just about everyone I could think of,' she laughs. 'But the next day I felt nothing. I had no inclination to get out of bed and face the constant pressure.'

14 D She admits to being a perfectionist, an attribute which saw her rise through the ranks in no time. 'It's a weakness, too,' she says. 'It can mean that you're reluctant to delegate and end up with the pressure of doing it all yourself.'

15 C 'I felt I should have been carefree at that age but the burden of responsibility was enormous. I felt trapped.

Use of English: CAE Part 4 Gapped Sentences

Page 54

1 To link this exercise with what has been studied, point out that these collocations all appeared in the reading text. Students should try the exercise without looking back at the text, but afterwards can check their answers in the text.

Answers

1 grudge **2** role **3** position/role **4** pressure **5** favour **6** contract **7** ranks **8** notice

2 While students are doing exercise 1, write the answers to exercise 2 in jumbled order on the board. Students should do this exercise by first referring to the reading text and then by matching the collocations to the definitions on the board.

a support or agree with something
b be given a series of promotions
c be an influence in a particular situation
d gain a (better) job in the same company
e be given the chance to work for a company
f have to deal with difficult or stressful situations
g inform your boss (usually in writing) that you intend to leave your job
h continue to dislike someone because they once treated you badly or unfairly

Answers

1 h **2** c **3** d **4** f **5** a **6** e **7** b **8** g

3 Relating this to the exam, make the point that the gapped sentences task sometimes tests collocation (at other times it merely tests knowledge of multiple meanings of a word). As it is the first time we have encountered the gapped sentences task, a little help is given – the missing words are all somewhere in exercise 1.

Answers

1 position **2** bear **3** face **4** favour **5** rise

Further practice activity in Teacher's Book
Write the following on the board. Here the words students wrote in exercise 3 feature with different word partners.

a) ______ a difficult challenge/an uncertain future/ the awful truth
b) ______ dramatically/to the challenge/to fame
c) a sitting/kneeling/upright ______
d) ask/expect/return a ______
e) ______ bad feelings towards/no relation to/some responsibility for

Answers

Answers to further practice activity in Teacher's Book
face rise position favour bear

Exam note:
In the gapped sentences task there are five sets of three sentences. For each set candidates find one word that can complete each sentence.

Listening 2: CAE Part 2 Sentence completion Page 55

1 This is a much used quote in English, and a common complaint people make when they are stressed. It could refer to the various people in the reading text on burnout. Ask this question to various students in whole class mode. Ask them about their studies, homework, tasks they have to do at home, and so on.

2 Remind students to use the time allowed profitably – during the pause in the CD they should read the questions and remember what kind of information they are listening for.

Alternative approach
If you would like to give your students more help with the task, ask them to close their books and put their pens down. Say that when the CD has finished, you are going to ask the whole class to say in their own words, five or six of the pieces of advice that the expert gives about time management.

Answers

1 (forward) planning
2 realistic
3 tiredness
4 (our) health
5 achieve perfection
6 self-discipline
7 (most) fulfilling
8 television

During feedback on the answers, if some students have missed an answer it can be useful to replay the relevant part of the CD. For this reason we have underlined the answers in the listening script.

Listening script 1.16

Time, ladies and gentlemen, is one of our greatest assets, and in this fast-moving competitive world, poor management of our time is a major cause of stress both in the workplace and at home. The first and most essential element of *effective* time management is **forward planning**. If you start the morning by mapping out what you hope to achieve during the day, you can go a long way to avoiding unnecessary frustration and wasted effort. Be **realistic**, though, in terms of what you hope to achieve ***in*** the time available, and think through carefully how and when you will achieve it. Unmet expectations will only serve to put you under more pressure, to create more stress – and you'll only have yourself to blame if that happens.

Of course, **tiredness** – rather than any lack of ability – can often present a major obstacle to our obtaining the goals we've set ourselves, or indeed to meeting the deadlines that others have set for us. If that's the case, stop, turn your computer off, take a break. If you feel you can't go on, or you're just too snowed under, don't make yourself ill. Work should always take second place to your **health**. It can be counterproductive to carry on regardless, particularly if the next day you have to phone in sick and take time ***off*** work.

And also, if time is ***against*** you, if you're pressed ***for*** time, be prepared to adapt to the circumstances – don't worry if what you produce is less than wonderful. We cannot, we *should* not always aim to **achieve perfection**. It slows us down, it reduces productivity and means we have no time for other tasks. Good enough is still good, and in all probability no one will notice the difference. And the same principles apply in the home as they do at work. A similar dose of **self-discipline** is needed when we take on the household chores. Limit the amount of housework you try to do in a day, lower your expectations and relax if the shirts you've just ironed still have creases. It *doesn't matter*.

Because ultimately, let's face it, what we all work for is to make time ***for*** ourselves, to free ***up*** time for the things we *really* want to do outside of work. It's essential to set ***aside*** enough time to pursue your interests, to do the things which are most **fulfilling** for you in life. Many people fail to achieve the right balance between work and relaxation and once again, stress is the outcome. And just a word of warning here – if by relaxation you understand slumping in front of the **television**, think again. It is a poor use of time, and it usually ends up making you feel more tired, and time-pressured than before.

Now, technology has done a great deal to ...

3 You might also ask individual students what bits of the expert's advice they thought were particularly useful/appropriate to them. Conversely, were there any pieces of advice that they disagreed with (eg the expert seems to be suggesting that sometimes you just have to do a job and not necessarily do it well).

Vocabulary: Time Page 55

Optional extra activity
By way of lead-in conduct a very brief brainstorming of collocations or phrases that include the word 'time', just long enough to change the pace and motivate the class. With a weaker class, you may need to give indirect prompts (eg think of football, think of work, try it with prepositions) or more direct prompts, so as to elicit phrases such as: time management, extra time, overtime, time for a break, arrive on time, time for bed, what's the time? etc.

1 Then point out the connection between the first activity (ex 1) and the listening text.

Answers

1 in **2** off **3** against, for **4** for, up **5** aside

2 When discussing answers, point out that the words in b) always need an article, ie a/the qualifying etc time. Students might need help with d). Peak viewing time and prime time refer to the time when the highest number of people are watching TV.

Answers

a half: *football*
b record-breaking: *athletics*
c flying: *aeroplanes*
d prime: *television*
e sale: *shops*
f harvest: *farming*

3 Students follow the instructions in their books.

Writing 2: Character reference

CAE Part 2

Page 56

1 In pairs, students look back in their books to the Language focus on Gerunds and infinitives, section C (page 51), and decide if each of the pairs of sentences is making a positive or negative comment.

Answers

1 a very positive way of saying something potentially negative – he's shy.
2 rather negative – she seems very lacking in self-confidence, though the writer is defending the nature of the applicant's work.
3 wholly positive
4 wholly negative
5 wholly positive

2 After reading the character reference, students should remind themselves of the job Lara applied for, by reading the advertisement on page 49.

Answers

The character reference is, on the whole, extremely positive. She clearly has relevant experience of 'correspondence and diary management', as 'she is familiar with all aspects of office work'. She has experience of booking travel. As an 'office manager' she seems fully qualified to take on the role of PA. 'Contact with business people at a high level' is not specifically demonstrated in the character reference, but this is compensated for by other qualities. All in all, it would seem Lara has a good chance of being selected for interview.

3a Make the point to students that, in any good piece of writing at this level, each paragraph should be clearly about something slightly different.

Answers

Paragraph 1: writer's relationship with the applicant and time he/she has known her
Paragraph 2: applicant's personal qualities and attitude to work
Paragraph 3: applicant's personal qualities and relationships with other people
Paragraph 4: applicant's relevant skills
Paragraph 5: writer's recommendation

3b Point out that many words and phrases appear regularly in job references, regardless of the nature of the job.

Answers

Suggested answers
I have known and worked with ... for ... years
... has shown great enthusiasm for her work
... has always managed to combine a ... nature with a ... approach
... has been a major asset to the company
have a tendency to ... + negative quality
this is a mark of her ...
... is one of her greatest strengths
... has excellent ... skills (see Wordlist for possibilities)
The whole of the last paragraph

3c Point out that it is very common for referees to put in such a negative reference towards the end. They wish to appear honest and truthful, so a letter of 'total praise' would seem over the top.

Answer

She can be sensitive to criticism and does have a tendency to take things to heart. However, this is a mark of her perfectionism, which generally manifests itself as a positive attribute.

4a The fun/quiz element in this activity could easily be exploited: ('See how quickly you can find the odd one out. You must be ready to justify your choices.')

Answers

2 reluctance: the only negative word
3 lack: the only one meaning 'not having'
4 become ill: this relates to health; the others relate to personality
5 poor: the only negative word
parenting: the others usually relate to the world of work
6 slapdash: the only negative word

4b Students now turn to the Wordlist at the back of their books.

Answers

Some adjectives are open to interpretation.

Positive

approachable	easy-going	outgoing
attentive	flexible	patient
caring	industrious	responsible
considerate	knowledgeable	self-assured
creative	likeable	self-confident
dedicated	loyal	sensible
determined	mature	single-minded
		trustworthy

Negative

arrogant	indecisive	slapdash
clumsy	insensitive	stubborn
conceited	moody	unreliable
disorganized	pompous	
impatient	self-centred	

5 Point out to students that it is normal for the opening paragraph to contain information about your relationship to the applicant and in what capacity you have known him/her.

Remind them to orientate the letter towards the particular demands of this job – the customers are *elderly people*, and the context is *tours of your country*.

Sample answer

To: Whom it may concern,

AR MUSTAFA

I have known Mr. Mustafa for a very long period of time. He was working with me over six years. His ability reflects in his promotion from a customer service assistant to a sales floor manager within a short period of time.

His keenness to learn and dedication to work is one of the main characteristics which paved the way to success. Although he is one of the hardest working people in the company, it never banned him from being kind and considerate to his colleagues. He was very friendly and helpful to customers as well as to colleagues.

He is an excellent communicator in his mother tongue as well as in English. With his great sense of humour he always keeps the atmosphere light. Sometimes it may be unsuitable for the situation, but never the less it acquired him affection of his collegues and customers.

He is very keen on travelling. He has done a degree in leisure and tourism while working in the company. His familarity with the Bangladeshi tourist attraction lead to his additional responsibilitie of organizing company's anual tour to the countryside.

In all those tours, he has proven himself as an excellent tour organiser.

In light of my personal experience with him, I am confident that he is well suited for the post in your company. I am happy to give this personal reference.

By Nariya Wareham

Examiner's comment
Content: Personal qualities are well described and this a satisfactory character reference. There is adequate, though not very detailed, information about Mr Mustafa's previous experience and relevant knowledge. There is clever mention of a negative point about Mr Mustafa's character, which is then turned to his advantage.

Organization and cohesion: The letter is well organized and paragraphed, although the short single sentence should not be a paragraph of its own. The letter would benefit from more overt linking devices.

Accuracy: There are some errors – in the use of verbs (*was working, keenness ... and dedication is*), in structure (*it acquired him*) and in the use of vocabulary (*banned*), but these do not impede communication.

Range: There is a satisfactory range of structure and vocabulary, and some evidence of ambition, especially in the second and third paragraphs.

Register: The register is appropriate and consistent: fairly formal, serious and respectful.

Target reader: The target reader would be reasonably well informed about Mr Mustafa's suitability for the post.

Mark: Band 3

Review 4 answers Pages 58 and 59

Word combinations

1 handed in	**4** viewing	**7** way	**9** great
2 bear	**5** set	**8** hate	**10** every
3 pressed	**6** available		

Gerunds and infinitives

1 going, trying, to get, to go
2 smoking, eating/to eat
3 noticing, asking
4 not to keep, to think
5 giving, to come, talk
6 agreeing, to help, to set, to do
7 to enter, cutting
8 to claim, seeking

Use of English: CAE Part 5 Key word transformations

Before doing the exercise refer students to the reading text on burnout on page 53. Ask them to underline 6–8 points of language (these could be structures, collocations, expressions). Students then compare their list with their partner's, and explain why they underlined these language points.

Then return to page 59, and point out that the transformations are all taken from the reading text.

Go through the example together. Point out that

- 'was reluctant to' is paraphrasing 'no one really wanted to'
- 'explain to me' is paraphrasing 'tell me'.

With item 1 stay in whole class mode, and elicit from the class:

- all the information here must be a paraphrase of 'My boss doesn't mind'

You may need to give similar help with other questions that students are finding difficult.

Remind students of the advice given in the previous unit:
The words you write must

- connect with what precedes the gap
- use the given word
- connect with what follows the gap.

After doing the exercise, students refer back to the text to find the answers.

Answers

1 makes no difference to my boss
2 was the brains behind
3 admit/confess to being
4 handed in/gave in my notice
5 had/felt no inclination to get
6 to step into his shoes
7 (to be) in favour of
8 is no such thing

Point out that noticing and recording language in reading texts is good preparation for transformations, for the Use of English paper in general, and for the exam as a whole.

5 Getting on

Content overview

Themes

This unit is concerned with relationships.

Exam-related activities

Paper 1	**Reading**
Part 2	Gapped text
Paper 2	**Writing**
Part 2	Essay
Part 2	Articles (review)
Paper 3	**Use of English**
Part 2	Open cloze (review)
Paper 4	**Listening**
Part 1	Multiple choice (short)
Part 3	Multiple choice (long)
Paper 5	**Speaking**
Part 2	Long turn
Part 3	Collaborative task
Part 4	Further discussion

Other

Vocabulary 1	Verb + Noun collocations
Vocabulary 2	Relationships
Language focus 1	Reference and ellipsis
Language focus 2	Relative clauses

Speaking 1: Long turn Page 60
CAE Part 2

As suggested in the Teacher's Book notes introducing the Long turn in Unit 1:

- Allow students longer than they would get in the exam, in order to exploit the material fully.
- Some students have difficulty in coming up with ideas when confronted with pictures. Very briefly elicit a few 'starters' (ideas which will enable them to get started) from the class, or be ready with a few ideas of your own.

Before students begin, look together at the 'Don't forget!' box.

- Remind students that the question is more than just 'talk about the pictures' – they must address the specific details of the question.
- Refer students to the adjectives in the wordlist, as instructed. Elicit the meaning of the more difficult ones:

a prickly relationship	(either person easily becomes angry or offended)
a rocky relationship	(in a bad state and unlikely to last very long – we also speak of a marriage being 'on the rocks')
an uneasy relationship	(either person is uncomfortable or anxious about the other)
a business/working relationship	(a relationship at work only, suggesting that the two people wouldn't necessarily get on well outside work)

1–2 Now students do the task.

Listening 1: Multiple choice
CAE Part 3

Page 61

Photocopiable vocabulary exercise on page 152.

Lead-in

- Write the following on the board:
  bride (bride)groom best man bridesmaid
- Ask students to define in pairs who these people are and what role they play in a wedding.
- Then students continue working in pairs and describe five wedding customs from their country to each other. When they have finished do a brief whole-class feedback, to try and get a total of ten customs.
- Relate the discussion to the listening, by asking a question such as, 'How has marriage changed since your grandparents were young?' Elicit the idea that in many countries more marriages are now failing and divorces are more common. At this stage, do not spend long on this – the idea will be more fully exploited after the listening.

1 Now ask students to look at the listening questions. Ask them how many people appear in the questions, and who is married to whom. (= Julie and Peter are one couple, Bryan and Chrissie are another.) Then tell them that there are two speakers (plus a presenter) in the listening. Ask who the two speakers are (= Julie and Bryan, see questions 1 and 5). To summarize, put on the board: Julie speaks about her relationship (with Peter), and Bryan speaks about his relationship (with Chrissie).

Answers

1 C **2** C **3** D **4** A **5** D **6** B

2 Give students as long as they need to discuss the points in groups of three, and allow the discussion to develop into other areas. Circulate and monitor. Write on the board any useful vocabulary that comes up or which students need to express their ideas:

eg In my country **society's attitudes** towards '**living together**' (ie cohabiting outside marriage) are now much more **tolerant** and **liberal**.

Have a few extra questions 'up your sleeve' to ask students:

- Do you believe in the concept of love at first sight?
- Do you believe that you are destined to meet your ideal partner?
- Can you speak about ideas of love and marriage in other cultures?
- What are the positive aspects of starting a young family? And the drawbacks?

Listening script 1.17

(P = Radio presenter; J = Julie, B = Bryan)

P: Now in this special programme on the state of marriage in Britain today, we ask two people about their experiences and views on the topic, Julie Sanders and Bryan Simpson. Now, you're both married – not to each other, I hasten to add! – so perhaps I should start by asking you both 'Why?, given that in this country over one in three marriages ends in divorce. Julie?

J: Well, I'd been *living* with Peter for just over a year – in fact, we'd recently celebrated our first anniversary in the flat – when suddenly, one evening, he got down on one knee and asked me to marry him. It was so romantic – I didn't have the heart to turn him down! No, but of course, we'd spoken about it before and we both agreed it was the right thing to do – a natural stage in our relationship and a way of making it official. And of course, our parents were delighted!

P: Was it a church wedding?

J: Oh yes, the whole works. I'd always dreamed of having a wedding dress and walking down the aisle. We had nearly 300 guests – it was all very lavish. Peter didn't share my enthusiasm at first – particularly when he thought of the cost of it all – but as the big day got nearer he worried less about the money and more about making sure it'd be the best day of our lives.

P: And you Bryan? You've done it twice, haven't you? Did you know that you are twice as likely to get divorced if you and your partner have done so already?

B: It doesn't sound too good, does it? But anyway, Chrissie – my current wife – and I got married more for the tax advantages than any need to make a public statement or keep our parents happy. At the time there were a whole load of benefits and allowances for married couples which we wouldn't have had access to if we'd just lived together. So it was just a quick registry office job for us – much cheaper and less fuss.

P: What about love? Didn't that come into it at all?

B: Yes, of course, but only in the sense that Chrissie was the sort of person I knew I could grow to love more, rather than someone I was besotted with and who'd end up disappointing me. And that's the way she saw things as well. There wasn't a great deal of passion in our romance but we do have a good marriage based on mutual respect and we still enjoy each other's company.

P: That's good to hear. Julie, you've been married for just six months now. How is *your* marriage working out? Has it changed your relationship?

J: Well, it's a little early to say, yet. We're still very much in the honeymoon period, I suppose. But it's not all domestic bliss – I notice that we do argue more than before, but it's usually about trivial things, so it's over and done with in about half an hour. So far we haven't had any fights over major issues – we haven't been throwing plates at each other, or anything like that.

P: Have you ever reached that stage in your marriage, Bryan?

B: Well *I* haven't, but I'm not sure how close Chrissie's come to it... No, but there have been some difficult times. Having my own business put a tremendous strain on my first marriage – having to work 12 hours a day, six days a week doesn't do much for a relationship. So I sold the business soon after I married Chrissie. Now *our* 'major issue', as Julie describes it, has been the children. With two it was fine, but three proved to be something of a crowd – at least until we got over the nappies and bottle stage. Now we don't feel quite so restricted by it all – we're not tired and irritable all the time.

P: And how do you both see the future? The average marriage lasts just over 10 years. Will you both last that long?

J: I sincerely hope so – we've just taken out a 25-year mortgage! No, I do feel very positive about the future. I can see the two of us being retired together. There'll be bad times, I know, but you've just got to work at it and be truthful with each other. Getting divorced is the easy way out – the hard bit is to stick at it and work through the problems.

P: Bryan?

B: Ask me in three years' time. There's just nothing certain about the future – least of all in this marriage business.

P: Julie, Bryan, thank you for coming in. After the break we'll hear from Marriage Guidance Counsellor, Margie Freeburn, who'll ...

Reading: CAE Part 2 — Gapped text

Page 62

Optional lead-in

Write on the board:

father to son father to daughter mother to son mother to daughter

Ask students which bond is the strongest? What feelings characterize the relationship in each case?

1 Establish whether it is to mothers, fathers or friends that students turn for help and advice.

2 Ask students to read the base text (on page 62) first. They should do this fairly quickly, without pausing to consider difficult vocabulary or to think about gaps. Remind students that the base text will give them most of the important information.

- Explain that you will help them with the first gap. Ask them to read the first paragraph of the base text again, in more detail. Elicit from students that we end the paragraph with the son back at home with his mother, feeling a little better after splitting up with his girlfriend.
- Explain that the first sentence in a paragraph of a text usually gives you a good idea of what the paragraph is about. (When we skim read in our own language we often just look at first sentences to see if a paragraph is interesting or relevant.) Ask students to read the first sentences of the paragraphs on page 63 until they find one which seems to follow on well from this point in the text (answer = F).
- Ask why the first sentence of A doesn't fit (= the mother has been relied on for advice, so A is saying the opposite). Ask why the first sentence of E doesn't fit (= Celia Pyper has not been named yet).
- Establish that F is the answer, and ask students to read the rest of paragraph F.
- Ask how the end of F fits in with the beginning of paragraph 2.

Answer

The writer (a mother) ends F thinking about her own experiences with her own mother. This connects with 'Girls I knew then ... '.

- Students continue in the same way, using this 'first sentence' technique. As instructed in the 'Don't forget!' box, they should underline the links they find.

Answers

Answers to Reading task

1 F **2** A **3** C **4** G **5** B **6** E

Answers

Answers to links

A 'These days, however' refers back to the final sentence in paragraph 2. The final sentence of A links forwards to 'that way' in paragraph 3.

C 'this reluctance' in C refers back to the final sentence in paragraph 3. The final sentence of C links forwards to 'They're also' in paragraph 4.

G 'As he got older ... he didn't' in G refers back to the final sentence in paragraph 4. The final sentence of G links forwards to 'these same tricks' in paragraph 5.

B the first sentence of B links back to 'tell me whatever happened to be on his mind' at the end of paragraph 5. The generational change described at the end of B links forwards to 'another important change' in paragraph 6.

E The fact that boys call their mothers a lot (end of paragraph 6) doesn't mean girls are stronger (start of E). 'something I expected' at the end of E links forwards to 'What I didn't anticipate' in paragraph 7.

Textual note:

short-term contracts: contracts between employers and employees are no longer 'for life' but often for a short time only, eg six months, two years.

downsizing: when companies reduce the size of their operations, resulting in the loss of jobs.

redundancy: when a person is 'made redundant' they lose their job, usually because the company can no longer afford to employ them.

return to the nest: 'the nest' here refers to the family home.

Reacting to the text

The speaking point here is somewhat different from that in the lead-in. Students are now asked to consider the aspect of generational change, as raised in the text.

Vocabulary 1: Verb + Noun collocations Page 63

1–2 This could be a homework activity.

Answers

1 express their feelings (para 2)
take pains (to do something) (para 6)
show physical affection (para 6)
show their emotions (para 6)

2 drift off to sleep: gradually fall asleep (para 1)
broken up with his girlfriend: ended the relationship with his girlfriend (para 1)
let down their defences: lower their (emotional) defences and open up (para 2)
go through many career highs and lows: experience good and bad moments in their career (para 3)
see through the mask: understand the truth behind the appearance (para 4)

Language focus 1: Reference and ellipsis Page 64

A Reference

This section should be done after the gapped text. If done in class, try it in pairs, so that partners have to negotiate each answer in English.

As with previous Language focus sections, if you feel the grammar is known, treat this section remedially. Students try the exercises, then read the Grammar reference section, then look back at their answers to check them and if necessary change them. If, however, you feel your class will struggle with the exercises, allow them to look at the Grammar section beforehand.

A1 Point out that reference words or phrases are the ones in bold. It is very important to know about them for the gapped text reading task, where they can help you decide which paragraph goes in each gap.

Students will need to refer back to the gapped text to get the answers.

Answers

1 **a** in my own student years
b sons leaving home at 18 to move into jobs for life.
c ways of putting up new defences
d encouraging boys to show their emotions
e the fact that boys call their mothers on mobile phones more than anyone else
f confide in their mothers

A2 Substitution is a very common device in spoken English, so this exercise is especially relevant to the speaking and listening papers.

Answers

1 so	**2** not	**3** do
4 ones	**5** those, one	**6** This

B Ellipsis

B1 Students will need to refer back to the gapped text to get the answers.

Answers

a midnight
b stumbled on motherhood's best-kept secret
c he, prevail

B2 Again, ellipsis is a common feature of spoken English, so this exercise is particularly relevant to the speaking and listening papers.

Answers

1 A Do you think you'll be home before midnight?
B I should be ~~home before midnight~~.

2 I asked him to play a tune on the piano and he said he didn't want to ~~play a tune on the piano~~.

3 She always comes to class on Tuesdays but ~~she~~ hardly ever ~~comes to class~~ on Thursdays.

4 He left without saying goodbye. I have no idea why ~~he left without saying goodbye~~.

5 A I have a feeling he was sacked from his last job.
B Yes, he might well have been ~~sacked from his last job~~.

6 He told me to apologize to her but ~~I'd already apologized to her~~ I already had (*or* I'd already done so).

In question 6 a very slight change of word order is also required.

B3 Students do the 'family of teachers' text in pairs or for homework.

Answer

Possible answer
For most of **her** working life my mother taught chemistry in a secondary school. She always said the reason she had entered the teaching profession was because her father had virtually forced her **to (do so.) Her parents were both teachers**, though she herself had no intention of becoming **one**. However, whereas my grandmother felt that my mother should only follow in their footsteps **if she wanted to (do so),** my grandfather was determined that she should teach for a living – **so she did**.

She'd actually like to have become a pharmacist and run her own business, but she wasn't sufficiently qualified (to do so). Apart from **this**, she might well have had problems raising the necessary capital, and if she'd asked her father to lend **it to her**, he probably wouldn't have (**done so**). I think my mother resented my grandfather for the pressure **he** had put on her, and **she** always encouraged me to make my own decisions. I **did (so)** – and now I work as a teacher, and my son **does too**!

Vocabulary 2: Relationships Page 65

1 Point out to students that the topic of relationships is full of idiomatic phrases as well as individual words.

Some of the seven phrases will already be known to students; those that are unfamiliar can be worked out from the context in the sentences.

Answers

1 a/b get	**2 a/b** put	**3 a/b** had
4 a turned	**4 b** turn	**5 a/b** took
6 a/b look	**7 a** kept	**7 b** keep

2 The question is whether the expressions themselves (in bold) are positive or negative, not the surrounding context of the sentences. So, for example, (5a) is actually positive, although the surrounding context here is negative.

Answers

1 a positive	**b** negative
2 a negative	**b** negative
3 a negative	**b** negative
4 a negative	**b** negative
5 a positive	**b** negative
6 a positive	**b** negative
7 a usually negative	**b** positive

3 It is important to personalize any such language input. The extra thought process involved in relating the meaning of the phrases to your own life and experience means that the target language has much more chance of being remembered as useful.

Speaking 2: CAE Part 3 Collaborative task

Page 66

Students should look at the pictures on both pages. Remind students to justify their opinions fully. Provide a few examples of your own to give students some ideas: eg the two plain-clothes policemen have a professional relationship where teamwork is terribly important – they may find themselves in life-threatening situations. So it is vital that they back each other up, as they are trained to do. The rally driver's relationship with the navigator is an interesting one. The driver is the one who takes all the glory, but the navigator is very much the unsung hero because without his skills in giving directions the rally driver would be lost … literally! The old woman is approaching an age when she is becoming much more dependent on others, and if she lives alone her contact with the young girl might be terribly important to her.

Remind students when you wish them to start considering the second aspect of the task. At this point they should begin to round up their discussion.

As a whole-class activity, briefly ask each pair what their final conclusion was.

Further discussion

Page 66

This part of the exam is testing candidates' ability to summarize, give opinions and interact successfully. The questions in this part are more abstract.

This is the first time we have met the further discussion, but both Coursebook and Teachers' Book have already given plenty of practice of this in every unit.

Go through the 'How to go about it' box together. Add the following points:

- Part 4 is the part of the speaking test where you are really given freedom to show what you can do. So you should use a full range of vocabulary and grammar.
- It is better to show ambition, take a few risks and make a few mistakes than to play safe and use basic English.
- It is fine to use personal anecdotes or refer to current affairs in order to answer questions.
- It is very important to realize that you are being assessed on your interaction with the other people in the room. In real life, speaking is all about listening to other people and responding to what they say.
- The conversation should be spontaneous and natural. Allow your partner time to speak and respond to what he or she says. Do not try to dominate the discussion.

Students do the task in pairs or threes.

Listening 2: Multiple choice

CAE Part 1

Page 67

Ask students to cover the questions 1–6 with a piece of paper. They should look at the six pictures on pages 66 and 67. Play the three extracts and stop after each one to ask which picture the extract refers to (= extract one refers to the picture of the director and actor, extract two to the men taking pictures in a car, extract three to the men driving a car).

Possible approach

Ask students to work in pairs. They cover the A, B, C options as they listen for each question. After they have heard each extract twice, they speak together and decide on their own wording of the answer, which they write down. Then they compare with the exam task and decide on the correct answer. To make it less easy to 'cheat', you might copy out the six questions (less the options) on a piece of paper and photocopy one for each pair. In the exam some students (particularly those who find it difficult to listen and read simultaneously) might benefit from such an approach – although in the exam, of course, there would not be time to write down the answer in this way.

Answers

1 B **2** C **3** C **4** A **5** A **6** B

Listening script 1.18–1.20

(I = Interviewer)

Extract one

I: Miriam – the curtain goes up on your new play next week – are you at all anxious or is opening night an occasion which no longer bothers you?

Actor: Well it depends on the production but in this case, I've been privileged again to have Malcolm Rush as a director. He doesn't care whether you're exhausted, mentally – physically – emotionally – it's immaterial – he'll just continue pushing until every scene is simply perfect. You don't just learn the part – you live it, which takes away any fears you might have of not being able to persuade an audience you're real.

I: Malcolm does have a reputation of being quite the dictator. No one dares voice their opinion, I hear.

Actor: Well I do. Malcolm is entirely willing to listen to your point of view once you gain his respect. When we're working on a play, it's a two-way process in which one person comes up with an idea – we see how it works out – and then we don't hold back on any constructive criticism. If you're relatively new to the stage, he's going to be tough with you – but once you've proved yourself, it's all about co-operation and being open to changes.

Extract Two

Anya: I have to say, Stephen, I was expecting more from this director. The whole thing seemed terribly formulaic to me – we have two mismatched cops, one of whom plays by the rules and the other is a rebel. Isn't this the kind of scenario we've seen too many times already?

Stephen: The tense relationship between the detectives is definitely a cliché, I admit, but I think the quality of acting is excellent enough to make this work far superior to others in the genre. And the plot, which is actually quite sophisticated, keeps you guessing all the way through. It's not just relying on stunts and explosions to fill up time.

Anya: Well the female characters – the wife and the girlfriend have more to say than usual. They do seem to be there for valid reasons – rather than decoration.

Stephen: And unusually for a commercial film, the two heroes – or anti-heroes if you like – do not suddenly develop great affection for one another. There's a level of respect – a recognition that the other man is a professional – someone you can depend upon to do the job and who will never be corrupted – but when it's all finally over – they want nothing more to do with one another. They just both find one another offensive in some way.

Extract three

I: So David, with the next rally less than twelve hours away, how confident are you of holding your position in front?

Driver: Well – the team has done an incredible job sorting out all the problems with the car – it's running at peak performance now. The big issue, as you may know, is that my co-driver, Scott King, broke his leg last week and so that's it – he's out for the foreseeable future. Fortunately for us Eddy Houseman stepped in at the last minute - though of course he's never partnered me before, which is a bit of a concern. At least the conditions are favourable – the worst of the ice has cleared – just a few patches left we can deal with.

I: Scott's been with you from the start, hasn't he?

Driver: Yes – people often underrate the co-driver's role – the glory always goes to the driver. But it's Scott who has the map and the notes – without him I'd be truly driving blind. You have to have complete faith that what he says is right – I have to know exactly how fast I can take a corner – and be sure that we don't end up rolling into a ditch. That's not to say he's always to blame for every crash! And I don't know how Eddy's going to deal with my temper – Scott's got used to it after all this time ...

Language focus 2: Relative clauses

Page 68

1 The most difficult point here is the difference between defining and non-defining clauses. This might seem unnecessarily technical to some students, but it is important, as it affects not only the choice of relative pronoun, but the punctuation as well. In exam terms, it is especially important to master this point for the Writing paper.

The Grammar reference section explains the difference very clearly.

Because of likely difficulties with this aspect of relative clauses, it would seem wise to do these exercises in class rather than for homework.

Answers

1

1 **a** Scott
b an occasion
c All that precedes it, ie the fact that you don't just learn the part, you live it.
d two mismatched cops
e the plot

2 **c, d** and **e** contain non-defining relative clauses
a and **b** contain defining clauses

3 *who* and *which* in **a** and **b** respectively

4 *which* or *that* – In a defining relative clause such as this, if the relative pronoun (here: *which* or *that*) refers to the object (*scenario*) of the verb in the relative clause (*we've seen*), the pronoun can be omitted.

2

1 I went walking with my husband at the weekend, **which** is something **which/that/***omit* we haven't done for a long time.

2 The novel is set in Kaunas, **which** at that time was the capital of Lithuania. The initial chapters focus on Vitas's father, **whose** fiery temperament had a lasting effect on the boy.

3 **What** I'd like to know is what happened to that boxer **who/that/***omit* she was seeing. Are they still going out together?

4 He left all his money to a woman **who/that** had never shown him any affection. The reason **why/that/***omit* he did this has never been fully understood.

5 Her mother, **who** hated city life, longed to return to the village **which/that/***omit* she grew up in and **where** she still owned a small plot of land.

6 Is there anyone **who's/that's** got a car or **whose** mum or dad could give us a lift?

Writing: CAE Part 2 — Essays Page 68

1 Point out that the three possible paragraph plans are all perfectly acceptable. It is probably easiest for students to read the model answer first and then the three plans.

Answers

Answer to question in Student's Book

1 C

Draw students' attention to certain features of the model answer.

- The last paragraph nicely restates the writer's position, but in very different words and without sounding repetitive. Essays which merely repeat at the end create a bad impression.
- It can also be nice to end with a slightly new point, so that the reader is left thinking at the end, and finishes the piece impressed.

- Note that the paragraphs are neither too long nor too short, and each is making a slightly different point.
- The essay also makes good, interesting points which are convincing to the reader (eg when we change jobs or cease to take part in a group activity, the friendships end).

2–3 Students work individually.

Answers

2

words and expressions which introduce a contrast
Despite this, however
by contrast
on the other hand
(This is not) however (the case)
whilst
nevertheless

words and expressions which introduce the writer's main points
The first point to bear in mind is that
A further point is that
Finally

other useful words and expressions for writing essays
evidence seems to suggest that
a recent survey found that
in addition
it would be wrong to argue that
it is generally agreed ... that
this is not the case with
to conclude
some argue that

3

Agreeing with a statement	Disagreeing with a statement
It cannot be denied that	It would be wrong to argue that
There can be no doubt that	It is simply not the case that
It is my firm belief that	I would dispute the claim that
It is true to some extent that	It is difficult to accept the idea that

4 Helping students with what they will say in their essays (and other pieces of writing) is a vital part of preparing them for the task and a very useful way of spending class time. Encourage them to use their own experiences to back up their opinions. Personalizing the material through direct questions, and picking up on what students say, can produce useful ideas. Here is an example for item 1.

- Do you have any elderly relatives? How do you feel about them? Do you feel less respect towards younger people? Who or what do you respect in your life? Is it the same for your friends – do you think they feel the same way? Who or what do you not respect in your life? Do you think you will complain about lack of respect from the young when you are older?

5 Students follow the instructions.

Sample answer

It is better to live alone than in the parental home.
Many young people cannot wait to own their own flat and they move from their parental home as soon as they can, even if it means to live alone. However, the price of flats is rising greatly and the size of flats is reducing, so is it really worth living alone than with your parents?

It cannot be denied that living alone gives you privacy and independence. There is no one to tell you what to do and you can come and go when you want. Parents still try to control your life, despite of the fact that you are more than twenty years old, so there is a big advantage to breaking up with them and having your own space.

Nevertheless, it is my belief that there are more advantages to keeping on living with them. The first point to bear in mind is that it is much cheaper: you may pay some rent to your parents but it is never as expensive as paying a mortgage or renting a flat on your own. Related with this is the fact of being able to save money while you live with them, so that one day it will be easier to buy your flat.

A further point is that always your meals are cooked for you, and your washing and ironing can be done too. If you live alone, you do not always eat healthily and you spend a large amount of time doing housework and shopping.

To conclude, it is true that living with your parents can put a great strain on your relationship with them, but there are more advantages than disadvantages.

Examiner's comment

Content: The content of the task is covered.

Organization and cohesion: The answer is well organized and there is evidence of use of a range of cohesive devices (*'The first point to bear in mind …'*, *'A further point is …'*).

Accuracy: Reasonably accurate with some grammatical errors (*'despite of the fact'*, *'always your meals are cooked for you'*) or incorrect choice of vocabulary (*'rising greatly'*, *'breaking up with'*).

Range: There is evidence of a good range of vocabulary and tense usage. (*'you may pay some rent to your parents but …'*, *'… put a great strain on your relationship'*).

Register: The register is appropriately formal.

Target Reader: Would be clear about the writer's opinion and their reasons.

Mark: Band 4

Review 5 answers Pages 70 and 71

Vocabulary

1 down	**4** to	**7** to	**10** through
2 on	**5** on	**8** down on	
3 on	**6** in for	**9** up with	

Reference and ellipsis

1 old one keeps
2 I hope not
3 and neither/nor is
4 but I do.
5 If so
6 It should be
7 I have already! or I already have! or I've already done so!
8 love to.
9 should have been.
10 he hasn't

Use of English: CAE Part 2 Open cloze

1 were	**6** which	**11** have
2 would	**7** without	**12** their
3 them	**8** it/this/that	**13** to
4 when	**9** What	**14** out
5 Despite	**10** over	**15** such

Content overview

Themes

This unit is concerned with intelligence/the brain/memory/sleep.

Exam-related activities

Paper 1	**Reading**
Part 3	Multiple choice (long)
Paper 2	**Writing**
Part 2	Reviews
Paper 3	**Use of English**
Part 3	Word formation (review)
Part 4	Gapped sentences
Part 5	Key word transformations (review)
Paper 4	**Listening**
Part 2	Sentence completion
Part 4	Multiple matching

Other

Speaking and reading

Vocabulary 1	Intelligence and ability
Vocabulary 2	Sleep
Language focus 1	Passives 1
Language focus 2	Passives 2

Speaking and reading Page 72

Photocopiable vocabulary exercise on page 152.

Lead-in

Individual students will bring different background knowledge of the people in the photos. Exploit this, by allowing those who can speak informatively about one of the people to do so. Ask 'What do you know about each of the famous people in the pictures?' This is likely to be done best in whole-class format, but a particularly mature class might share their knowledge in groups.

Biographical notes:

Einstein – (German) widely regarded as the greatest genius of the 20th century. Famous for the theory of relativity (1905), which revolutionized atomic theory, and the way we now view time and space.
Beckham – former captain of England football team, married to pop star 'Posh Spice'.
Monet – Impressionist painter. 'Impressionism' was a movement in the world of art originating in

France in the late 19th century. Impressionists conveyed the impression of a scene rather than minute detail, and looked at the world in a freer, livelier, more colourful way.
Rowling – English writer famous for her 'Harry Potter' books, about a boy who has magical powers and attends a school for witches and wizards. Famous for her 'rags to riches' story – she was a single mother with no writing experience, whose Potter manuscripts were initially rejected by many publishers.
Darwin – English biologist famous for the theory of evolution by natural selection (1859). The idea that life is subject to natural laws guaranteeing the survival of the fittest initially caused a great controversy, since it seemed to diminish the role of God in the creation of the universe.
Streep – American actress widely regarded as the best of her generation. Starred in eg *The Deer Hunter* and *Sophie's Choice*.
Curie – Polish-born French physicist, who studied radioactivity and discovered radium.

1 Then give students one minute to work individually, on the basis of what they know and what they have just learned about the people, and rank them in order of intelligence.
Finally allow five minutes or so for pairwork discussion.

2 Students read individually and answer the question in their books.

Answer

Gardner would rank them all the same.

Reacting to the text
There are some difficult but important ideas to engage with in the three pairwork questions. Question 1 is dealing with the idea that Gardner's theory is just taking to an extreme something that we have always known – that different individuals have different talents, which should be respected and nurtured. Question 3 is dealing with the idea that school curricula tend to promote the opposite idea from that in the text – ie that students should be given as wide an education as possible and should only specialize later.

If some students have difficulty getting to grips with these ideas, prompt them with further questions such as:

(Q1) Do we know all this already? What do you like about Gardner's theory? Do you agree with Gardner that intelligence cannot be measured merely by 'pen and paper tests'?

Listening 1: Multiple matching
CAE Part 4

Page 73

1 If you are doing the listening on a different day from the 'Multiple Intelligences' reading, ask for volunteers to recall the key ideas of the reading text. This will serve as a lead-in to the listening.

Students do the listening task.

Answers

1 D **2** C **3** H **4** A **5** G **6** G **7** H **8** D
9 E **10** B

2 There are various ways in which this could be done.

- A novel approach would be to use the listening (pausing after each speaker) as a vehicle for discussion. Students have, say, one minute to react to what each speaker says.
- Students could look at the statements A–H in task two, and decide which three they think are most important and why (rather like a collaborative task).
- Students could be asked specific questions, eg in pairs from a worksheet. Questions might include:
  Is home-schooling legal in your country?
  What are the advantages of home-schooling?
  What are the disadvantages?
  Why might parents send their children to boarding school?
  Would you ever consider sending a child of yours to such a school?
  What kind of adult would you expect a boarding school child to become?
  What are the pros and cons of single-sex schools?

Listening script 1.21–1.25

Speaker 1
I went to – if you like – 'normal' school Monday to Thursday – and I didn't particularly excel in anything – and if that'd been my sole form of learning experience, I probably wouldn't be where I am today – I mean playing in front of huge European audiences. You see, on

Fridays I went to an independent school, where they set up a project for the day – say something on volcanoes. You learnt the usual stuff but then they encouraged you to respond in your own way. So for example, the arty kids would make a sculpture, the practical-minded kids built models – and I used to get the instruments out and compose something – just in the corner by myself at first – but then I gained confidence. For me, that's what education should be about – getting kids to express themselves, to use their imagination as a means of developing their abilities.

Speaker 2

I think I got into this profession partly as a reaction to my *own* teachers – I wanted to show them how teaching *should* be done. You know, there's nothing worse than when a teenager has a go at something and then they're criticized for getting it wrong. It humiliates them – makes them reluctant to speak out in front of who they see as the brainy kids. My colleagues and I all have the attitude that participation should be rewarded. See – rather than just telling them, 'You're wrong' it's better to help them out with a few more leading questions that'll direct them to the right answer. In that way you're sending the message that it's better to have a go even if their answer isn't quite right than sit there in silence and be excluded.

Speaker 3

There was never any doubt that we were going to send Andrew to boarding school– it's a tradition that goes back four generations in our family – although Andrew is back with us at weekends and I only ever returned for the holidays. The academic advantage is clear – with far smaller classes you get greater individual attention. That allows you to really master a subject. But also, the reason why this kind of private education system works is that the whole ethos is about becoming self-sufficient – it is up to the individual student to ensure they spend a good amount of time on their homework or studying in the library. It is up to them to be in class on time and keep their rooms in order. That kind of discipline is invaluable when it comes to the real world.

Speaker 4

For the last thirty years or so, the majority of schools have allowed boys and girls to study side by side. Whereas their integration within the classroom may benefit them in terms of their social development, the studies we have carried out show that boys consistently underperform when learning alongside girls. Our investigations were based on observations within classrooms that we visited as well as the examination results from 100 schools over the last three years. Many parents find the notion of educating their son or daughter separately from members of the opposite sex rather old-fashioned, but I believe that school should provide the opportunity for a learner to do as well as they possibly can. While not every child may be naturally gifted, it is possible to develop their intelligence to a far greater extent in the right learning environment.

Speaker 5

My father was rather unconventional and he took it upon *himself* to educate me at home. This often involved visiting castles, art galleries, and of course, the wonderful Science Museum. And that's where it all began for me: I was fascinated by the models of atoms and by the early microscopes. I would read up about the stuff I'd seen at home and my father would always say 'When you're ready, we'll have a little test and see what you can remember,' but there was no strict schedule. He knew that it takes *time* to *absorb* information. In my laboratory I have to do everything with extreme care and it is vital you do not *rush* things, but the end result makes it all worthwhile. The same approach should be applied to education.

Language focus 1: Passives 1 Page 74

This section is largely self-explanatory. Students can work through the material in pairs, but input from the teacher is likely to be needed at stage 4.

Answers

1 **a** J. K. Rowling **b** Claude Monet **c** Marie Curie **d** Charles Darwin **e** Meryl Streep

2 **a** She is of course famous for writing/having written a series of books.
The stories, which have been translated into
b These masterpieces of Impressionism were all painted at the end of the 19th century by the man who is/was generally regarded as the leader of the movement.
c He was introduced to her by a Polish acquaintance
the study she had been commissioned to do by the Society for the Encouragement of National Industry.
d He arrived at Salvador, Brazil, aboard the HMS Beagle ('arrive' here is an intransitive verb. Only transitive verbs can be used in the passive.)
and he was plagued/he was to be plagued by fatigue and intestinal sickness
e she should have been awarded an Oscar for her part in *Silkwood*
complaints about radiation sickness are ignored by the management

3 **1** c (teachers) **2** d **3** b **4** a

4 **b**
b These masterpieces of Impressionism: passive

c He: passive
d During his travels there he: active (*contracted*) then passive (*was plagued*)
e This dramatic film/whose: passive

5 b
b the man who is generally regarded as the leader of the movement
c Polish acquaintance ... the Society for the Encouragement of National Industry.
d fatigue and intestinal sickness
e the management of the plutonium factory where she works

Practice
Using the information in the Grammar reference, students work in pairs to complete the task. They should think in particular about what the 'given information' is.

Answers

1. Change to passive; agent required.
   The item was written by Steven Ward, former Olympic athlete and manager of the Crowfield sports centre, which sponsored the event.
2. No change. The second sentence begins with given information: 'This development'
3. Change to passive; no agent required.
   The event could be held in the 2,000-seater Mulberry Hall Function Room in Scarcroft Road.
4. Change to passive; agent required.
   The survey was carried out during the busy pre-Christmas period by first-year students at Holmbush Business College, who designed their own questionnaire as part of their course work.
5. Change to passive; no agent required.
   I have recently been promoted to the post of Chief Accounts Clerk, in charge of a staff of five.

Vocabulary 1: Intelligence and ability
Page 75

1 Ask any other questions that occur to you, eg (a) which one is used of someone who knows a lot about computers or technical matters? (= whizzkid) (b) which one suggests the student has a very particular talent? (= gifted)

Answers

1 a a whizzkid
b brainy
c I'm a dab hand at painting
d I'm (an) ace at tennis
e I'm hopeless at cooking

2 Students should use any of the language which applies to them, and obviously change the examples accordingly.

3 Point out that there are plenty of other adjectives that could possibly collocate with the nouns, eg a good skier, an ok skier, a confident skier. But the collocations here are particularly strong ones.

4 Also emphasize that such collocations enrich students' vocabulary, and would impress any examiner if used in one of the productive papers (writing and speaking)!

Answers

4 a practically **b** largely **c** absolutely

5 Students follow the instructions in their books.

Writing: Reviews Page 76
CAE Part 2

1 Take this as a whole-class activity. If students do not recognize the actors:
Russell Crowe is an Australian actor famous for 'tough-guy' roles, such as the lead in 'Gladiator'.
Judi Dench is a British actress whose films include: 'Shakespeare in Love', 'Chocolat' and 'Die Another Day'.

2 Ask students to look at the question only and to highlight or underline the three elements of this task:
- compare and contrast
- similarities and differences
- which recommend and why

Elicit from them that in a review:
- 1st person style is acceptable
- personal opinion is typical – good or bad
- it is ok to sound enthusiastic
- the style is often informal – but be careful; it must be suitable for the target audience

Exam note:
The review task is usually more than simply 'write a review of a film/book you have seen recently'. There will be other elements involved, such as a comparative element. It is vital to answer this question according to the precise instructions given – writing out 'pre-prepared answers' which don't fit with the instructions means you have not answered the question and cannot get any marks.

Now ask students to read the model answer. As they read they should answer the question:
'How does the writer feel about the two films?'

(He or she is positive about both of them, but seems marginally to prefer 'A Beautiful Mind'.)

3 Now ask students to focus on the paragraphing. Remind them that in good writing, each paragraph, although connected to the previous one, is about something slightly different.

Answers

Paragraph 1:
Basic information on content of two films, including overall opinion and comment on acting performances.
Paragraph 2:
Similarities between two films, including further comment on plot and opinion on Russell Crowe's appearance.
Paragraph 3:
Differences between two films, including further opinion on Kate Winslet's acting and use of flashback technique.
Paragraph 4:
Overall strengths of films with personal recommendation.

All paragraphs include the writer's opinion.

Make the important point that the clear paragraphing in the model answer shows to the examiner that this candidate was well organized and had written a clear plan.

4–5 Now focus on the language used. Students work in pairs.

Answers

4 adjectives in text
entertaining afternoon's viewing
moving portrayal
remarkably convincing
very credible (Kate Winslet)
to good effect (adverbial phrase)
powerful acting
visually appealing
plausible
a definite must-see (noun)

4 adjectives in Wordlist
Some adjectives are open to interpretation

Positive
action-packed, atmospheric, compelling, credible, entertaining, exhilarating, fast-moving, gripping, impressive, innovative, memorable, moving, powerful, stunning

Negative
clichéd, disappointing, excruciating, implausible, overhyped, predictable, sentimental, tedious, unconvincing

5
Both focus on
common to both films is the fact that
'Iris' differs from 'A Beautiful Mind' in this respect, relying instead on
unlike the more linear American film
more visually appealing but no less plausible

Then students do the vocabulary exercise in the Additional material section (Coursebook, page 206).

Answers

1 resemblance	**3** lines	**5** difference
2 terms	**4** similarities	**6** genre

6 This might be done as homework. Students should organize their ideas into logical paragraphs and use some of the language from exercises 4 and 5 above.

Sample answer

The exciting world of spies is beautifully reppresented by James Bond films. In Sean Connery's 'Dr No', James Bond fights against a scientist who utilises atomic energy for the motive of diverting rockets and missiles. In Pierce Brosnan's last edition 'Die another day', the enemy holds a powerfull weapon, a satellite with a diamond crown that functionates as an enormous laser.

Common to both films is the way James Bond saves the world from terrible disasters. Another similarity is the exotic and atractive settings. 'Dr No' takes place in appealling crystal water beaches of Jamaica and 'Die another day' moves from picturesque 'La Habana' to the very impresive views of Iceland. But the more great similarity of all, made in propurse of course, is that in both films there is a comparable scene of Ursula Andress in the first one and Halle Berry in the second one, which coming out of the water dressed in exactly the same bikini.

What sets one film apart from the other is the gap of time between both of them. Old James Bond was sciovinist and even a bit racist instead Pierce Brosnan's Bond treats Halle Berri as an equal and as well behaves it could be said as a perfect gentleman. It is also noticeable in respect of the gadgets they use, there is no comparasion between the Giger Counter (to measure radioactivity) used by Sean Connery and the invisible car of Pierce.

Both films are action-packed and compelling, which makes the perfect choice for a diverting evening's viewing, however, if you prefer a visually appealling experience, but I have to say maybe less plausible also, then 'Die another day' is the film for you.

By Donatella Fiore

Examiner's comments

Content: The writing successfully addresses the different parts of the question. The task is well fulfilled and certainly analytical rather than merely descriptive.

Organization and cohesion: The writing is well organized and introduces similarities and differences in an appropriate and logical manner. There is clever use of paragraphing, each paragraph being clearly about something different.

Accuracy: There are a number of mistakes which suggest a lack of control: *'which coming'* and *'more great'*.

Range: There is a range of tense and vocabulary usage, including some impressive language such as *'Common to both films is …'*. However, this ambition is not always successful *'a diamond crown that functionates as an enormous laser.'*

Register: The register is appropriately semi-formal, as befits an arts review in a newspaper. It correctly addresses the reader directly and gives the personal opinions of the reviewer.

Target reader: Would be informed and would consider using the piece in the magazine.

Mark: Band 3

Use of English: CAE Part 4 — Gapped sentences

Page 77

Students do the task as instructed.

Possible approach

You might adopt the following approach to Gapped sentences tasks that are done in the classroom:

- Divide the class into small groups. Give some groups sentence 5.1 to look at, some groups sentence 5.2, and other groups sentence 5.3.
- Each group has two minutes to come up with as many words as they can to fit each gap. Record all this information on the board. Hopefully the correct word (= thought) will appear on the board in all three sentences, so you can simply ask 'Which word appears in all three sentences?'

Answers

Possible answers to approach in Teacher's Book

5 As we boarded the ship, the ... **feeling/thought/idea** ... occurred to me that I would probably never return to my country and see my family again.
Some people take risks while they're driving, with no ... **concern/thought/respect** ... for the safety of other motorists.
We ... **thought/looked** ... over the offer very carefully and after a week or so we decided to accept.

Students might find this approach helpful when they do these exercises individually.

Answers

1 mind **2** bright **3** slow **4** head **5** thought

Remind students that collocation is often a feature of this task. Encourage them to note down any collocations they did not know or find especially useful.

Reading: CAE Part 3 Multiple choice

Page 78

Photocopiable vocabulary exercise on page 153.

1 If no ideas are forthcoming, use the following to start things off:
It might cause problems with a line manager if a sufferer was always falling asleep at work.
There might also be certain professions that sufferers would be barred from for security reasons.

2 Students skim read the text to see if their predictions come up. Allow no more than a minute for this.

3 For variety, practise the important skill of *locating the answer in the text*. Explain that with multiple-choice reading, students need to find the place in the text where the 'stem' seems to be located (the stem is the first line of the question, as opposed to the four options).
Students must be able to do this successfully. Having found the location, they then need to do a detailed read of that section of text in order to answer the question.

Do the first two together, then give the rest of the task to students in pairs (answers below).

Answers

Answers to activity in Teacher's Book

1. A quick read shows that the first paragraph deals with schools and the second with work, so the answer is likely to come from these two paragraphs.
2. The location is already specified in the question.
3. This is cued by 'When I arrive for our interview' (line 63).
4. Surprise is expressed in line 88, so the answer is likely to come from that paragraph.
5. This is more difficult to locate, but a skim read of the paragraph beginning line 101 shows references to 'socially' and 'horror movie' (see options).
6. Line 118 speaks of joining the police force, so the answer is likely to come from that paragraph.
7. The location is already specified in the question.

Finally, students do the exam task.

Answers

Answers to multiple-choice task

1 C 2 A 3 B 4 D 5 C 6 C 7 B

Vocabulary 2: Sleep

Page 79

There are many idiomatic expressions in English containing the word sleep. Exercise 1 asks students to find some from the reading text. In exercise 2 we do some wordbuilding, looking at other expressions.

Answers

1 a snooze
b nod off, fall asleep, doze off

2 A
1 good **2** soundly **3** deep **4** fast
B
1 rough **2** wide **3** sleepless **4** light

Optional extra activity
Write the following on the board. Students must work in pairs and decide on the meaning of each of the expressions in bold.

1 The seating on the plane was a bit cramped and **my leg went to sleep** after about an hour.
2 We had to **have our dog put to sleep**: she was suffering too much.
3 Don't decide now – go away and **sleep on it** and we'll talk about it again tomorrow.
4 Yes, I failed the exam, but I'm not going to **lose any sleep over it**.
5 It's about time the Council **woke up to the fact that** people in wheelchairs cannot walk up and down steps.
6 It was quite a change, moving from the busy capital city to a **sleepy village** of just 200 people.

Answers

Answers to extra activity in Teacher's Book

1 **my leg went to sleep**: I lost the sense of feeling in my leg
2 **have our dog put to sleep**: take it to the vet, who gave it drugs so that it would die without pain
3 **sleep on it**: delay making a decision until the next day, after you've had time to think about it
4 **not lose any sleep over it**: not worry about it
5 **woke up to the fact that**: realized and understood
6 **sleepy village**: one that is quiet and where not very much happens

3 Students follow instructions.

Language focus 2: Passives 2 Page 80

The focus here is on more difficult aspects of the passive voice, rather than on tense manipulation.

A Reporting verbs

A1 Ask students to turn to the reading text on narcolepsy on page 78 of their books. Write on the board:
An incurable sleep disorder that ______________ at least 2,500 people in the UK.
Sufferers _________________ inebriated or lazy.
It ______________ the result of a genetic mutation.

Tell students to look at the first column of the text and complete the missing words.

Then ask them to turn to the Language focus on page 80. Here they will see the answers to this board exercise in bold print.

These are examples of reporting verbs. The structure is 'noun (or noun phrase or pronoun) + be + past participle + infinitive'. The use is for generalized opinions or facts. This structure is practised in 2.

Answers

A

2 **a** The Prime Minister is expected to announce his resignation later today.
b The 22-year-old striker is understood to be considering a move to a Spanish club.
c The band are rumoured to have sacked their (or is rumoured to have sacked its) lead guitarist.
d He was alleged to have been selling stolen goods.
e She is reported to have been paid over £2 million for her part in the film.

B *Have/Get something done*

B1–2 These can be done using volunteers as a whole class activity.

Answers

B

1 **a** We're painting the house at the weekend.
We're doing it ourselves.
b We're having the house painted at the weekend.
We're paying someone to do it for us.
c We're getting the house painted at the weekend.
We're paying someone to do it for us. (slightly more informal than b)

B

2 **a** I had my watch repaired last week.
Someone repaired my watch because I asked/paid them to.
b I had my watch stolen last week.
Someone stole my watch. I did not ask them to! This use of the structure is for unpleasant events (usually) over which the subject has no control.

C Other passives with *get*

C 'Get' is especially common in the strong collocations listed. It can also be used as an alternative to the auxiliary 'be' in most passive sentences – but students should handle with care, as this use is restricted to informal speech.

Practice

Answers

Possible answers

1

c have had/got this dress/suit
d to get lost/to have got lost
e would have/get your eyes

f of having/getting my nose
g got caught
h to get/have the car
i had/got our house/flat
j should/ought to/'d better get/have your hair

2 Listen out for and encourage use of the correct passive forms during this brief practice activity.

Listening 2: Sentence completion

CAE Part 2

Page 81

1 Discuss students' knowledge and any personal anecdotes on the topic first.

Optional gist listening activity

In order to help students with the main content of the text, put the following key words from the listening on the board:

swinging watch, brain, magnets, cigarettes

Ask for volunteers to suggest how these four things might be talked about in the listening. Then play the recording in order to check this information.

2 Give students plenty of time to read the questions carefully. Check the meaning of any difficult words ('coined' in 4 means 'invented'; 'props' means things that hypnotists use as part of their 'act'). Select a few questions at random and ask things like:
Which question is likely to have a date or year as its answer? (= 1)
Which question is likely to have a type of scientist as its answer? (= 4)
Which two questions are likely to have the names of medical conditions as their answers? (= 2, 7)

Now play the recording.

Answers

1 1778	**5** switch off
2 deafness	**6** magical symbols
3 tubs of water	**7** lose weight
4 surgeon	**8** psychological

Textual note: chloroform – a kind of gas once used by dentists to put people to sleep.

Listening script 1.26

We've all seen images of the TV hypnotist who manages to get members of the audience doing outrageous things in front of the cameras – shy accountants doing Elvis impersonations or reserved librarians declaring their love for items of furniture. But there is a serious side to hypnotism – and a history.

Born in 1733, the Austrian physician Dr Anton Mesmer moved to the French capital in 1778 at the age of 45, taking with him a revolutionary new healing method. 'Mesmerism' was based on the idea that each living body contains a potent therapeutic force which he called 'animal magnetism'. Mesmer claimed that he – or any other trained individual – could control this force to cure a range of conditions including deafness, rheumatism and even paralysis. His success had members of high society *flocking* to his dimly-lit rooms for treatment. Surrounded by astrological symbols decorating the walls, patients were told to sit in tubs of water, while Mesmer used iron bars and other gadgets to harness their magnetic force and effect a cure. At a time when anaesthetics were unknown to medicine, mesmerism was used by some early 19th century practitioners to relieve pain during operations.

The word 'hypnotism' was first used in 1841 by the surgeon, James Braid, who defined mesmerism as 'neurohypnology', or the science of sleep. In fact, it was the Englishman Braid who first used the familiar swinging watch to hypnotize his patients. The watch may seem something of a cliché, but it does serve a practical purpose. Imitating what happens when we dream, hypnosis causes the left brain, the side associated with logic and reason, to switch off, allowing the right brain, the side of fantasies and imagery, to take over. To achieve this, hypnotists get the left brain to focus on something monotonous such as the swinging watch, often accompanying this with a low droning voice – the typical 'Your eyes are getting heavy, you are falling into a deep sleep, a very deep sleep.' Many other aids have been used to hypnotize people, though, including chloroform, magnets applied to the head or magical symbols painted on card.

Once the right side of the brain is in control, it will respond to the hypnotist's suggestions in a dream-like way, treating everything he or she says as if it were true. Hypnotherapists claim that by making suggestions in this way they can do such things as cure insomnia or encourage patients to lose weight. Apparently, people can be made to believe that chocolate tastes of petrol or that beer smells of rotting food. Of course, this type of treatment has its detractors, sceptics who say it is the person's existing decision to change and not hypnotism that has the effect. However, it is now widely believed that hypnotism does have its place in medicine, and is especially effective with illnesses that have a psychological basis – stomach problems, skin disorders and chronic headaches, to name but a few.

Some of these problems may have their origins in childhood, and age regression, when the patient relives their childhood, is another area of hypnotism ...

3 Students follow instructions.

Review 6 answers Pages 82 and 83

Use of English: CAE Part 3 Word formation

1	infections	**6**	visualizing
2	unfortunately	**7**	disorganized
3	participants	**8**	comparison
4	analysis	**9**	fictional
5	spatial	**10**	systematically

Vocabulary

1	poor	**5**	promising	**8**	fast
2	strong	**6**	get	**9**	sets
3	gift	**7**	badly	**10**	choose
4	bright				

Use of English: CAE Part 5 Key word transformations

1 to be fully assessed
2 taken aback when he was/at being/by being
3 thought to have made
4 house done up
5 being taken for granted
6 has been put off
7 fewer/less than six people are required
8 be weak at speaking

CAE Paper 3

Use of English

Part 3 Word formation
Part 4 Gapped sentences
Part 5 Key word transformations

Part 3: Word Formation Page 84

1 Go through the 'What to expect' box together. Also point out that students should think hard as they are doing the task about what part of speech the gapped word is. This should be clear from the surrounding text. In this text some help is given in this respect – the words around the gaps which give the necessary context are shown in bold.

Also emphasize to students the importance of reading the whole text, understanding what it is saying and keeping in mind the argument of the text as it develops. This is particularly important when a negative prefix is tested.

Students try the task.

Answers

1	definition	**5**	beliefs	**8**	unbearable
2	emotional	**6**	theoretically	**9**	length
3	variety	**7**	tolerance	**10**	accompanies
4	psychological				

2 Either go through the answers to exercise 1 in detail and at the same time do exercise 2 in whole-class mode or allow students to compare their answers to exercise 1 in pairs and then try exercise 2.

During feedback on the answers to 1 and 2, point out that

- in question 8 the answer is 'unbearable' not 'bearable'. If one follows the line of argument in the text starting with the sentence containing gap 6, it is clear that a negative is required.
- in question 9 an 'internal' change is made to the word in bold. Students should be aware that although most of the questions require the addition of a suffix or prefix, this 'internal' change is also possible.

Answers

1 'definition' is a noun.
2 'emotional' is an adjective
3 'variety' is a noun. There is a spelling change: 'y' at the end of 'vary' becomes an 'i'.
4 'psychological' is an adjective
5 'beliefs' is a noun in the plural form
6 'theoretically' is an adverb
7 'tolerance' is a noun
8 'unbearable' is an adjective. The prefix 'un' makes it negative.
9 'length' is a noun. There is a spelling change: 'o' in 'long' becomes an 'e' in 'length'
10 'accompanies' is a verb. It uses the prefix 'ac'.

3 Remind students about the importance of reading the whole text. If they have read and understood something of the whole text (of course it is hard to do with some of the words taken out!), it will be much easier for them to do the questions. If they do not read the whole text first, they can easily be caught out and get the answer wrong.

Ask the whole class what we learn about moths, and perhaps list this on the board:

Answers

Answer to point in Teacher's Book
We learn that:
moths are a kind of insect similar to a butterfly.
moth numbers are falling in Britain.
this in turn endangers their predators in the food chain.
moths are disliked – people think they are night creatures which damage clothes.
in fact this is only partly true.
there is a campaign to raise awareness about their plight.

Now students do the exam task.

Answers

1 entitled	**5** expertise	**9** establishment/ establishing
2 halved	**6** threatens	**10** unavoidable
3 finding	**7** perception	
4 enthusiasts	**8** diversity	

Part 4: Gapped sentences Page 85

Help is given here underneath each question, so students can do this task in pairs without input from the teacher.

Note that any gaps which involve the use of a collocation are shown in bold. Draw students' attention to these.

Answers

1 ahead **2** aim **3** figure **4** open **5** will

Part 5: Key word transformations Page 87

Read the rubric and the 'How to go about it' box with the students. Remind them that in the exam if they change the given word or do the task in seven or more words they are throwing away marks. So it is important to check their answers, as it is surprisingly easy to do these things, no matter how good one is at English! Also remind them that they should check their spellings, as everything must be spelt correctly.

Do the first question as a whole class, going through the 'Help' questions before you agree on the answer.

For the remaining questions, students work in pairs.

Answers to Help questions

Set 1 speak / gerund / in
Set 2 gerund / *do*
Set 3 it's not a surprise / noun
Set 4 past / take
Set 5 speech / on – of
Set 6 stop + gerund / make
Set 7 wish + *had* + past participle / pay / to
Set 8 today's / adverb / comparative forms of adjectives and adverbs, *more* and *less*, verbs

Answers

1 speaking/talking about herself in
2 losing (some/a little) weight would/will do
3 as no surprise
4 have taken more care in/while/when
5 a speech on behalf of
6 until it stops/has stopped making
7 I had paid more/greater attention to
8 considerably better in today's test than

Content overview

Themes

This unit is concerned with health and fitness.

Exam-related activities

Paper 1	**Reading**
Part 1	Multiple choice (short)
Paper 2	**Writing**
Part 1	Letter
Paper 3	**Use of English**
Part 1	Multiple-choice cloze
Part 4	Word formation (review)
Paper 4	**Listening**
Part 3	Multiple choice (long)
Paper 5	**Speaking**
Part 3	Collaborative task
Part 4	Further discussion

Other

Vocabulary	Health
Word formation	Verbs
Language focus	Reported speech
Listening	Passive smoking

Reading: CAE Part 1 — Multiple choice

Page 88

Photocopiable vocabulary exercise on page 153.

1 This is not an exam-type task. Students can react in any way they wish – through personal experience, anecdote or feelings. If no ideas are forthcoming, prompt with other lines of questioning, such as 'This unit is about health and fitness; what aspect of this topic is illustrated in the three pictures?'

2 Do not allow this to become a detailed read, and students should not look at the exam-style questions yet.

Answers

Text A matches with picture 3
Text B with picture 1
Text C with picture 2

3 Students do the task.

Answers

1 A 2 B 3 C 4 C 5 B 6 D

When discussing the answers, you might focus on Question 2 from the first text. With such questions, students should first locate the quoted bit of text from the question, then find and underline the options. Then they should match one of the options to the question. The two phrases here are very similar in meaning.

You might also focus on Question 4 in the second text. Here the question focuses on the whole extract – so there is more than just one place one could underline as containing the answer. Ask students to supply evidence for the writer's scepticism: things like 'I was a little taken aback at first', 'Oh please, don't do that anymore', 'feeling eerie and ill at ease', all suggest scepticism indirectly, then in the final paragraph, there are more direct references to scepticism – 'but the next day I was back to normal and I never got that sensation of instant energy again', and especially the whole of the last sentence.

Reacting to the texts

Be ready to ask further questions as and when required, and if suitable for your class:
Do you know if such trials exist in your country?
Have you heard any news stories about them?
Why is the pharmaceuticals company taking this action?
What alternative therapies have you heard of? How do they work?
Have you ever required emergency attention at a hospital?

Vocabulary: Health Page 90

A Health problems

A1–2 This section should be done after doing the reading texts, as the first task involves finding words from the text.

Answers

A 1	A 2
1 chronic	1 tooth, bone
2 pressure	2 ankle, wrist
3 allergic	3 nose
4 blinding	4 shoulder, hip, jaw
5 infections	5 ribs, thigh
	6 glands, lips, feet

The speaking section can easily be expanded if enough interest is being shown in the topic:
How many days have you missed from school this year?
Do you tend to get certain types of illness and not others?
Do you tend to get ill at the same time each year?
What influence do you think the weather has on your health?
How many times have you been in hospital in your life?

B Phrasal verbs

B1–2 There are a number of useful phrasal verbs on the topic of health. These are all taken from the reading text. Students should try this exercise first without looking at the text. They use the text only to check their answers.

Answers

B 1

1 carrying out	3 got round	5 ease off
2 set up	4 taken back	6 put down

Use of English: CAE Part 1 Multiple-choice cloze Page 91

1–2 Background information

This phenomenon is growing rapidly in many countries. Governments and doctors cautiously welcome it, hoping that it will save large amounts of money in unnecessary visits to doctors. However, the difficulties involved in diagnosing patients who one cannot examine directly are obvious.

Answers

1 A	4 A	7 A	10 B
2 C	5 D	8 A	11 C
3 C	6 D	9 C	12 C

Note: In question 8 a medical complaint is a secondary meaning of 'complaint' – a synonym of 'condition'.

Draw students' attention to the 'Self help' box. Encourage them to analyse each text they read for useful vocabulary around a topic. Use of English texts can be particularly useful. From this text, they might record the following:

0 fall ill
1 come out in a painful rash
2 a mild fever
be diagnosed as having + illness (eg shingles)
3 the doctor prescribed + medicine etc
4 relieve the pain
5 medical consultation
8 medical complaint
10 contract + disease (eg malaria)
basic medical facilities
12 serious illness

It can also be very useful, while feedback is being given, for teachers to focus on a few carefully chosen wrong options. They too provide useful input and wordbuilding possibilities.

Here are some examples:

1 We use *passed out* when somebody has *fainted*, or lost consciousness.
4 *Lighten* sounds tempting, but is not the right answer, as it's not used with 'health'. It occurs commonly in the expression *lighten your (work)load*.
12 We say that an illness is *fatal*. *Deathly* is quite rare, but does occur in the common collocation 'a deathly hush' – meaning a sudden silence.

If you are in any doubt, a good dictionary will reveal plenty of such information about the use and collocations of such words.

3 Students follow instructions.

Speaking 1: Collaborative task
CAE Part 3
Page 92

At this stage in the course, do not be bound by the time constraints of the exam. The task should prove relevant and interesting, so allow students enough time to explore their knowledge of this topic fully. Extend the discussion element by getting feedback from various groups/pairs on their 1, 2, 3 choice.

Useful language

Point out that in such a task, where your focus is on doing the task correctly, it is easy to rely on some familiar expressions and say them again and again. Write on the board:

very important a big effect very effective

In order to impress the examiner, it is necessary to show a good range of vocabulary (and grammar). Often the key to this is collocation. It is collocation that can enrich and improve students' English.

In 1, 2 and 3, students will work on this.

Answers

1 a utterly **b** elementary

2 a *significant* implies a much greater effect than in the case of the other three. Preposition: *on*
b *reasonably* suggests that it is less effective than in the case of the other three. Preposition: *in*

3 a *pay, to* **b** *take, of*

Speaking 2: Further discussion
CAE Part 4
Page 93

Remind students:

- to give full answers to the questions, justifying their opinions and developing their arguments. They should not feel worried about being judged on the 'quality' of what they say – it is their language which is being assessed.
- that they should respond to what their partner says, and pick up on their ideas. Part of the assessment is based on how well the students interact.

As students do the task, circulate and collect good ideas that different pairs come up with. Share these with the whole class when the activity is finished.

Listening: Multiple choice
CAE Part 3
Page 93

1 Students follow instructions.
2 Ask students to read the six questions only and ignore the options for now.

Elicit that we know the following information:

- There are two speakers, Dr Evans and Lynnie. From the pronouns, we know that Dr Evans is the male voice and Lynnie the female one.
- We know that Dr Evans gives the treatment at special parties.
- We know that Dr Evans and Lynnie both have the treatment.

Remind students that in the long Multiple-choice listening there are two or more speakers who interact. Questions will reflect this. Point out that we can predict that questions 1, 3 and 6 will come from Dr Evans' turns, and 2, 4 and 5 from Lynnie's.

This simple process will help students to locate the answers in the text.

Now play the recording. See below for a way of simplifying the task.

Extra help

If your students still need extra help with this difficult task, photocopy the task with the A–D options taken out. Students close their books and answer the six photocopied questions in pairs, discussing what they have heard and what the answer seems to be. Finally let them return to their books and see which A–D option best corresponds with the answer they have written.

Answers

1 C 2 A 3 A 4 D 5 B 6 D

3 Take this as a whole class activity if the topic is likely to be unfamiliar, or in pairs if you think students will have plenty to say on the issues.

Other questions that might be asked:

- Can you name any celebrities who have undergone cosmetic surgery or had botox injections?
- Have you heard of any occasions when such operations have gone wrong?
- The doctor seems to have no doubts, but do you think what he is doing is ethical?

Listening script 1.27

(P = Presenter; DE = Dr Evans; L = Lynnie)

P: In search of a more youthful appearance, many people nowadays are turning to Botox, the botulism toxin which is purified and used in small doses to remove unwanted wrinkles. With me is Dr Duncan Evans, who regularly turns up at parties to inject the guests with the toxin, and Lynnie Highfield, one of Dr Evans' patients and a regular Botox party-goer. Dr Evans, perhaps I should begin by asking why this treatment takes place at parties and not in a surgery?

DE: That's very simple, really. It's easier, and more convenient, for people to go to a social gathering at a friend's house, than to give up their valuable time getting into central London. When I first started out in this business, I'd often be asked to go to the homes of the rich and famous, the type of people who didn't want to get caught by the press going into a clinic. Now, though, it's mainly people who've simply got too much going on in their lives to justify making the journey in.

P: Is that your case, Lynnie?

L: Yes, it is. Plus of course we have a good time. I've been to several parties in the last couple of years and you tend to meet up with the same people. That's largely because the benefits of the injection tend to wear off after three or four months so we all keep going back for more.

P: Is it painful?

L: Nowhere near as painful as having your legs waxed, I can tell you! Just a slight discomfort as the needle goes in, that's all. And there are no serious side-effects – or so Dr Evans tells us – just some minor bruising and an outside chance of getting some fluey, cold-like symptoms.

P: So Dr Evans, how does it work? Why would anyone want to have a poison injected into their body?

DE: Well, yes, poison it most certainly is, and a deadly one at that. But injected in small quantities into the forehead it does nothing more than paralyse the muscles that cause frown lines and wrinkles. Different people use it for different reasons – to make them feel better, to look younger, to enable them to get work on television – whatever. Of course, I need to set a good example if I want to convince people of the benefits of the treatment, so I regularly hand over the needle to my wife, who does it for me. She's a qualified nurse, so I have every confidence in her.

P: Does it work for you?

DE: Well, I make a living, if that's what you mean, but perhaps I should have started younger – as you can see, I've still got one or two faint lines there.

P: And how about you, Lynnie. Why do you have the injections?

L: For me it's a way of growing old gracefully. I mean, we all use moisturizer, we all take care of ourselves. I think it's just an extension of that. Many people might baulk at the price, but I think it's fairly affordable. It's certainly worth doing, anyway. I look upon it now as normal maintenance – something that needs doing on a regular basis. I also like doing meditation, as well. I want to feel beautiful on the inside as well as on the outside.

P: And have other people noticed the effects?

L: Yes, they have. And they've grown used to my new look now, of course, but when I first went for treatment, they didn't say, 'Oh, you do look younger', which is of course why I had it done. It was more of a 'you look less stressed' or 'you don't look so depressed'. Before the treatment, you see, I had these terrible hereditary lines, a kind of constant frown, which made it look as though I was permanently unhappy. I was always saying, 'I'm fine. Really. It's just the way I look'. Now I don't have to make excuses for my appearance any more.

P: You must be very proud of your work, Dr Evans, knowing the effect it can have on people's lives. And it's fun too, I imagine.

DE: It's certainly a wonderful feeling seeing people grow in confidence and self-esteem. I'm not a great one for being charming and chatty when I'm working, though – that would just be too draining. Dealing with twenty-odd patients in one evening is not normal, by any stretch of the imagination, and it takes a lot out of you. But no one seems to notice that. I'm obviously so fresh-faced and young-looking ...

P: Now it's funny you should mention that, because I've been dying to ask you about your age ...

Language focus: Reported speech

Page 94

A Direct and reported speech

A1 Do this as a whole-class activity, and elicit the answers.

Answers

A 1 Tense changes: present perfect in direct speech changes to past perfect in reported speech.
Other changes: use of 'if' when reporting yes/no question; changes to pronouns and possessive adjectives (*my* to *her*); changes to time adverbials (*now* disappears in the reported speech version).

A2 This can be done in pairs. If your students are familiar with reported speech, eg from having done the First Certificate exam, the information in the note in the answer box will be relevant.

Answers

A2

1 admitted, had sold, pointed out, had given
2 predicted, would be, warned, might be
3 concluded, had to, reminded, didn't/did not, would go
4 announced, intends, stressed, has not/had not

Note
This 'back tense' effect is standard and common, but native speakers sometimes mix past reporting verbs with present following verbs.
In 1 *has sold* and *has given* are also possible – present perfect would suggest this is either recent or new information.
In 2 *will be* is also possible if the protest has not yet taken place.
In 3 *must/have to, don't, will go* are also possible if the speaker is thinking of the future.

B Alternative verb patterns

B1–2 Remind students of the need to show a good 'range of grammar' in productive papers (writing and speaking). Students often overuse 'said' as a reporting verb, but there are many common alternatives. This exercise focuses on the grammar of these alternatives.

Answers

B 2
1 C **2** B **3** A **4** D

B3 As you receive answers from students, put some of them in mini sentences. eg 'threatened to do something ... yes ... He threatened to strangle her.' Encourage students to do the same. Each mini sentence must be a different context. Amusing ones are especially welcome!

Answers

B 3

threaten: B	persuade: A
recommend: A, C, D	ask: A, B, D
encourage: A	offer: B
demand: B, D	

C Verbs and dependent prepositions
Using these alternative reporting verbs means getting right the prepositions that go with them!

Answers

C
1 for **2** on **3** of **4** against **5** to

Practice

1a Play the first five lines of the recording only, pausing after 'risk of heart disease'. Write the example on the board to show what kind of notes students should take. Then play the rest of the recording.

1b Show how the reported speech in the second example relates to the information in the first example. Then students do the same for two more of the points in their notes.

2 While comparing, each student should check the grammar of their partner's sentences.

3 Students speak in pairs and give reasons for their choice.

Answers

Possible answers
Answers may include the following main ideas:
The man claimed that 50% of smokers would die of a smoking-related illness.
The woman claimed that passive smoking was not a risk.
The woman pointed out that smokers tended not to eat a lot of fresh fruit and vegetables, and that this could also cause lung cancer.

Listening script 1.28–1.29

Male doctor

We know that non-smokers living with smokers inhale small amounts of nicotine. This poses a risk to their health, as they are probably taking in a proportionate amount of the life-threatening components, too. It's difficult to predict exactly how great the danger is for passive smokers, as that depends on the exposure, but studies have shown that passive smokers have a 20 per cent increased risk of heart disease.

The fact is that half of all active smokers will die of an illness related to their smoking and that tobacco will most certainly be one of the biggest causes of death in the world's population this century. It is nonsense to suggest that passive smoking has zero risk.

Female doctor

Passive smoking poses no risk at all. Researchers have been into homes and recorded nicotine levels in the blood of passive smokers. The figure is too small to be of any real danger and it cannot possibly cause a 20 per cent increased risk of heart disease.

Research has also shown that smokers do not include fresh fruit and vegetables in their diet and have a high intake of saturated fats. This in itself can lead to a higher risk of getting lung cancer. Obviously, people living with smokers will share their lifestyle and diet. That's what causes them to fall ill, not the passive smoking.

Word formation: Verbs Page 95

This section is best done after the listening in the section on reported speech. If done in class, it could lead into the Word formation exam task in the review at the end of the unit.

1 This should be done as pairwork. It is important for students to write down the verb forms, as well as underlining the odd one out. Point out that they may need to make changes to the spelling in order to make the affixes fit. In the example, this applies to summary → summarize.

Point out also that the affix 'ise' is also acceptable. British English tends to favour the 'ise' spelling, and American English the 'ize'. Both would be correct in the exam.

Answers

1
1 classify exemplify simplify identify <u>generalize/ise</u>
2 differentiate <u>qualify</u> captivate evaluate assassinate
3 characterize stabilize familiarize <u>dominate</u> computerize
4 strengthen sadden <u>enrich</u> deafen heighten
5 enlarge <u>widen</u> ensure endanger encourage

During or after the task, encourage students to think about putting some of these words into phrases or small sentences. At the same time you can check on the meaning of some of the more difficult ones. A possible question would be: 'Now, are there any of these words that you wouldn't be able to use in a sentence yourself?'

This could be done by asking individual students for one such word each. Then either supply a context yourself, or get the rest of the class to do so.

2 This could be related to the Word formation exam task. 'If the word 'cook' appeared in the exam, as one of the bold words to the right of the text, how many different prefixes can you think of to go with it?'

Check also that students understand the meaning of the prefixes. Ask the following:

- Which three have a negative sense? (= un-, dis- and mis-)
- Which of the three is often about doing things wrongly (= mis-)
- Which one means 'do again'? (= re-)
- Which one has a sense of 'do too much'? (= over-)
- Which one has a sense of 'greater or better than'? (= out-)

Answers

reappear, disappear
reread, misread
renumber, outnumber
reload, overload, unload
rehear, overhear, mishear
reuse, overuse, misuse (disused and unused – both adjectives)

3 Now the material is recycled. Some of the affixes or verbs in 1 and 2 are put in gapped sentences.

Answers

1 evaluated	**5** familiarizing/ising
2 deafening	**6** outlived
3 disqualified	**7** validated
4 outnumbering	**8** ensures

4 Try to 'visit' as many pairs as possible to check that the sentences students have made are producing the correct target language.

Writing: Letter Page 96
CAE Part 1

1 You might also ask students who have some experience of fitness clubs how this one compares with the one they know. Check the following vocabulary items:

- cardiovascular – exercising your heart and lungs
- treadmill – an indoor running machine (see photo)
- manicure – care of the nails
- waxing – ladies removing hair from their legs
- aquarobics – aerobics in water (see photo)
- Step – a fitness programme based on stepping on and jumping off benches

2 Read the task together, pausing to check on any potentially problematic vocabulary. After reading discuss the likely level of formality the situation demands.

Answers

A member of the health club is writing to the General Manager, so one would expect the register to be more formal than informal. However, students should not go too far; the Manager's letter is semi-formal, with its use of bullet points and 'Kind regards'. The most important thing is that the register should be consistent throughout the letter.

3 This can be done with the whole class.

Answer

appreciative, friendly, polite and constructive

Point out that it is often not appropriate to reproduce the tone established in the handwritten notes. Here, appreciative, constructive comments are needed. The tone should not be too negative and complaining.

4 Emphasize that students will also have to compare and link different bits of input information in this way in the exam.

Answers

purchase of equipment for the gym ⟶ take on extra instructors
building of a second sauna ⟶ extend changing room

5 This could be done as homework.

Useful language
Remind students of the importance of demonstrating a range of vocabulary in writing tasks, and not relying on one repeated reporting verb (often 'said').

Exercise 1 focuses on this, and exercise 2 on use of collocation for the same purpose.

Answers

1 *demand*, *insist* and *warn* would not be in keeping with a polite, friendly, constructive and appreciative tone; *reckon* would be too informal for this task.

2

1 suited (*suitable* would be possible)
2 short
3 complete

Sample answer

Dear Mr Roberts,

The reason of this letter is to present my opinions about the changes to the club that the management proposed and also to propose additional changes.

To begin with, if you purchase some extra equipment for the Gym, it is not essential and would take up more space than the one currently available. So I suggest hiring more instructors so a greater variety of classes can be offered to the members.

It could be nice to have a second sauna. However, I should point out that this improvement is not what the club is in the greatest need of. More useful maybe to extend the area dedicated to changing facilities, provided they are big enough to fit everyone in.

Finally, for improving the snack bar, I believe that buying a second microwave and some other cooking facilities would allow people to enjoy a wide range of dishes. The acquisition of a wide screen TV makes for a cost I feel to be not afordable.

I expect the proposals to be useful for you when you make the final desicion and look forward to know what do you think for them.

Yours sincerely,

Olaf Johansson

Examiner's comment
Content: The writing addresses the main points successfully.

Organization and cohesion: At paragraph level the letter is well organized and coherent – the various pieces of information from the different input texts have been cleverly combined. Some sentences and phrases, however, read somewhat awkwardly eg *'a cost I feel to be not afordable'.*

Accuracy: There are minor problems in accuracy eg *The reason of this letter, look forward to know.*
Range: There is evidence of a good range of vocabulary and tense usage. (*'The acquisition of a wide screen TV ...', '... is not what the club is in the greatest need of*).

Register: The register is generally appropriately formal.

Target Reader: Would be well informed and clear about what is expected.

Mark: Band 4

Review 7 answers Pages 98 and 99

Use of English: Word formation
CAE Part 3

1 tiredness
2 combinations
3 noticeably
4 unwanted
5 purifies
6 sharpens
7 moisturizing/moisturising
8 growth
9 immunity
10 memorize/memorise

Vocabulary: Health crossword
Across: **2** complaint **6** foot **7** ankle **9** headache **11** rash **12** thigh **13** nose
Down: **1** stomach **3** pain **4** tooth **5** ill **6** fever **8** muscle **10** drug

Reported speech
1
1 having **2** about **3** need **4** them **5** of

Possible Answers
1 She insisted we go and visit them some time and assured us we would love it there.
2 He apologised/apologized for not phoning earlier and explained that he had been very busy.
3 He warned her that it was a very dangerous part of town and urged her not to go there on her own.
4 She recommended he wear gloves on the run the next day, and reminded him to do some warm-up exercises beforehand.
5 He predicted it might rain at the weekend, but promised to take them all to the funfair if it didn't.

8 This is the modern world

Content overview

Themes

This unit is concerned with technology/inventions/computers/the future.

Exam-related activities

Paper 1	**Reading**
Part 2	Gapped text
Paper 2	**Writing**
Part 1	Reports
Paper 3	**Use of English**
Part 1	Multiple-choice cloze (review)
Part 4	Gapped sentences
Part 5	Key word transformations (review)
Paper 4	**Listening**
Part 2	Sentence completion
Part 4	Multiple matching

Other

Vocabulary 1	Amount
Vocabulary 2	Verbs formed with *up*, *down*, *over* and *under*
Language focus 1	Determiners and pronouns
Language focus 2	Modal verbs 2
Language focus 3	Talking about the future

Optional lead-in activity

- Write the following on bits of card: dishwasher, electric toothbrush, plastic, exercise bike (a stationery bike on which you exercise in your house/garage), television.
- Put students in groups of five and give a different card to each person.
- Give them one minute to work silently and individually. They must think up some reasons why their object was the most useless invention of the 20th century.
- In their groups they must put forward their arguments. They have two minutes to do this.
- When they have finished, the other people in the group have time to criticize the arguments made.

Alternatively, if you think your students will have difficulties thinking up their own ideas (point 3), first put them in five groups. Give each group the same card. They then have two minutes to brainstorm ideas. Then they go into new groups of five people, each with a different card in order to present their case individually.

Listening 1: Sentence completion

CAE Part 2

Page 100

1 Speaking point

Take this as a whole-class brainstorming activity.

Answers

Possible answers

Uses for a mobile phone: work, phoning friends, text messaging, taking photos, calling for help, calculator, games, alarm, Internet, storing information, impressing friends

Some reasons why people don't have them: don't want to have to carry round something fragile and valuable, find them an anti-social nuisance, don't know how to use them ('technophobes'), think they're too expensive.

2 Activity to assist with 'cueing'

- It is important not to miss the 'cue' for each answer – this means the information in each answer which tells you when to expect the answer in the script.
- To make this point, explain that they will be listening for three whole minutes to someone talking, but the questions only require them to focus on eight bits of information. So clearly there is plenty of content in the script which they do **not** need in order to complete the task. This task is partly about listening for the information you need, and discarding the information you don't need.
- It is therefore important to underline or highlight the key words in each sentence. The 'cue' for the first question is likely to be *The first category*.
- Put this to the test. Play the first few lines of the script; when students hear a reference to *The first category* they should put their hands up. Then stop the recording and ask which words have cued the first answer (= *four main types*). Do not focus on the actual answer yet.
- Establish that the words in the script which cue the answer (*four main types*) will usually be an approximate paraphrase of the idea in the question (*The first category*) rather than the exact same words.
- Then give students a minute or so to highlight the key words for questions 2–8.

At this point, **either** students do the exam task **or**, if you feel they need more help, continue with the cueing activity as above for questions 2–8. With pens down, tell students to focus on the cues rather than the answers. Proceed as per the last bullet point above.

Answers

Answers to cueing activity

2 Style bandits
3 Hedonists and resisters ... simplicity
4 colours
5 Food colours
6 UK teenagers
7 Ring tones
8 High prices

Answers

Answers to exam task

1 rational/(a) rational buyer
2 art object
3 low cost
4 personality
5 childhood
6 50%/fifty per cent/half
7 in the charts
8 easy to remember/memorable

Listening script 1.30

Radio presenter

Fashion accessory, work tool or just in case of emergencies? Mobile phones mean different things to different people, and information about who uses them and why is of great interest to the companies that produce them. One leading manufacturer has divided customers into four main types.

First, there are the 'rational' buyers, those who use their phones for email and Internet access, as well as making calls. This kind of buyer puts performance and extra features above style and appearance. That's more the priority of the second category, the so-called 'style bandits', who look upon the mobile phone more as an art object than a communication device. These people are willing to pay whatever it takes to ensure their phone projects the right image.

The final two categories, the 'hedonists' and the 'resisters', are similar in one respect, but very different in another. Both want easy-to-use phones at low cost, but the 'hedonists' are young, fun-loving people whose phone seems permanently attached to their ear, while the 'resisters' are against mobile phones but feel they have to own one.

Whatever type of user you are, you can guarantee the manufacturers have designed a mobile phone to suit your needs.

They'll also have produced a handset or a replacement cover in a colour to suit your personality. According to psychologists, the colour of a mobile phone speaks volumes about its user. Yellow, for example, is a bold, bright colour which appeals to the lively, energetic type, whereas someone who is calmer and more reflective may choose green or brown. Many people are attracted by food colours, like honey, apple or marshmallow, which, it seems, can stir up memories of our childhood and all the good things associated with it.

Colour, of course, is not the only feature we have a choice in – ring tones can also be personalized. You can download them from the Web, buy them on a scratch card or order them over the phone. Incredibly, over fifty per cent of teenagers in the UK have paid for a ring tone at some point. It's a lucrative business – in Europe alone it is worth hundreds of millions of pounds each year.

Ring tones cover every musical genre including themes from the Bond movies, classical music, country dancing and, for the teenage market, whatever happens to be in the charts. And because that changes every week, it's hardly surprising that teenagers are spending more on ring tones than anyone else.

At the top end of the market there's another type of personalization available to users. Companies are paying huge sums for mobile phone numbers that are easy to remember. Numbers with a repeated pattern, such as 450 450 will cost around three hundred pounds, but a string of the same digits like 555 555 or a run of consecutive numbers – 123 456 – can fetch upwards of twenty thousand pounds. In China, eight is a lucky number, and Chinese businessmen are apparently offering incredible amounts of money for any number with a series of eights ...

3 Speaking

Here the discussion broadens out into other issues. Refer to other points you may have heard about mobile phones, such as the rumoured health risks involved. Another interesting point is the way they have changed society. For example, there are far fewer public phones around these days, as there is an expectation that most people will prefer to use their mobile.

Language focus 1: Determiners and pronouns Page 101

Ideally this section would be done in the next lesson after the listening.

Explain that determiners and pronouns are commonly tested in the Use of English paper.

1 Play the listening recording from the previous section, so that students can complete the gaps (the recording needs to be played, as otherwise there are several possible right answers).

Answers

1 one respect
2 in another
3 Both want
4 own one
5 Many people
6 every musical genre
7 another type

2 Take this as a whole-class activity rather than pairwork.

Answers

1 determiner
2 pronoun
3 pronoun
4 pronoun
5 determiner
6 determiner
7 determiner

3a Make sure the correct sentences are all said aloud, so that models of correct English are heard by students.

Answers

3 a Grammatically incorrect words:
1 All **2** every **3** Several

3b Read out the example and then extend as follows:
'Some mobile phones enable you to log on to the internet.'
'No mobile phones have built-in printers.'

Then students supply sentences for 1, 2 and 3.

(Further examples if more help is needed:
No outfield player is allowed to handle the ball in football, except when the ball is out of play, or when taking throw-ins.
Each player is allowed to handle the ball in rugby.
Neither player is allowed to handle the ball in tennis, except when serving.)

4 Students continue in pairs.

Answers

4
1 every many
2 another one month
3 no many

Practice
1–2 The practice stage is best done in pairs.

Answers

1
1 Every other year *or* Every two years, each other *or* one another
2 most of them play, none is very welcoming
3 there's every likelihood, no intention
4 on the other hand, as much/many as twenty hours

2
1 lot, little
2 none
3 every
4 Either
5 All, any
6 few, most
7 one
8 each

3 These expressions are commonly used by native speakers, and certainly make for impressive use of English! The distinctions between them in meaning are often quite subtle, so before students do the task in exercise 3, highlight the meaning/features of use of the following:

second to none (2) means 'the very best'.
When we say *every single one* we use emphatic stress (louder, higher pitch, slower delivery).
either way (4) means 'Whichever alternative you take'.
When we say *all too often* (5) we are making the point that this fact is regrettable/unfortunate.
a good few (6) means 'quite a lot of'.

Vocabulary 1: Amount Page 102

This section looks at useful phrases and collocations (*at low cost, huge sums of money etc*). As well as being useful for the productive papers, these are sometimes tested in the key word transformations task (Use of English Part 5).

1–2 Both exercises can be done in pairs.

Answers

1
1 no limit
2 full refund
3 great deal
4 small discount
5 high cost
6 large/high number

2 Possible answers
1 The details of a competition.
2 A mail order company explaining the rights of customers who are not satisfied with a product they have ordered.
3 A newspaper article about a forthcoming event such as a concert or sporting contest.

4 A shop offering discount to customers who pay in cash rather than by credit card.
5 A company explaining to retailers the reasons for a recent price increase.
6 A warning letter to an employee whose work or behaviour has been the subject of complaint.

Gapped sentences

Page 103

Students do the task in their coursebooks.

Possible approach
If they are having difficulties with any particular question, write down six or so words on the board that fit in the individual gaps. Then students choose which one goes in all three sentences. For example, in exercise 1 you would write 'high happy cash full wonderful great' on the board, then students have to put these words in each gap (answer = gap 1.1 high full great; gap 1.2 happy full wonderful great; gap 1.3 cash full. 'Full' appears in all three gaps so must be the answer. 'Great' appears in two of the gaps, but that isn't enough, because it doesn't work in gap 1.3.

Answers

1 full **2** deal **3** cost **4** high **5** limit

Note that in previous gapped sentence exercises we have given help to students by showing collocations in bold print. From this point on, we give less help, but students should still underline and record useful collocations (eg at full speed, paid in full, deal with complaints).

Gapped text

Page 104

Photocopiable vocabulary exercise on page 154.

1 Take this as a whole-class activity and brainstorm ideas.

2 Put the following questions on the board, and give students just one minute to read the base text only (not the gapped paragraphs on the next page):

What picture do you get of the writer? What key information do we learn about him?

Answers

Answers to questions in Teacher's Book
He is old-fashioned and unwilling to change his ways.
He is probably a writer by profession – he did some research in the library.
He sounds like an 'arty' person, surrounded by books and music.

Explain that the tone of the piece is jokey and ironic. One of the ways the writer achieves this effect is by his use of invented words. Put the following on the board:

Internot   snail mail   internaut

The writer thinks the new 'language' of computers (dot coms, email etc) is ridiculous, and makes fun of it with these invented words. Ask students what they mean:

Answers

Answer to question in Teacher's Book
Internot – someone who hasn't got access to the Internet.
Snail mail – letters sent by post.
Internaut – someone who uses the Internet.

If you think your students will have difficulty with the text, put the following Help box on the board:

1 The text immediately after the gap suggests that gap 1 has ended with a long list of things that you can do on the Internet.
2 You are looking for something that links back to 'friends' and forward to 'snail mail'.
3 The paragraph you need is likely to continue and finish the writer's story about the library.
4 The text before the gap talks about computers being 'unattractive and bulky'. The text after the gap talks about the writer's own equipment.
5 The paragraphs before and after the gap both deal with music.
6 The paragraph you need is likely to be an example of 'quaint, old-fashioned way(s)'.

Now students read and do the task.

Textual notes
word processor – a rather old-fashioned machine, an electronic typewriter.
the whole kit and caboodle – jokey way of saying 'everything'.

Answers

1 C **2** G **3** B **4** F **5** E **6** A
D not used

Reacting to the text
It is helpful for the students if your own role during such fluency exercises has a single, pre-planned focus, such as:

- circulating and helping with ideas
- circulating and listening for errors – which you will deal with after the activity
- circulating and listening for 'language you needed but didn't know'. During feedback the aim is to widen and enrich students' vocabulary, especially phrasal verbs ('you said x but you could have said y').

Vocabulary 2 Page 106

Verbs formed with *up*, *down*, *over* and *under*
Ask students to close their books. Write the three examples on the board minus the prepositional part of the verb:
The world is being _____ run by people ... worrying about _____ dating and _____ grading.
We can now _____ load our music from the Net.
Companies are constantly _____ cutting each other.

Link this to the gapped-text reading students have just done – explain that the three examples are taken from it. Ask if anyone can remember the full form of the verbs. They will need to put in a preposition in order to do this.

Students can then open their books to check the answers.

Then they complete the six sentences in pairs or threes. There are a number of such verbs formed by combining a preposition and a verb – more can be found in a good dictionary – but the ones focused on here are particularly common. Tell them you will look at the meaning of the words after the exercise, as the examples given will show how they are used. Give extensive feedback as follows:

Answers

1 *overthrown* This is the only use of the word – a government/dictator etc being overthrown. The meaning is something like 'remove from power'.
2 *downsizing* This is the main use of the word – when a company reduces the size of its operation, in the interests of cost and efficiency.
3 *overrule* This means something like 'use your superior authority to change a decision' – could be anyone in a position of higher authority eg a police inspector, a Head Teacher etc.
upheld When a decision that has been questioned is confirmed as correct.
4 *undertook* In this context could mean 'promise', but also has the sense of 'made themselves responsible for'.
5 *undergone* In this context could mean 'had' but generally means something like 'go through an unpleasant process'.
downplaying Could also be 'playing down', meaning something like 'make it appear less important than it is'.
6 *uprooted* This means 'leave a place where you have settled down'.

Language focus 2: Modal verbs Page 106

1 Go through the examples with the whole class.

2 Give detailed feedback as follows:
(**0** notice that *will* and *shall* can both be used for offers.)

Answers

1 Refusal You could say 'It refuses to start' or 'he refused to move it'. Here *wouldn't* is simply the past of *won't*, so we have present and past refusal.
2 Willingness An unusual use of *will* which may surprise students – in this case you can use *will* with 'if'.
3 Habit This use of *would*, meaning 'used to', is well known, but *will* can be used in the same way.

4 Assumption This is assumption, because the phone rings and the speaker assumes the caller is Mike.
5 Annoying behaviour *Would* is used when there is a sense of frustration from the speaker and a feeling of 'How typical!'.
6 Request for advice/instructions Note that *will* is not normally used in this case.

3 This exercise might also be done while going through the answers for exercise 2.

Answers

1 car
2 television
3 Nintendo GameBoy
4 telephone (receiver)
5 oven
6 fridge/freezer

4 Draw students' attention to the fact that the 'it' objects referred to in exercise 2 were all domestic appliances, machines or other electronic devices. In their own sentences, students can either choose a different object or one of the same objects but with a different context.

Writing: Reports

CAE Part 1

Page 107

1 Discuss these questions in whole-class mode. Ask individuals in what ways they have used computers and other technological aids for language learning and whether they have found them useful.

2 Ask a few students which features of the centre appeal to them.

3 Point out that students are now going to write about a multimedia centre in another language school.

Check students have grasped the facts by asking the following:

Where is this situation based?	(a language school)
Who are *you*, the writer?	(a helper in the Multimedia Centre)
Who is Alan Shields?	(the Director)
Why has Alan written you?	(to ask you to write a to report on the Centre)
Who wrote the four comments on the right?	(different users of the centre)
Why did they write these comments?	(they were sent a questionnaire)
Who sent the questionnaire?	(you, the writer)
What information goes in the report?	(student's opinions and your suggestions for improvements)

- Alan's letter asks for a summary of what the other users say. So it is not enough merely to repeat the four comments from students. They will need to be paraphrased as far as possible, and ideally grouped/presented in a different way.

Go through the 'How to go about it' box with students, and remind them of the following points made in Unit 3 of the Teacher's Book.

- Writing a report in essay or letter format would be misunderstanding the task. Therefore, while candidates are not expected to write in perfect report format, they will impress if they can use underlinings/headings/bullets etc.
- Reports also tend to have a clear beginning, stating the purpose of the report, who commissioned it, what its scope is etc and a clear conclusion at the end.

Point out that there are two possible ways of organizing the report:

i) First summarize students' comments. Then make suggestions for improvements in later paragraphs. This would be standard procedure in a report.

ii) Deal with both elements in the question at the same time. This would mean having more thematic paragraphs, such as:

<u>Introduction</u>
<u>Audiovisual equipment</u>
Films are not international
CD players are poor quality
Suggested solutions

<u>Misuse of/lack of sufficient computers</u>
You can't always get on a computer because some people are writing emails.
Suggested solution

<u>Number of people/Conditions</u>
Too hot, crowded, too noisy
Suggested solution

Praise
Like the DVD library
Listening material is excellent

Alternatively, the first two sections could be joined under the heading 'equipment'.

Finally elicit from students that the task requires a fairly formal register – you are writing a report for the director of the school. Note that the language in the questionnaire notes is informal (eg 'shame the CD players are so bad'). Such language will need to be made more formal.

4 Students write the report.

Multiple matching

Page 109

1 Students focus first on the comments in task one and speak about them briefly.

Then check students know the meaning of the feelings in task two. (Indifference = the speaker doesn't really care/doesn't have strong feelings about something.)

2 Play the recording. Students do the exam task.

Answers

1 D	2 A	3 H	4 C	5 B
6 D	7 C	8 F	9 G	10 B

Listening script 1.31–1.35

Speaker 1

I think a lot of the science fiction scenarios of miniature computers the size of a matchbox and phones you can wear like a button on your jacket are going to be too impractical to be put to general use. You only have to look at a wide-screen TV to realize there's little chance of that happening. My own belief is that electronic gadgetry will actually take over our living space – you won't be able to move in your own home for fear of knocking into some device or other. That's a big shame, really – life was so much simpler before, so much more free of clutter. And I'm not talking about the dim and distant past here, but a relatively recent one.

Speaker 2

There's little doubt that the average lifespan will be greater, but I can't help feeling more than a little concerned about the quality of life we'll be leading when we reach the end of our days. I'm not sure, for example, that we'll have achieved what we need to in terms of finding cures for certain degenerative diseases such as Alzheimer's or Parkinson's. There's a great deal of enthusiastic talk about genetics and how absolutely marvellous it is that we've mapped the human genome Now that's all very well, but I'm afraid I just can't see myself, or anyone else for that matter, playing tennis at the age of 120.

Speaker 3

It always irritates me when people go on about population growth and how it's getting out of control and so on. If you look at the figures, you'll see that predictions of exploding populations made twenty or thirty years ago are simply not coming true. It's probably the same people that worry about the number of vehicles on the roads, as well. Let's face it though, fifteen years from now most of us will be working from home on a computer, which means fewer people getting stuck in jams on their way to work, and a consequent reduction in pollution. Now that's definitely something worth looking forward to, isn't it?

Speaker 4

They sent me on a computer training course last month – at my age! We had a right laugh about it in the office, I can tell you. Still, you've got to keep up with it all, else they won't keep you on, will they? There seems to be more and more technology every day – it's going to change the way they do things here completely, you know. In fifteen years from now you won't recognize the place at all. Of course, I'll have left long before then, and I'll probably be enjoying a long and healthy retirement somewhere. But it does make you wonder whether they're up to something – you know, Big Brother and all that. I've always been suspicious of change, me. Can't help it.

Speaker 5

Where I live, you'd be forgiven for thinking the size of the population is mushrooming. Every weekend there are more and more houses going up, and you see more and more traffic on the roads. But what's happening, of course, is that the existing population is financially healthier than it used to be, so more and more people can afford to buy themselves a second home in the country – which is where they're all driving out to on a Friday evening. And because the price of land is so expensive, these places are gradually shrinking in size – so much so that by the time I've raised enough money to buy my own place, I won't be able to swing a cat in it. Sounds funny, but it's a real nuisance, I can tell you.

3 Speaking

In addition to the general question in the Coursebook, get students' reaction to any points in the listening which you think will be of interest to them/may be affecting their own lives/they may have heard about in the media (eg the phenomenon of people buying second homes).

Language focus 3: Talking about the future Page 109

1 In order to introduce the concept of 'same or different' needed for the next exercise, elicit from the class that sentences with *going to* and *will* (taken from the listening) are saying the same thing. However, the sentences with *I'll have left* and *I'll probably be enjoying* are saying different things.

Answers

1 a I'll probably be enjoying
b I'll have left

2 Suggested procedure: students discuss each one in pairs. Then they read the Grammar section. Finally they check the answers they have given, and change any if necessary.

Answers

1 D *I hope she passes* means 'I want her to pass'. *I expect she'll pass* means 'I think she'll pass'.
2 S No difference
3 D *Will you come* is a request or invitation. *Will you be coming* is a polite way of asking about someone's plans. The speaker is suggesting that the other person, the 'you', will already have decided whether to come or not.
4 D *The parcel should arrive* means it is expected to arrive. *The parcel might arrive* is simply suggesting a possibility.
5 S No difference, although whereas *due to* refers to only one train, the present simple can be used to refer to the regular daily/weekly service.
6 S No difference. Note that these two structures are more common in the past: *I was about to/on the point of.*
7 D *She's bound to get the job* means 'she's certain to get the job'. *She's likely to get the job* means 'she'll probably get the job'.
8 D *He's confident of success* means 'He thinks he will succeed' ie it is his opinion. *He's assured of success* means 'He is certain to succeed' ie it is the speaker's/other people's opinion.
9 D *They're planning on getting married* suggests they are more decided than in the other sentence.
10 D *The Government is to spend* means 'The Government will spend'. '*The Government is expected to spend*' is less certain.

3–4 This should be done individually, before comparing in exercise 4. The sentences can either be generally true in real life or true in the students' personal lives.

Alternatively, students could gap the parts of their sentences which refer to the future. Their partner completes the sentences. Then in exercise 4 both partners discuss the choice of tenses/structures in each of the sentences, and if necessary correct them.

Review 8 answers Pages 110 and 111

Determiners and pronouns

1 another
2 other
3 others
4 few
5 little
6 every
7 each
8 all
9 much
10 either

Use of English: CAE Part 5 Key word transformations

1 made the most of
2 are second to none
3 be driven/used every other
4 of every single one of/made by every single one of
5 would not/wouldn't keep changing
6 would often compete with one
7 probably have been/got held/caught
8 has no intention of making/has no wish/desire to make

Use of English: CAE Part 1 Multiple-choice cloze

1 B **2** C **3** B **4** B **5** A **6** D **7** B **8** C **9** C **10** D **11** C **12** B

9 Going places

Content overview

Themes

This unit is concerned with holidays and travel.

Exam-related activities

Paper 1	**Reading**
Part 4	Multiple matching
Paper 2	**Writing**
Part 2	Contributions: guidebook entry
Paper 3	**Use of English**
Part 3	Word formation (review)
Part 4	Gapped sentences (review)
Paper 4	**Listening**
Part 2	Sentence completion
Part 3	Multiple choice (long)
Paper 5	**Speaking**
Part 2	Long turn

Other

Vocabulary 1	Doing things alone
Vocabulary 2	Anger
Language focus	Creating emphasis
Word formation	Alternatives from the same prompt word

Reading: CAE Part 4 — Multiple matching

Page 112

Photocopiable vocabulary exercise on page 154.

Lead-in

Ask students to look at the pictures and tell their partner which of the activities they would rather do alone, and which with a group.

1 In case students need help with ideas, here are some of the pros and cons of holidaying alone.

✓ It enables you to experience a place yourself, so everything is much more personal and meaningful.

✓ You have plenty of time to think and take in the experience, without having to do what somebody else wants to do all the time.

✓ You experience a greater range of emotions – more highs and lows, a greater sense of excitement, achievement and the thrill of overcoming danger.

✗ You are seeing wonderful new things and it is a shame not to have someone there to share your experiences.

✗ Everything is much more dangerous, and the consequences of losing something become much more serious.

✗ If you are travelling in a group, you stand more chance of seeing all the important sights.

2 By now students should be thoroughly familiar with the multiple-matching task, so focus on something slightly different from before – distraction.

- Write question 15 on the board. Tell students the answer is E, and see how quickly they can find the answer in E (first two sentences of second paragraph).
- Then ask them to look at B and D. Say, 'There is something in both of these which might make you think they are the answer to 15 if you are not careful' (they are 'distracting' for 15).
- Ask them to find this distracting information.

Answers

Answers to 'distraction' task in Teacher's Book

B We did some sightseeing, went to night clubs ... (end of second paragraph)

D The trip itself combined culture, relaxation and travelling ... (end of second paragraph)

Emphasize to students the point of this activity – to make them aware that at first sight you may think you have the answer to a question (eg because you have found a similar idea or similar key words), but you then need to read very carefully and in a detailed way in order to check whether you have actually found a match.

Now students do the reading task.

Answers

1, 2 A & D in any order **3** C **4** E **5** A
6 B **7** C **8, 9** B & E in any order **10** D
11 A **12** C **13** A **14** B **15** E

Reacting to the text

Students follow instructions.

Vocabulary 1: Doing things alone
Page 114

Optional extra activity
Students underline any words or expressions in the reading which relate to doing things alone or being alone, eg going it alone.

Answers

Answers to extra activity in Teacher's Book
Introduction: go solo, with nobody but yourself to please, single travellers, blazed their own trail;
A: I'd never been away myself
B: I went on my own to Tenerife, the only single person, go on a singles holiday
C: I booked myself onto an expedition, everyone had come independently, I had a tent to myself
E: travelling alone, do their own thing as individuals

1 If you are not doing the optional extra activity, make the link with the reading text by saying that some of these expressions occurred in it.

Answers

1
1 self-made
2 single-handed
3 self-reliant
4 solitary

2 We now focus on useful phrases and expressions on the theme. This should be done as a pairwork activity.

Answers

The following words to be crossed out:
1 with, with, at **2** by, on **3** with, by

3–4 These speaking points are for pairwork. Students should try to use some of the expressions from exercises 1 and 2.

Listening 1: CAE Part 2 Sentence completion
Page 114

1 Package holiday – a holiday organized by a travel agent, for which you pay a fixed price that includes the cost of transport, accommodation and some meals.

Some ideas to get students started:
✓ Package holidays are much easier and more convenient.
✓ They should be safe and reliable if anything goes wrong.
✗ They tend to involve cheap charter flights, which are often subject to long delays.
✗ The hotels they use have a reputation for being in built-up tourist areas.

2 Give students the meaning of *temperance* before they listen (an old-fashioned word meaning the practice of not taking alcoholic drinks). Establish that Thomas Cook is the leading travel agency in Britain.

Then play the recording.

Answers

1 wood turner
2 (village) missionary
3 (newly invented) train
4 (society) meeting
5 (ever) package tour
6 middle classes
7 traveller's cheques
8 postal services

Listening script 1.36

Presenter
Now on *The Travel Guide*, we go back in time to trace the origins of the good old package tour. Roger, you've been doing some research on a Mr Cook.

Roger
That's right Debbie, Thomas Cook, the man who founded the global travel agency with the same name. Now Thomas Cook actually had quite a few jobs before he hit on the idea of organizing package tours. He started out as a market gardener, then he handed in his notice and became a wood turner, and he also tried his hand at printing. What many people don't know about Thomas Cook, though, is that he was a very religious man and in 1828, when he was just 20, he started working as a Bible-reader and village missionary in the Leicester area. And it was this religious streak that led him to become a member of the Temperance Society. In case you don't know, the Temperance Society was an organization whose members were against drinking alcohol in any shape or form – no beer, no wine, no spirits.

'But what's all this got to do with the tourist industry?' you might ask. Well, one day he said to himself 'wouldn't it be great if we could use the newly invented train to help us in our mission to get across the idea of temperance?' and in 1841 he got together about 600 temperance supporters in Leicester and packed them off on the 8.15 to a temperance meeting 15 miles away in Loughborough – all for the modest price of one shilling. And it was such a popular idea that he did it again the year after, and the next two years after that, too. But it wasn't until 1845 that he actually thought about making a profit from his idea. That's when he organized a pleasure trip to Liverpool, with the option of going on to Dublin, the Welsh coast or the Isle of Man. And that was the first ever package tour.

After that excursion, the world was his oyster. By the early 1860s he'd moved upmarket and from his travel firm in London was arranging tours for the English middle classes to different parts of Europe – especially Italy – Tuscany mainly, famed for its beautiful scenery, its history and its artistic heritage. He booked them into the best hotels, gave them a guidebook for the trip and issued them with 'circular notes' – what we know today as traveller's cheques. They could cash these in at any hotel and bank which Cook had made arrangements with – well over a thousand different places in the 1880s. By then he'd already organized his first world tour – that was in 1872 – and he was now taking on responsibility for postal services and military transport for England and Egypt.

Thomas Cook died in 1892 at the age of 83, leaving behind him the beginnings of a major global industry – oh, and a pub in Leicester, which is named after him.

Cheers, Mr Cook!

If necessary, give the following explanations while going through the answers:
Wood turner – wood turners use tools to shape wood as it rotates on lathes. Typically they make round wooden components such as chair legs, bed posts, flag poles.
Missionary – a person sent to a foreign country to teach the Christian religion to people who live there.
Cheers – a friendly expression spoken by people before drinking an alcoholic drink.

3 Speaking
In monolingual classes this activity should focus on the tourist industry in the students' country, with local news and anecdotes.

Background ideas for teachers to work in to the discussion (or to brainstorm in a whole-class activity):
Thomas Cook was a 'philanthropist' ie he wanted his 'invention' to be for the benefit of humankind.
Travel enables people to:
- broaden their horizons
- learn about other cultures and ways of life
- experience life in all its richness and see great things
- become independent (especially when young).

But mass tourism has attracted a bad reputation for:
- creating cheap ugly hotels which spoil the local environment
- the hedonistic behaviour/noise/litter etc of some of the tourists
- the complete lack of interest in the country which some tourists display.

Benefits of tourism:
- it can bring much needed money into the local economy
- it's relatively cheap, so it has enabled many people to experience foreign travel.

Language focus: Creating emphasis

Page 115

This is an important point of language input at advanced level. It is likely to be met in texts, especially listenings, it is likely to be needed by students in the speaking and writing papers, and it may well feature in the cloze tasks in Use of English.

Exercises 1–3 will probably need to be presented, while 4 and 5 can be done through pairwork.

1–2 Point out that in each case we are choosing to emphasize certain facts, as speakers often do in English (we also do this with the passive voice). These facts are
- his religiousness
- his religious streak
- the date.

Note that question 2c is particularly difficult. You might decide to give students some help with this, such as giving them the first word (He).

Answers

1 a he was a very religious man
b this religious streak
c wasn't until 1845

2 b This religious streak led him to become a member of the Temperance Society.
c He didn't actually think about making a profit from his idea until 1845.

3 This use of *what* is often used when you are explaining to somebody what you have done.

Answers

a an action or series of actions; a noun
b the only thing that
c a prepositional phrase; a moment in time

4 In the example we are choosing to emphasize the amazingness. The speaker of this sentence would also put stress on the word *amazing* (louder, higher pitch, longer time on the word).

For variety drill the pronunciation of the answers, putting stress on the information that is being emphasized.

Answers

1 I'd like to know is how old she is.
2 did was (to) start up his own business.
3 was the music (that) I enjoyed most about the film.
4 was in June (that) they got married, not July.
5 when he took his hat off that I recognized him.
6 until I spoke to Jerry that I found out she'd moved.
7 I did was (to) switch it on.
8 he ever thinks about is his precious car.

5–6 In order to activate this language, do this as a quick classroom exercise, with the emphasis on speech, rather than leaving it to be done as homework.

Contributions: guidebook entry

Page 116

Ask students if they know anything about Edinburgh. (It is the capital city of Scotland and houses the Scottish Parliament. Tourists know it principally for its famous castle and its arts festival 'The Fringe'.)

1 You might choose to explore this question with a few volunteers in the following way:
At home which do you appreciate more – the city or the country? Would this be different if you were a tourist abroad? Many tourists say they are going on holiday to escape their busy city lives, but then find themselves drawn to cities. What might interest tourists about cities?

2 Instruct students not to pause to consider difficult vocabulary at this stage. Give them no more than a minute to read. Then they should give reasons to a partner.

3 Point out that brochures typically contain a number of set expressions. These are useful and impressive, and students can re-use them without feeling that they are descending into cliché.

Answers

1 destination	5 past	8 distance
2 walkway	6 sands	9 life
3 picnic	7 air	10 countryside
4 views		

4 This 'remind yourself' activity might also be left to a later point in the lesson.

5 Now students have the opportunity to look at the text again in more detail. It is probably not worth collecting 'answers' on this, as there is a certain amount of personal preference involved. The point is that students are going into the writing task with some useful language they can use/adapt for use.

Textual notes
Georgian and Victorian – historical periods in architecture (Georgian 1714–1830, Victorian 1837–1901)
539 feet – 163 metres
the Royal Observatory – a building from which scientists watch the stars, planets and weather

6 Students use the extract on page 116 as a model, remembering to write their answer within the word limit.

Multiple choice

Page 118

1 Take this as a whole-class activity. If no ideas are forthcoming, suggest the following: the pace of modern life, more stress, more cars on the roads, faster cars, tendency in society for people to be less tolerant of others.

2 Ask students to focus only on the questions (not the options). Elicit what we know about the structure and content of what we are going to hear:

- A road safety expert called James is being interviewed.
- We begin with James talking about why drivers

become angry.

- James then moves on to talk about another category of road rage – revenge rage.
- He then considers how people get angry on other forms of transport.
- Finally he considers solutions – one involving an experiment with grass, one involving a hi-tech car.

Now listen to the recording.

Answers

1 A 2 B 3 D 4 A 5 C 6 C

Listening script 1.38

(P = Presenter; J = James)

P: It started with road rage in the nineties, then we had air rage, and now it's trolley rage, surf rage, movie rage and even dot.com rage. Anger, it seems, is all the rage these days.

But why? With us is James Frith, head of road safety at the British Automobile Club. James, what makes people so aggressive on the roads?

J: Well, it's all about control, really. Once people get in their car, they feel a false, a dangerous sense of security and control. They're in their own little world, their own safe environment where they can deceive themselves into thinking they're better drivers than they really are. But this of course contrasts with events that happen outside the car, events over which they have absolutely no control whatsoever.

P: And when they lose control, they lose their temper, right?

J: That's right. For instance, most people set deadlines for their road journeys, and if someone threatens to prevent them from meeting that deadline, from not getting where they want to, when they want to, they blow a fuse. And that's when we get road rage, or in many cases now, revenge rage.

P: Another rage! What's revenge rage, James?

J: Well, it's similar to road rage, but less active. People get worked up inside, but just think nasty thoughts about other road users, without actually doing anything. They imagine, for example, going after someone who's cut them up and forcing them off the road. The problem is they get so caught up in their angry dreams of revenge that they fail to concentrate on the essential task of driving safely. And there's more of a risk of them causing an accident themselves than there is for the driver who has offended them.

P: And who are these angry people, these so-called 'road' and 'revenge ragers'?

J: We carried out a study recently and we found it was mainly 18- to 25-year-old men who committed acts of road rage, and these people often had criminal records, histories of violence or drug or alcohol problems. In the case of 'revenge ragers', people who merely fantasize about violent acts, they are more evenly spread across the age groups and between the sexes. The majority, though, are low-mileage motorists, those who only average between 30 and 60 miles a week. And the people who are most likely to trigger revenge rage, the ones who cause these people to lose their temper, are inexperienced youngsters who drive quickly, elderly drivers and drivers of big articulated lorries or vans.

P: Makes you wonder why people don't just get the bus! Surely that's a calmer, more comfortable way to travel. Or is there bus rage, too?

J: Not exactly. But people do get fed up, don't they, when the bus just crawls its way along the route because the driver's busy taking people's money, giving them change or answering questions. And other road users don't respect the bus lanes so you can end up in the same congestion, the same anger-inducing situations that you tried to avoid by leaving the car at home.

P: So what is the solution? How can drivers keep their calm on the roads?

J: I'm not sure there are any easy answers. But in one experiment, Dr David Lewis, the man who coined the term 'road rage', gave 25 stressed-out city drivers a kit containing real grass and a spray of grass scent. He told them to park their cars, take off their shoes and socks and enjoy the sensation of grass beneath their bare feet.

P: The point being ... ?

J: Well, changes in their heart rate and blood pressure were measured and they were clearly more relaxed with the smell and sensation of grass around them. Now, you'd expect a higher proportion of calm drivers on country roads because there is considerably less traffic, but it's the combination of silence in the car, the smell of our immediate environment and what we can feel that can really help calm us down and have a positive influence on our driving habits.

P: So can we expect grass kits to be on the market soon?

J: Possibly. I'm sure the research will be put to some use. What we do have already, though, is a kind of back-seat computer. Engineers have developed a hi-tech car which criticizes drivers when they are behaving rashly or have poor control of the car. A message comes up on the control panel. It also praises them for good road manners when they are driving considerately. If the driving becomes too erratic, the car stops.

P: Sounds like a good idea.

J: As long as drivers don't rely on it. We're always interested in technology that helps drivers' control, but not technology that takes it away from them. Certainly, though, we've all been in that situation with someone in the passenger seat telling us to calm down – it can be annoying, but very effective. And if this works in much the same way, then fine – though I can see stressed-out drivers becoming even more irate when their car suddenly stops.

P: Yes, indeed. Now, James, some of our listeners have written in with their own suggestions as to how we can maintain our composure in the car. Alan Hammans writes in from Tooting telling us how he uses spoken-word tapes ...

3 Speaking
The questions can easily be amplified if students are short of ideas: Considering both trains and buses, is public transport cheap/quick/reliable/comfortable enough for people to use it in preference to cars? Speak about anti-congestion schemes in operation now or in the past in your city/country or that you have heard about abroad.

This speaking section could broaden out into a wider discussion of driving, cars and public transport, if students show interest.
Further questions could be asked, such as:

- If you are a car driver, what annoys you about other people's driving habits?
- What is 'joy-riding' and what causes it?

Vocabulary 2: Anger Page 119

Expressions from the text feature in exercise 1. Then in exercises 2 and 3 we move on to other expressions on this topic.

1 Students consider the degree of formality. The meaning of the expressions is very similar.

Answers

1 more informal: blow a fuse, get worked up

2–3 Students complete the gaps in pairs. In exercise 2 the target words are all adjectives; in exercise 3 they are all nouns.

Answers

2

1 heated	**3** cross	**5** berserk
2 irate	**4** seething	

3

1 top (note that this is particularly informal)	**3** outburst
	4 steam
2 rage	**5** tantrum

4 Students consider the questions in pairs.

Long turn Page 120

Students look at the pictures and familarize themselves with the task. Remind them that:

- the second partner (student B) should remain silent during the first long turn, but should listen carefully to what is said, as (s)he will have to comment appropriately on what the first partner (student A) has said.
- In the exam itself the procedure is slightly different – student A is given *three* pictures to talk about, and student B listens. Student B also sees these pictures.
- When the roles are changed, a new set of pictures are given. In the exam these are on a different theme to the first set. Again the listening partner sees the pictures which the speaking partner is talking about.

If you feel that you are at a stage in the course where you would now like to impose more actual exam conditions on students, you could instruct Students A and B which three pictures they should each look at.

Useful language
While students look at the pictures, ask them to find expressions in exercises 2 and 3 from the Vocabulary section on Anger which best describe each situation. (There are no right answers for this – except that *throw a tantrum* is only applicable to the picture of the young child.)

Keep students focused on language to be used, by referring them to exercise 2 in the Useful language section on page 121. Do this before students attempt the exam task.

Explain that sometimes the Part 2 task requires candidates to use their imagination and to speculate what has happened/is going to happen.

Answers

2

1 might have	**3** looks as	**5** very likely
2 may well	**4** fair chance	**6** looks like

Now students do the task.

- If your students need help with ideas for pictures, allow some preparation time – in groups of three they could brainstorm ideas for each picture, before reassembling into pairs for the exam task.

As a whole-class follow-up activity, ask a few pairs how many of the expressions for speculating they used. If they missed any out, ask how they might have incorporated them into what they said.

Word formation: Alternatives from the same prompt word Page 121

Our focus in this word formation is on the fact that for each prompt word there are at least two alternative grammatical possibilities. In other words, any word chosen as a prompt word will have some distraction.

1 Ask students what two alternative words could serve as distractors here.

Answers

composition, composer

Obviously these would be completely wrong, given the context. A composer is a person who writes music, while a composition is a piece of music, a poem or an essay.

2 Point out that sometimes it is grammar that will help you – from the context it should be clear what part of speech is needed. However, sometimes there are two possible nouns or two possible adjectives that can be formed from the prompt word. In this case, collocation may help you decide which one is correct. In exercise 2, we focus on this. The collocates in bold will help students decide on the correct alternatives.

As you go through the answers, you might also look at how the wrong words are used:

Answers

1 a timeless (an untimely death/end)
2 adopted (adoptive is not common in English – it is mainly used in 'adoptive parents')
3 deceptive (deceitful is used when talking about people wilfully deceiving others: eg deceitful person, his deceitful attempt to persuade her … deceptive seems to be used with 'things' or rather abstract concepts eg deceptive appearance, deceptive pace)
4 supporting (a supportive friend/colleague/boss)
5 appreciable (an appreciative audience)
6 identity (identity is about 'who you are' and identification is about papers. You show identification to prove your identity)
7 consulting (a consultative committee/role)
8 entries (entrance = a door or the act of coming in – make a spectacular entrance)
9 hardship (hardness is a neutral word – the hardness of a metal)
10 advisory (It is advisable to = a good idea to)
11 imaginable (an imaginary game/situation) (an imaginative child)
12 respective (a respectable person is considered by society to be good and proper, a respectful person is one who feels or shows respect)

Review 9 answers Pages 122 and 123

Use of English: CAE Part 3 Word formation

1 destructive
2 regardless
3 residential
4 composure
5 respectful
6 easily
7 inconvenience
8 relating
9 irritable
10 background

Vocabulary

1

A

2 e fly into a rage
3 a let off steam
4 b throw a tantrum
5 f blow a fuse
6 d go berserk

B

2 f fend for yourself
3 e leave you to your own devices
4 c keep yourself to yourself
5 d have a mind of your own
6 a go it alone

2

1 let off steam
2 fend for herself
3 went, berserk
4 keeps himself to himself
5 throws a tantrum

Use of English: CAE Part 4 Gapped sentences

1 spots
2 entry
3 worked
4 view
5 cross

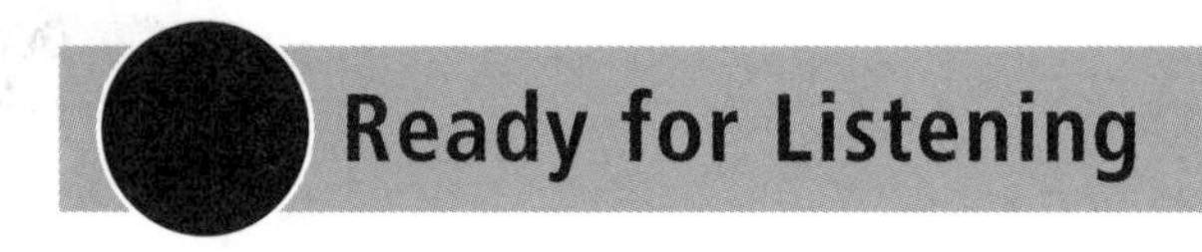

Ready for Listening

CAE Paper 4

Listening

Part 1 Multiple choice (short)
Part 2 Sentence completion
Part 3 Multiple choice (long)
Part 4 Multiple matching

In this section we look at each task from the point of view of the exam, covering advice and strategies. In particular, we look at 'distractors', that is, other words in the script that students might be tempted to write as answers. With Part 2, we show where a student has gone wrong in completing the answers.

Part 1: Multiple choice Page 124

1 Go through the advice together. Compare what happens in Parts 1 and 4.

Part 1	Part 4
Three short extracts	Five short extracts
Exchanges between interacting speakers	One speaker
Unrelated themes	One connecting theme
Each extract is repeated before the next one is played.	All five extracts are played once, then repeated.

2 Students do the exam task in their books.

Answers

1 A 2 C 3 C 4 B 5 B 6 A

3 This could be done as a pairwork activity. The answers are in the listening script.

Listening script 2.1–2.3

(I = Interviewer, L = Lecturer, A = Andrew, J = Jennifer)

Extract 1

I: Donald – TV 1's programme on global warming has stirred up a lot of debate in this country. Do you think it is in any way irresponsible to present the views of a minority of scientists who say that global warming doesn't exist?

L: Well, the first thing any journalist learns is that you must have a balanced approach to reporting. That means allowing the public to hear both sides of an argument. At the same time, we know that a real balance does not exist. You wouldn't for example, give as many column inches to the enemy opinion in a war. The same goes for the global warming debate. Realistically – far more attention is given to the scientific view that climate change *is* happening – and not to the few voices that deny it.

I: But don't you think that people watching the programme may now decide it's pointless taking steps to save the environment?

L: If the media really had that much influence – people would already be behaving in a far more environmentally friendly way. At the end of the day, people are slow to change their habits if there's no immediate effect. Only government regulations will stop people using cars so much, or make them recycle ...

Extract 2

I: Andy, your company Kiss Chocolates was established a good twenty years before you took over. What made you suddenly decide to make a leap into chocolate-making?

Andy: Actually a combination of random events. I was made redundant in 2002, and although I absolutely loved advertising, it was a relief to leave because it meant that all the uncertainty about whether the job would last was gone. At the same time, my wife had just happened to come across the chocolate shop and was buying a gift box when she overheard the owner mention her desire to retire. We both thought the product was excellent – and we both knew there would always be a demand for chocolate.

I: Yes, indeed! And there are probably a lot of people listening who are very envious of you. What's the best part of the job for you, Andy?

Andy: Well the product is certainly hard to resist! (laughs). But because people come in to buy the chocolate as a gift – as a token of love or of appreciation for another person – you never have to face anyone in a bad mood. That's what makes it all so rewarding for me – even more than the prospect of long-term financial security.

Extract 3

J: I have to say that I found *The Children of Hurin* completely absorbing, far more so than I expected. But it's hardly uplifting, is it?

A: No. Even from the early pages, one has a great sense that all is not going to end well for the central character, Turin. He *is* a hero in the sense that he is a brave, honourable man on a mission, but fate delivers him one cruel blow after another. As events unfold, you can see how tragedy is inescapable.

J: Now the book is based on various manuscripts that JRR Tolkien never completed before he died. And it's taken his son Christopher thirty years to put them together as a single cohesive story.

A: That's right – and overall, he really has produced a thing of beauty. Readers will notice, however, that one passage may be written in some kind of ancient English and then the next in a more contemporary manner – as you'd expect in a book pieced together from manuscripts written over a fifty-year period, and that can be a little distracting. Tolkien's characterization is sometimes underdeveloped but not so this time, as Christopher has given us a hero who we can identify with...

- In extract one, we have underlined two lines in particular for question number one, but it might equally well be argued that the answer is coming from the whole of the lecturer's speech. This is an important point to show students. Some questions will test the gist (= general meaning) of a longish speech or even of the whole piece.
- In extract three students meet an 'agreement' question. Again, draw attention to this, as students may be unfamiliar with this question type. Obviously with this question, they must listen to what both speakers are saying. The agreement will probably be contained in the **content** of what they are saying, rather than with obvious phrases of agreement, such as 'I agree with you that ...'.

Part 2: Sentence completion Page 125

1 Read through the information with the class.

2 Look at the 'What to expect' box and ask students to try the prediction exercise in the first bullet point.

Answers

Possible answers

2 clearly the name of a course
3 a verb (clue – subject here refers to the person being sculpted)
4 noun – likely to be something like personality or celebrity
5 a material
6 could be *standing, seating, leaning* etc
7 a period of time
8 a noun similar to *cosmetics*

Be sure to go through the next bullet point. An example of distraction occurs in the second question. Tell students they will hear both the name of Amanda's university course and the name of a subject she specialized in at school. Degree course refers to university, not school, so it is important for students to listen out for the correct information and not be distracted by other information.

Now students do the task.

Answers

1 basement
2 Fine Arts Sculpture
3 take measurements
4 newsreader
5 metal
6 sitting/seated
7 five months
8 oil paint

Listening script 2.4

Well, hello everyone. My name's Amanda Tyler and I've come to tell you something about my work as a waxwork sculptor. Um ... I spend nearly all of my time hidden away with my colleagues in the studio of the wax museum. It's a rather sad room with no windows down in the basement, so it makes a really nice change to be here with so many people and so much natural light!

I suppose I became interested in sculpting at school, where I was doing an A-Level in art and design. My teacher was very encouraging and she advised me to go on and specialize at Loughborough University on their impressively titled Fine Arts Sculpture course. Um ... I have to say I never imagined that once I'd graduated, I'd be working in a museum with the likes of Eminem, Bill Clinton and Ronaldo!

Well, firstly, I'd like to tell you a little bit about the process that goes into making a waxwork figure. Um ... The first and perhaps most enjoyable stage is when we take measurements of our subject – that's the person we want to make a model of. This is a real highlight of the job, as you get to travel and meet celebrities. It's not easy though, getting them to sit still for two hours or more while you struggle to get the information you need!

Now, as you can't have failed to notice, I have on the table the head of the well-known TV newsreader, David Wainright. He's not looking too good, is he? But that's because we're still in the early stages. At the moment he's made of clay which I've moulded onto an 'armature'. That's this thing here, which is basically a frame built out of wire netting. Back in the studio I have an armature for his whole body – that's got metal rods as well, which I've cut to size for his arms and legs.

It's important to show each individual in a pose which is normally associated with that person. So a politician, for example, might be in a standing position, giving a speech; when I've finished him, dear old David here will be seen sitting behind a huge desk; and in the museum we've got the athlete Carl Lewis running across the finishing line.

The whole thing is a very slow process. It can take me about three or four weeks just to get the clay model stage we have here, and I may need as much as five months to make one figure – from the time I start to the time it's ready to go on display.

So what's next? Well, from this clay model I'll make a plaster mould and fill that with hot liquid wax. And when it's cooled, hey presto, we have our wax head. Um ... Then it's time for the eyes. What we do is select two acrylic eyeballs that are roughly the same as the subject's. Then we touch them up by hand with watercolours to get a more exact copy. That's usually my job. Then I hand it over to our make-up artist, who uses oil paint together with more conventional cosmetics for the rest of the head.

The hair is probably the most laborious part and can take weeks. This is the tool we use – unfortunately it can only insert two hairs at a time, so you can imagine ...

Finally, ask students for their own experiences of waxwork museums. Do they find such places interesting or not?

3 Refer students to the Additional material section. Here they will see the answer sheet of a student who has made a lot of silly mistakes!

Answers

2 a, d, e
3 a, b
4 e, g
5 b
6 h
7, 8 The answer to 7 has been left blank (c). The answer to 8 has been recorded as the answer to 7 (f).

Part 3: Multiple choice Page 126

1 Refer students to the 'What to expect' box. Explain that for this part we will concentrate on distraction – that is, why the other three options are tempting but wrong.

2–3 Students follow the instructions. Do not play the CD yet. Students should read from the listening script.

Answers

3
0 C Sandra: *I reckoned I'd probably be the first to have to leave.*

4 Students continue to read from the listening script, discussing why the other options are wrong. Give detailed feedback as follows:

Answers

Suggested answers

A *We are only told by Sandra that the company 'weren't making enough money'; she does not comment on her salary.*

B *Sandra says 'they were a young, dynamic group' but she does not say she was too old.*

D *She says 'I'd never felt so comfortable working in a team as I did with that group of people'; she does* **not** *say 'I never felt comfortable working in a team'.*

5 Now students do the exam task.

Answers

1 B **2** D **3** B **4** A **5** B **6** C

Listening script 2.5

(I = Interviewer; S = Sandra; D = David)

I: On this week's *In Partnership* programme we talk to Sandra Peyton and David Sadler, who together run the successful media company Advert Eyes, specializing in the making of TV commercials. Sandra, if I could start with you. What were you doing before you set up in partnership with David and what made you change?

S: Well, I was directing – er, drama mostly – for a small satellite TV company. It was an interesting, experimental time for me – they were a young, dynamic group and seemed to be going places. But these were troubled times for the business in general and they just weren't making enough money. Anyway, things weren't looking too good for me; as I'd been the last to arrive, I reckoned I'd probably be the first to have to leave.

I: So you jumped before you were pushed, so to speak.

S: That's right, and that was a great shame, because I'd never felt so comfortable working in a team as I did with that group of people.

I: David, you had a similar background, didn't you?

D: Yes, I'd also made a name for myself directing TV drama, but with the much larger Trenton TV. I left them because they were moving in a different direction to where I wanted to go. But the experience proved invaluable for the future – I can see that now.

I: In what way?

D: Working in close collaboration with others is an integral part of this business – that's always been clear to me – but I came to realize that you can't rely on other people to make things work. It's a tough old world and ultimately it's down to you – it's a question of attitude. Things only happen if you let them – and if you only see grey skies and gloomy days ahead, that's what you'll get.

I: So the whole thing focused you for your future with Advert Eyes.

D: That's right, I did a lot of growing up with Trenton.

I: Well, tell us how you met each other, Sandra.

S: We were introduced at a party by a mutual friend. I remember I was very wary of David at first. He already had quite a reputation in the business – his past work spoke for itself. And he looked so serious, so apparently indifferent to everything. He mentioned some vague idea he had for setting up a business, something to do with advertising – but that wasn't what struck me most. I just couldn't get over how animated, how passionate he became when he talked about – well, everything really. It was difficult not to be carried along by his words.

I: So when he asked you to join him, you had no hesitation in accepting?

D: Well, it was actually Sandra who asked me. And I was the one who had no hesitation. My colleagues at Trenton had warned me against going into business with a complete unknown – they said it was too much of a gamble. But when I met Sandra, it was like looking into a mirror. Here at last was someone on my wavelength, someone who looked at life through the same camera lens. And anyway, I felt it was time to do something different, to live a little dangerously.

I: And has it been? Dangerous, I mean.

D: Anything but. Funnily enough, though, it's turned out that we do have quite a lot of differences, but these have all been to our advantage. Sandra, for example, has much more of a business brain than I do.

I: Is that right, Sandra?

S: Well, yes, it seems to be a hidden talent of mine. But I've had to learn the hard way. Raising money, for example, was an absolute nightmare – we just couldn't seem to get the finance.

I: That must have been quite disheartening.

S: Well, no, you can't afford to let things like that get you down. It was no good getting upset about it; throwing a tantrum in a bank manager's office is never a good idea – you might need to go back there one day. No, I just couldn't work out what the problem was, given our experience and the way the advertising market was shaping up at the time. We were just a small concern, asking for a small amount of money.

I: But you obviously got the money.

S: Yes, I met an investor who understood what we were about – and then, once we'd made a couple of ads, money was easier to come by.

I: David, how does, er advertising work compare with TV drama? Is it very different?

D: Well, for a start there's more money around than for normal TV work, and that can be very liberating. But the market's understanding of quality may not be the same as yours and you find your creativity stifled. Yes, it's our own company, and it may seem a creative business to an outsider. But an advert is not your own baby in the same way that a TV drama might be. There are too many people who have a say in what you do and what goes into the advert.

S: Yes, I'd go along with that, although for me, running a business can be incredibly creative.

I: So what does the future hold for Advert Eyes. What are your plans for the company?

S: Well, we can't really say too much at the moment. It's not that we're not willing to, it's just that we're not entirely certain how things will work out ourselves.

D: That's right. The normal thing might be to look at some type of long-term growth for the business, but at the moment we're concentrating on consolidating our position, rather than branching out. Who knows what the future will bring?

I: Sandra, David, the very best of luck for the future. There we must leave it. Thank you.

S and D: Thank you.

6 Having underlined the correct answers, students now discuss in pairs why the other options are wrong.

Answers

1

A *This idea comes up but is denied in 'but I came to realize that you can't rely on other people to make things work'.*

C *This is a misinterpretation of 'It's a tough old world'. This is not the point being made.*

D *The opposite is true – 'Working in close collaboration with others …'.*

2

A *David's 'reputation in the business' was undoubted, but it was not that which impressed her.*

B *Definitely not – he looked serious and indifferent.*

C *No, these were vague and didn't strike her.*

3

A *His colleagues warned him that it would be a risk, but there's no reference to him enjoying risks.*

C *We don't know this; we are only told she was a complete unknown.*

D *Again we don't know this; we are only told she has a good business brain.*

4

B *The idea of being depressed is there, but what Sandra is saying is that there's no point in getting depressed.*

C *She then goes on to make the same point about being angry.*

D *Sandra says 'We were just a small concern …'. Concern here is nothing to do with worrying; it's a noun meaning 'enterprise' or 'business'.*

5

A *This is a likely idea given the context, but is not present in the text.*

C *The opposite is true. He finds the large amounts of money available a positive point.*

D *The point made about the clients is that they get too involved and stifle his creativity, not that they have unrealistic expectations.*

6

A *This idea is suggested but then contradicted by 'It's not that we're not willing to …'.*

B & D *For both of these, the opposite is true – 'the normal thing might be to look at some type of long-term growth for the business, but at the moment we're concentrating on consolidating our position, rather than branching out.'*

Part 4: Multiple matching Page 127

Photocopiable vocabulary exercise on page 155.

1 This is the task with five short extracts and a common theme.

2 For a detailed task strategy see Unit 4 (page 46 in Teacher's Book). This discusses how to tackle the complicated business of listening twice and having two separate tasks to perform.

3 This use of the listening script gives variety to the normal way of checking answers, and is suggested at various other places in the main units as well.

Answers

1 C **2** D **3** A **4** G **5** F **6** E **7** H
8 B **9** D **10** G

See the script for the correct underlined parts.

Note that for exercise 4 the answer to task two, question 9, comes before the answer to task one. This is common practice in this part of the paper, but in other parts, answers will come up in the script in the same order as they appear on the question paper.

Listening script 2.6–2.10

Speaker 1

I could barely string two sentences together when I first arrived, and now I'm reasonably fluent. In that sense, then, I've achieved what I set out to do – just by being here and mixing with the locals. I've met some great people since I got here, especially the family I'm living with. But there's a big downside to all this. I decided to come here on my year out because it's so different to all the other places I could have gone to. Plus it seemed so exciting when I came here two years ago. However, that was on holiday and I realize now that living here is actually rather dull. I really wish I'd gone somewhere on the mainland now – my girlfriend's having a great time there.

Speaker 2

My father studied here as a young man so I knew quite a lot about the country before I came. And when the head of my company's overseas operations told me our branch here wasn't doing too well, and would I please go and sort things out, I was very happy to accept. My husband came out shortly after I did and like me, immediately fell in love with the place. The pace of life suits us to a tee and the food is just out of this world. Ultimately, though, we're home birds and when this posting's over we'll want to go back to be nearer our grandchildren – if we ever have any, that is!

Speaker 3

I was working in the dullest job you can imagine – 9 to 5 every day on the computer, answering customers' email queries. But it was thanks to that job that I got to know Patti, who was over on a work exchange programme in another department. She only stayed for three months, though, so after that nearly all our contact was by email. Of course, you can't keep something going like that indefinitely, so I took the plunge and moved out here. Life is fine – despite the overcast skies and regular downpours! I have to admit, though, it does get me down sometimes. I'd like to get back home more often, but it's just too far.

Speaker 4

I only wish I'd made the break earlier. It's so vibrant in this part of the world – there's so much more going on. I think if I was still back home, I'd be so depressed, what with the current climate there and so on. The fact is I was in a bit of a rut. I was sick of the same old thing, day in, day out and I thought, 'There's got to be more to life than this'. So I looked into the price of property in different parts of southern Europe, and this area was one of the cheapest. It didn't take me long to settle in – the language isn't much of a problem and I've even got myself a little part-time job. Keeps me out of trouble!

Speaker 5

A few years ago I set up in business with a friend of mine. Then I decided to go it alone and bought out my partner's share. Unfortunately, before long things started to go wrong and I was up to my eyes in debt. Call it cowardice, but I just couldn't deal with it and I moved out here. It got me out of a mess, but I can't say I'm having the time of my life. I know a lot of different people here, but I just don't seem to fit in with them. We share the same language – more or less – but we're worlds apart in most other respects. One thing's for sure – if ever I do go back to face the music, it'll be for good.

4 In question 6, which relates to the first extract, the answer was E. But one could see why the student might have been tempted to put D. He or she has heard the word 'exciting' in the script and wrongly jumped for D, without listening to the surrounding context. If we assume this student has acted in the same way for questions 7–10, the question is, what information is there in each extract to tempt him/her into thinking that A, C, B and H are the correct answers?

Answers

7 Speaker 2: *we'll want to be nearer our grandchildren*
8 Speaker 3: *I'd like to get back home more often*
9 Speaker 4: *I'd be so depressed, what with the current climate there*
10 Speaker 5: *if ever I do go back to face the music, it'll be for good*

Content overview

Themes

This unit is concerned with houses, accommodation, neighbours, country living, housework.

Exam-related activities

Paper 1	**Reading**
Part 3	Multiple choice (long)
Paper 2	**Writing**
Part 2	Information sheets
Paper 3	**Use of English**
Part 1	Multiple-choice cloze
Part 2	Open cloze
Part 3	Word formation (review)
Paper 4	**Listening**
Part 4	Multiple matching
Paper 5	**Speaking**
Part 2	Long turn

Other

Vocabulary 1	Describing rooms and houses
Vocabulary 2	Metaphorical meanings
Vocabulary 3	Noise and sound
Language focus	Participle clauses

Optional lead-in activity

Put the following words on the board.

igloo caravan palace bungalow
hall of residence castle
wigwam monastery old people's home
barracks chalet guesthouse
villa tent shed wendy-house summer-house

Students go into groups of three. They must define all the words. Student A chooses a word to define, then Student B, then Student C, then back to A etc. This is a fun activity which works on fluency and wordbuilding.

Vocabulary 1: Describing rooms and houses Page 128

1 It is a common feature of spoken English to combine certain adjectives (I'm nice and comfortable, a hot and sticky day, a cold and frosty morning). There are many such fixed expressions on the topic of houses.

Answers	
1 c cheerful	**4** b dingy
2 e airy	**5** d cosy
3 a tidy	**6** f cluttered

Check the meaning of any difficult words (*cramped* means there is not enough room, *cluttered* means that there is too much stuff in the room, *dingy* means dark and dirty; in the expression *dark and dingy* it suggests the room is rather dirty and depressing, and not cheerful or bright).

2

Answers		
a lit	**c** decorated	**e** situated
b furnished	**d** built	

Having given the answers, 'play' with them a little in order to recycle them. For example, ask questions such as:
Which one might suggest a romantic dinner for two? (a softly/dimly lit room)
Which one means 'perfectly located'? (ideally situated)
Which one tells us that there isn't much furniture in the room? (sparsely furnished)
Which one tells us that the owners have just repainted it? (newly decorated)
Which one might hurt your eyes? (a brightly lit room)

3 Students are most likely to remember and find useful those expressions that relate to their own situation, so it is important not to hurry through this personalizing exercise.

4 See how many of the different ways to express speculation students can remember (it looks as if, it looks like, this room may well, this room is very likely to, there's a fair chance this room is). Then students do the task.

Optional extra activity
To create further opportunities for fluency, ask various pairs to report briefly their feelings about the pictures to the rest of the class. This will also give students maximum exposure to alternative ideas they did not think of and, of course, reporting involves summary skills, another useful skill for speaking.

Use of English 1: Open cloze
CAE Part 2

Page 129

As a lead-in, brainstorm different types of housework (doing the dishes, sweeping the floor, dusting the furniture, doing the washing, ironing, doing the hoovering, making the beds etc).

1–2 Students come up with their own ideas, then read the text quickly to compare with the ideas in the text.

Answers

2 Housework is strenuous, boring, repetitive and never-ending. It is also unpaid and women, who still do most of it, often go out to work, which means they cannot do it as thoroughly as they might like.

Ask for a volunteer to paraphrase what Nicholas Emler says about 'open-ended tasks'. Ask if students agree with this psychological view on why housework is stressful.

3 Students try the task in pairs, answering the questions in the box as they go.

Answers

1 to (The verb 'suggest' would need to be in the third person singular form for a relative pronoun to be possible.)
2 are
3 is
4 without
5 how
6 for
7 no
8 out
9 from
10 some (Only a determiner is possible here as there is no definite or indefinite article. Determiners were presented in Language focus 1 in Unit 8.)
11 lot
12 too
13 may/might/could/can
14 we
15 under

After giving the answers, select certain vocabulary from the text you judge to be useful and put it on the board, eg

It may come as no surprise
There is evidence to suggest that
suffer from mood swings
pride yourself on
a spotless home
out of fashion
the vast majority of men
shy away from.

Ask students to close their books for a brief spoken exercise. In pairs they must use each expression either in an invented sentence of their own or recall how it was used in the original text. When everyone has finished, run through them quickly to check that the meanings used were accurate.

4 If appropriate, there are various other questions you might ask:

Do you think it is right for parents to give pocket money in return for doing household chores?
At what age do you think this should first be done?
What kind of basic chores might be suitable for young children?
Are men fully involved in housework in your country?

Reading: Multiple choice

CAE Part 3

Page 130

Photocopiable vocabulary exercise on page 155.

1 This can be taken as a whole-class activity, in order to control input of useful vocabulary, such as:

I can't imagine life without ...
collect water from a well
contaminated water
candles
a log fire

Note: 'Running water' means water *on mains supply*, ie it comes out of your taps.

2 The 'news value' of this article is that we are shocked to hear that someone still lives in this way in Britain today. The text explores the unusual combination of circumstances which has produced this almost unbelievable story.

This is a well-balanced piece of writing, written in such a way that we feel a mixture of sympathy for and frustration at Albert's situation. We sympathize with Albert because of his

- humble modesty
- love of the countryside and the simple pleasures of life
- determination to provide for himself and his wife without outside help

but we despair at the unnecessary living conditions Albert has forced upon himself through his own independence, pride and obstinacy.

Before students do their detailed read, point out that the text contains a lot of descriptive words and phrases which embellish the text, making it sound nice and poetic. Such words contribute little to the actual *meaning* of the text and do not need to be fully understood in order to do the questions.

3 Now students attempt the multiple-choice task.

Answers

1 C **2** A **3** C **4** D **5** C **6** B **7** D

Reacting to the text
Students discuss in pairs or small groups.

Vocabulary 2: Metaphorical meanings

Page 132

At advanced level, students can be expected to have to meet and deal with more subtle aspects of language such as metaphor. If you are in a monolingual situation, give examples from your own language to demonstrate that this feature of language is surprisingly common.

Present in exercise 1, do together with whole class in exercise 2, use pairwork in exercise 3.

Answers

2 Land that *rolls out* or is *rolling* (adj) has gentle slopes, continuing for some distance. There is of course no real movement, as in the literal sense.

A view or landscape that *sweeps* over an area, stretches over or covers that area in a long, wide curve. The movement of a broom as it *sweeps* the floor can also be in a long wide curve.

If you *choke*, you are unable to breathe because your throat is blocked. If a ditch, pond, river etc is *choked with weeds*, water cannot flow easily because the weeds are blocking it.

Literally, *fringed* means 'containing fringes', threads that hang from a piece of cloth or clothing to decorate it. Hills, lakes or coastlines that are *fringed with trees* have a strip of trees running around them or along their edge.

A *sea of mud* is a large area of mud.

The *heart of the countryside* is the central part of it, furthest away from large towns.

3 A

1 thunders	**3** sits	**5** nestles
2 towers	**4** hugs	**6** stretches

B

1 tide	**3** stream	**5** eyesore
2 roar	**4** nightmare	**6** patchwork

4 This could be done in spoken pairwork, or students could write a descriptive paragraph.

5 In a multilingual class, students will have to share their knowledge of their host country.

Language focus: Participle clauses

Page 133

As well as appearing frequently in reading texts, participle clauses may well feature in the Use of English paper. Students may also need to produce them, especially in the Writing paper.

This section draws upon the multiple-choice reading text, so it should not be done out of sequence.

1 This information should be presented by the teacher.

Answers

So this man, (who was) living on a labourer's wage, clearly believed he was just locked out of the lifestyle.

2 Students work individually to see how quickly they can find the corresponding information in the reading text.

Answers

a Having become rather frail and vulnerable in recent years, he and his wife were heavily reliant on the good nature of one neighbour ... (line 32)

b Fleeing from Estonia in 1946, he came to Britain ... (line 53)

c Shocked beyond belief by what they saw when they visited the house, these people began to put pressure on the council ... (line 74)

d 'That's the good thing about the country,' he says, looking out over the familiar prospect. (line 88)

3 Elicit answers from the class.

Answers

As the Grammar reference explains, the subject of a participle clause is usually the same as the subject of the main clause in a sentence. Sentence (2 a) shows that a participle clause can be given its own subject to avoid ambiguity.

1 Sentence (a) suggests that the police were driving home from the pub when they stopped him.
Sentence (b) means that the police stopped him as he was driving home from the pub.
Sentence (b) is more likely.

2 Sentence (a) means that Elisa took over all the manager's responsibilities because the manager was ill.
Sentence (b) suggests that because she was ill, Elisa took over all the manager's responsibilities.
Sentence (a) is more likely.

Practice

Exercises 1 and 2 should be done in pairs.

Answers

Possible answers

1

1 *After* he won the silver medal in the 100 metres, he went on to take gold in the 200 metres and long jump.

2 Don't look now, but the woman *who* is sitting next to you is wearing shoes *which* are made of crocodile skin.

3 *If* it is drunk in moderation, red wine is thought to protect against coronary disease.

4 Mr Brown, *who* was wrapped in a blanket and looked tired after his ordeal, was full of praise for the rescue services.

5 *When* he reached for the sugar, he knocked over his glass *and* spilt wine over her new dress.
6 *Because* he had never been abroad before, Brian was feeling a little on edge.

2–3
(Students may have alternative answers for exercise 3.)
1 Living within walking distance of the centre, I rarely use the car. *City*
2 Cycling in to work the other day, I saw a deer. *Rural area*
3 Having never had so much peace and quiet before, we found living here a little strange at first. *Rural area*
4 Situated at the back of the building, our bedroom has some superb views over the rooftops towards the docks. *City*
5 Played at full volume, it really annoys the neighbours. *Either*
6 Being a little off the beaten track, our house is not that easy to find. *Rural area*
7 The children having all left home, we decided to move away from the hustle and bustle. *Rural area*
8 Although not known for its tourist attractions, our neighbourhood does have one or two treasures waiting to be discovered. *City*

3 Students follow instructions.

Use of English 2: Multiple-choice cloze

CAE Part 1

Page 134

As a lead-in ask a couple of volunteers to describe their neighbours in as much detail as possible.

1 Students answer the question in pairs.

2 Before they attempt the exam task, direct students to the 'Don't forget!' box.

Answers

Answers to questions in the 'Don't forget!' box
What has caused the decline in communication between neighbours in Britain?
longer hours spent working at the office, together with the Internet and satellite television
What has been one of the effects of this decline?
a rise in burglaries and vandalism

Answers

2

1 B	**2** A	**3** D	**4** A	**5** C	**6** B
7 C	**8** D	**9** C	**10** A	**11** B	**12** B

Note:
- Neighbourhood Watch is a popular scheme, usually in wealthier areas of Britain. Stickers advertising the fact that 'this is a Neighbourhood Watch area' appear on walls and in house windows in the area, as a deterrent to burglars. You might ask if students know of similar schemes in their country.
- 'calling on' in number 11 here means 'asking' rather than 'visiting'.

Extra activity in Teacher's Book – analysing the answers
When you have given the answers, ask students to close their books. Write on the board:
next-door n________
acts of v_______
n________ ties
the breakdown of c________

Ask students if anyone can remember these collocations, which were tested 'the other way round' in the text.

Answers

Answers to extra activity in Teacher's Book
next-door neighbour
acts of vandalism
neighbourhood ties
the breakdown of communities

Students open their books again. Point out that four of the questions were testing collocation (1, 4, 9, 10). Then see if they can find which question was testing an idiom? (=12, keep an eye on), and which a phrasal verb (=11, call on). Finally direct them to Question 8, and point out that this involved a grammatical element – only the key goes with the following preposition. Students can expect to be tested on similar things in the exam.

3 Discourage students from getting on to the issue of problems and disputes with neighbours as this is the topic of the next activity.

Listening: Multiple matching
CAE Part 4

Page 135

1 This listening follows on thematically from the gapped text, so it should not need introducing.

Answers

1 F	2 H	3 A	4 B	5 D	6 F
7 G	8 H	9 A	10 D		

Focus on the following useful language from the listening script:

1 (Speaker 1) leave the engine running
2 (Speaker 2) I was just about to ... when ...
3 (Speaker 2) I was getting nowhere
4 (Speaker 3) We tried to reason with him, but ...
5 (Speaker 4) I did my back in
6 (Speaker 4) get off to sleep
7 (Speaker 4) a laid-back kind of guy
8 (Speaker 5) We rowed like we'd never rowed before.

Notes

1 A use of 'run' students might not be familiar with, but very common in this expression.
2 The meaning here is 'on the point of'
3 Another very common spoken expression, meaning making no progress.
4 'Reason' here means 'talk sensibly'
5 This is a colloquial way of saying 'I injured my back'.
6 Students probably know 'go to sleep' but perhaps are not familiar with this. They mean the same.
7 A nice phrase to describe a relaxed person, who doesn't normally get stressed or angry.
8 This simply means we rowed a great deal, but, used with other verbs, it is a nice way of embellishing a story or anecdote: (I cried like I'd never cried before!)

Listening script 2.11–2.15

Speaker 1

We used to live above a gym. I say 'used to' cause they had to close it down and go somewhere else. Some of the neighbours got together, see, and got someone from the Council to come round. It wasn't so much the music because the place was pretty well sound-proofed. It was more all the coming and going – especially at night, around 10ish, when it shut and the people would all leave at the same time and then one engine after another would start up. In the winter they'd leave them running for a bit – time to defrost the windows I suppose – and the neighbours said it made too much of a racket. I can't say I noticed it much, though – live and let live, I say. We've all got to make a living somehow.

Speaker 2

Well one day I was upstairs in my office and was just about to start on a new chapter when I heard this – noise. At first I thought someone was actually in pain and I leapt up to the window– but then I saw my neighbour Sheila and I guess a couple of her friends in her back room. What they were doing, see, was practising for the local amateur operatic group. The din was unbearable and it completely put me off my writing. And I've got deadlines to meet that I cannot put off and I was getting nowhere! It went on every morning for a fortnight and then just suddenly stopped. Perhaps they went to practise elsewhere. I live in dread that it'll start up again.

Speaker 3

Nothing but trouble, that man. Fancy bringing a cockerel to live in a residential area! That sort of thing you'd expect in the countryside, but not here. Being a cockerel, it would start at 5 – this awful racket and it'd wake up the baby and she'd start wailing so there was no way we could ignore it. We tried to reason with him but he said we were making a fuss over nothing. Then that afternoon there were a whole bunch of hens clucking around his back garden too. It got so bad that we realized the only course of action was to take him to court. Which we did and we won. It was expensive but worth it. He was ordered to have the cockerel destroyed or sell it. Whatever he did – we can now sleep peacefully.

Speaker 4

One of the benefits of working as a builder – all that physical activity knocks you out for the night. But since I did my back in and had to take a desk job, it's harder for me to get off to sleep. This woman down the road has a teenage son, and every Friday and Saturday night their house seems to be the meeting point for all their mates. They hang around in the road and maybe they don't realize how far their voices carry – or maybe they just don't care. Why can't they have a conversation indoors? I used to be a laid-back kind of guy but now I feel angry a lot of the time. That's not how I want to be – and I resent the effect it's had on me.

Speaker 5

Night after night he'd have it blaring out at full volume – news programmes and reality shows mostly – and all we could do was sit there, seething. He said he couldn't hear it if he had it on any lower. Deaf as a post, he was. It really brings out the worst in you, something like that, and it put a tremendous strain on our marriage. We were so stressed out by it all and we rowed like we'd never rowed before, often about the silliest of things. Anyway, we got so sick of it all, we sold up and bought a place in the country. Shame really, 'cause I like having people around me and there are days here when all I have for company are the pigeons and other birds we have nesting up in the trees across the road.

2 Pairwork, but if the teacher can tell some interesting anecdotes about neighbours, it will encourage students to open up, or may remind them of a little story they can tell.

Vocabulary 3: Noise and sound
Page 135

1 Remind students also of the common expression 'a terrible row' /raʊ/. 'Row' can mean quarrel or noise.

Answer

a loud unpleasant noise that lasts for a long time

2–3 These exercises are very suitable for pairwork.

Answers

2

1 *hushed*: very quiet; the other two describe a loud voice.
2 *unmistakable*: very easy to recognize (compare '*unmistakable smell*' in Unit 3); the others describe a sound which is/appears quiet.
3 *excessive*: too loud; the others describe noise which continues for a long time.

3

1 *goes off* (a gun, bomb or alarm *goes off*)
2 *rustle open* (leaves or paper *rustle*)
3 *hoot* (car horns *hoot*)
4 *engine* (*rowdy* describes people and their behaviour)
5 *groan* (*piercing* describes high-pitched sounds)
6 *ear* (ears can be *deafened* but not *deafening*: *deafening silence* is used when it is very noticeable that nothing was said or done)

4 Now we recycle some of the vocabulary from the previous exercises.

Answers

1 hushed voice
2 distant sound/ constant noise
3 noise dies down
4 rowdy fans
5 deafening silence
6 door slammed shut

5–6 Students' notes should consist of the English for the sounds they have heard. This should produce some excellent high-level vocabulary (creaks, slams, hushed, growls etc – see listening script below). Then they go into pairs and agree on what has happened. Once they have agreed, they write down their version of events. Finally, they compare with at least one other pair in the room. You might also get feedback from different pairs as a whole-class activity, highlighting any differences between people's stories.

Answers

Possible answer
Detectives enter a building where a gang of counterfeiters are making money. The criminals argue amongst themselves, one shoots another, the detectives rush in, fight, and the leader of the gang warns detectives to get back.

Listening script 2.16

1 door creaks open
2 door slams shut
3 'Keep quiet' – hushed voice
4 dog growls
5 'Oh dear' – squeaky/high-pitched voice
6 'Shh – listen!' – hushed voice
7 distant/constant sound of machinery
8 bell rings
9 noise of machinery fades away
10 muffled sound of angry voices (in other room)
11 unmistakable sound of gunshot
12 high-pitched scream
13 deafening silence
14 dog whines
15 people bursting into room, shouts and fight scene – terrible racket
16 booming voice 'Get back'

7 Typical favourite sounds, if no ideas are forthcoming: waterfalls, grasshoppers on a summer's evening, newly-opened wine being poured into a glass.

Writing: Information sheets
CAE Part 2
Page 136

Elicit from students that information sheets are usually free and produced by organizations (schools, colleges, companies, clubs etc) to:

- give information and/or advice
- explain how to do something
- describe how something works.

1 Read through the task together.

Ideally, in Part 2 tasks students should be moving from:

content points ⟶ plan ⟶ final version

In other words, the content points should form the basis of the plan, and a final version should be written directly from the plan (obviously there is no time to write out a draft version).

Answers

Yes. The three headings cover the three content points, but, cleverly, different words are used.

2 Students could work individually then compare thoughts with a partner. With a weaker class, you might like to give more help, and point out that one of the sections is not up to the standard of the other two.

Answers

The student's ability to use a wide range of vocabulary and structures is demonstrated in all but the section entitled 'Where do I look?'.

Examples of complex language in the other sections include:
no easy task
hard to come by
to help you on your way
outside their price range
a matter of personal choice
the vast majority of students
within easy walking distance of the school
flats here ***may*** *be slightly more expensive,* ***but*** *you save on ...*
be sure to ask for a receipt
things might not work out as planned
the flat may not live up to your expectations

3 Point out that a wide variety of things could be leaflets, and that the degree of formality will vary slightly depending on the subject matter.

Answer

The answer contains many examples of more informal language, including contractions, informal punctuation (dashes and exclamation marks), phrasal verbs and direct address (the use of *you* and *your*). This is entirely appropriate for the task, helping to create the impression of a friendly school which welcomes its new teachers.

4 Point out that linking is an important criterion in the assessment procedure.

Answer

As one would expect from a piece of more informal writing, linking expressions are short, individual words (or dashes). Note the absence of linking words in the section entitled Where do I look? (see 2).

What's available?
as, *and*, *also*, *further*, dash, *though*, *but*

What happens next?
Before, *this*, *also*, *since*, *and*, *Finally*, dash

5 Brainstorm ideas for events from the college committee (welcome party, a newcomers' fair with representatives from college clubs and societies present, walks and bike rides to familiarize new students with the locality, film show etc).

Note that the overall purpose of the information sheet is to be welcoming to new students and to help them integrate. It requires some other general advice about meeting new people during the rest of the year. For this task, it would seem likely that the bullet points already form the likely structure of the piece.

Then brainstorm ideas for the information sheet on stress (missing your family and friends, adapting to a new country, getting behind on work/not keeping to deadlines/being poorly organized, having relationship problems or difficulties with accommodation etc). For this task, two frameworks would be possible. Either each paragraph deals with a different cause of stress and also contains a suggestion on how to deal with it, or the various causes of stress appear in one or two paragraphs, followed by various suggestions, also in one or two paragraphs.

Sample answer

College's Welcome Week

WELCOME WEEK will take place in two weeks time and a number of events have been organized to help you integrate in the life of the college.

This year's events
As it has been proved at former years, the best way to integrate all different cultures co-existing in our college, is to get closer to every single one of them. For achieving this goal, the college will set up 4 thematic tents at the University's garden from 7th–12th September (11am to 6pm) where you will find several stands representing countries that belong to the same continent. Students coming from the same country will be in charge of decorating their stand, cooking some typical dishes and preparing some performance related to their own culture.

We have up to 30 different countries this year, all them have sent their programs. This will give you the opportunity to meet people and break down some cultural barriers from the beginning.

In addition, two discotheques are organized; one on Friday 10th September with a mixture of music to suit everyone's tastes, and another on Saturday 11th, which we encourage participants to come in fancy dress. Both events will take place in the Main Hall from 8.00pm and are completely free from charge.

Meeting people throughout the year
As far as what to do after WELCOME WEEK is concerned, you will have a wide range of activities to choose. Come to the International Centre office and we will give you all the information about different courses, pubs, clubs and so, where you will find your place here in our college.

Examiner's comment

Content: The writing addresses the main points successfully.

Organization and cohesion: Clearly organized and paragraphed, with attention paid to use of cohesive devices.

Accuracy: The writing is quite accurate, with a few slips such as the use of *'for'* as infinitive of purpose, *'free from charge', 'and so (on)'*.

Range: The range of vocabulary is quite impressive (*'break down some cultural barriers', 'suit everyone's tastes'*) and there are some fairly complex, well constructed sentences, showing a range of grammar.

Register: The register is appropriate for the context and the student audience: the use of direct address (*'you will find', 'This will give you the opportunity'*) ensures a more friendly, personal tone.

Target Reader: Would be informed about the events of Welcome Week and what to do in order to meet people throughout the year.

Mark: Band 4

Review 10 answers Pages 138 and 139

Vocabulary

1 c	**2** f	**3** b	**4** g
5 d	**6** a	**7** h	**8** e

Participle clauses
Looking through a newspaper one day, he saw a cottage for sale in a picturesque rural area. Situated in a small village near the church, it had a conservatory and a large garden containing fruit trees; it seemed perfect. Not known for his decisiveness, Charlie surprised everyone by putting down a deposit on it the very next day. Having seen it once, he immediately made up his mind to buy it.

Having moved into the cottage, he soon realized it was not the peaceful rural idyll he had expected. Chiming every hour on the hour, the church bells kept him awake at night. Also, the village being in an area of outstanding beauty, coachloads of tourists arrived every weekend disturbing the peace and quiet. Worst of all, objecting to the presence of outsiders in the village, the locals were very unfriendly towards him. Having lived there for six months, Charlie decided to move back to the city.

Use of English: Word formation
CAE Part 3

1 disagreeable
2 privacy
3 satisfying
4 ensure
5 freely
6 safety
7 curiosity
8 procedure(s)
9 setting(s)
10 ineffective

11 A cultural education

Content overview

Themes

This unit is concerned with culture, including: art, music, writing, photography.

Exam-related activities

Paper 1	**Reading**
Part 2	Gapped text
Paper 2	**Writing**
Part 1	Proposals
Paper 3	**Use of English**
Part 2	Open cloze (review)
Part 3	Word formation (review)
Paper 4	**Listening**
Part 1	Multiple choice (short)
Part 2	Sentence completion
Paper 5	**Speaking**
Part 3	Collaborative task
Part 4	Further discussion

Other

Reading and speaking: Gap Year

Vocabulary 1	Sight
Vocabulary 2	*Read* and *write*
Language focus	Inversion
Word formation	Nouns formed with *in, out, up, down, back*

Listening 1: CAE Part 1 — Multiple choice

Page 140

1 Pre-listening discussion questions

Notes for teachers' information

Photo 1: The man with a tattoo is a New Zealand Maori. It used to be common for Maori men to have many tattoos. These were an essential part of their culture and would have shown their ancestry, indicated which tribe or *iwi* they came from, and marked important events and rites of passage.

Photo 2: These Chinese gold miners are in Australia. The gold rush started around 1850 and many Chinese went to Australia to make money to send back to their families. Many had to walk hundreds of miles to get to mining areas – often as the result of unscrupulous ship captains taking their money but leaving them in the wrong place. The living conditions were very basic, but worse than this was the racism they encountered. They were often the victims of verbal abuse and physical assault.

Photo 3: These children are attending summer camp in North America. Summer camp is very much a cultural tradition in the USA and some children return to the same camp year after year. Although 'first-timers' may feel anxious about being away from their parents, there are many activities to keep them stimulated ranging from learning to fish, making crafts, and of course, learning new songs around the camp fire.

Begin in whole class mode and elicit basic information about the three pictures: a Maori man, children at a summer camp, Chinese gold miners. Then ask the class for any other information they can supply about these three sets of people.

Then students go into pairs to answer the four questions.

2 Students listen and do the exam task.

Answers

1 B **2** C **3** C **4** A **5** A **6** B

Listening script 2.17–2.19

(I = Interviewer)

Extract one

I: Diane – It's quite traditional for American children to go to camp every summer, isn't it? But what makes non-Americans – I mean young people from other countries – want to work there?

Diane: Well I think a big draw is the chance to see America – the camps are situated in beautiful locations, and the chance to go travelling after camp's over is also very appealing to applicants. But once our foreign staff actually arrive at camp – they're often surprised at how multi-cultural it is. You could be working alongside someone from Denmark, Australia, Ireland ... It may be the first time you've met someone from these places and you can find out how much in common you really have. It's a real education.

I: And if someone listening to this programme wants to apply to work for Summer Camps USA, how can they go about it?

Diane: They should look out for our advertisements in *The Globe*, the international student magazine, or they can apply online. But I must advise people that working at camp is not the equivalent to a luxury holiday in a hotel. While it is a very satisfying experience – it may feel a little like military camp at times. That's not to say that you're taking orders and have no say – it's all very much about team work. It's more to do with the hours

– you're often on duty for long periods – including night supervision of the children.

Extract two

I: James – I believe we both had great-great-grandparents who came to Australia as gold miners in the mid-nineteen hundreds. But did you know much about that era before you did the documentary?

James: I'm ashamed to say not much. You know, I've always seen myself as a Chinese Australian – but that was more to do with family values and the traditions of our culture. And we grew up relatively wealthy – and with a good education and I've achieved a good level of success, thanks to that. But I know now that I took it for granted. Making the film showed me just what hardships our ancestors went through, and the sacrifices they made, so we could be where we are today. I learnt an awful lot.

I: From your own experience – and going by the interviews you carried out for the programme – do you believe that Chinese Australians are now seen as 'genuine' Australians?

James: I think we've come a long way. Our communities used to be hidden from view but now they're much more integrated. We're not just working in cafes and market gardens anymore! And it's no longer the case that Chinese parents are insisting their kids become doctors or lawyers. You've now also got Chinese Australians performing as musicians, artists, writers – that was a rare sight not so long ago. But it still occasionally happens that when I'm introduced to a European Australian, they like to compliment me on my good English. It doesn't occur to them that my family may have been here longer than theirs.

Extract three

I: Jeremy, an exhibition on tattooing – it's not really regarded as mainstream art, is it?

Jeremy: Well, not in the West, no. But one of the reasons for putting the exhibition together is to break down people's preconceptions about this art form. There's this stereotype of tattoos being worn by sailors or people trying to show they're non-conformist in some way – but certain cultures have long been wearing tattoos to show exactly where they *do* fit in society – and they're seen as sacred, rather than merely fashionable. The exhibition really does provide a fascinating look at the history of tattooing.

I: A large part of the exhibition is dedicated to the Maori people of New Zealand. Were their tattoos purely decorative?

Jeremy: Well, as with other Polynesian cultures, tattoos for the Maori people were actually an indication of a man's rank in society – his degree of authority within a tribe. But unique to the Maori was how facial tattooing indicated a man's ancestry – the design on the left side of his face showed his father's side, and the right, his mother's. Such markings would also make a warrior more attractive to women. But that isn't to say that women weren't also tattooed – but it tended to be a design on the chin or just an outline around the lips. There's also a collection of tools on view – the bone chisels they used and ...

3 If students are interested, these questions could branch out quite considerably – has anyone attended a summer camp? What were their experiences? If not, could the idea of summer camps ever catch on in your country? How else do school students spend their summer holidays? What other kinds of people have tattoos or body painting? Why do they want them? Is this practice socially acceptable in your country? What about body piercing?

Vocabulary 1: Sight Page 141

1 Put the word 'sight' on the board, and ask students to make some phrases containing the word to talk about the picture of the tattoos. (eg What an amazing sight! The sight of these tattoos is very impressive!)

Then focus students on the five questions in their books. They work individually and check their answers in the listening script at the back of the students' book.

Answers

a look **b** view **c** sight **d** look **e** view

2 Students work in pairs to complete the gaps.

Answers

1 sight **2** eye **3** view **4** look **5** vision

Focus on a few of the phrases in exercise 2. Ask the class:

Which phrase means

- examine? (have a look at)
- seen without an instrument? (visible to the naked eye)
- saw quickly? (caught sight of)
- appeared? (came into view)
- don't let anyone see you? (keep out of sight)

3 Point out that these are other expressions, not from the previous exercises. If explanation is needed, X-ray vision is the ability, celebrated in certain comics or cartoons, to see through things like buildings.

Reading: Gapped text Page 142

CAE Part 2

Photocopiable vocabulary exercise on page 156.

1 The second and third points could be done as a brainstorming exercise in small groups. Possible ideas:

audience behaviour – should

- be quiet and serious
- listen carefully and concentrate on the music/ acting
- sit still
- clap in the right places
- keep head in same place so person behind doesn't have view blocked
- not rustle sweet papers or do anything to distract
- not whistle or tap feet to the music

2 Give the following clues (they might be written on the board, for example) if you feel that help is needed during the task:

1 The Fidget-Bottoms family have not yet been introduced, nor has the idea of anti-social behaviour.
2 Look for a forward link to the writer kicking the seat.
3 Look at the forward link – there is likely to be a contrast with the relaxed attitude towards formal behaviour shown today.
4 Just before the gap we have a list of anti-social behaviour.
5 Look for a backward link to the last sentence before the gap.
6 The paragraph before the gap speaks of our changing listening habits – that we can now listen to music at home so easily.

When everybody has finished, vary the way of giving answers.

- This time give the correct answers immediately.
- Get students to re-read the whole task in the correct order.
- Then they go into pairs, and take turns to describe the links in English.

Answers

1 E **2** G **3** A **4** F **5** C **6** B D not used

Background notes

English commonly borrows words and phrases from French. A *laissez-faire attitude* is explained in the following lines of the text (*you come as you please and behave as you please*).

Chopsticks is a rather facile (= easy and childish) piece of piano music.

Reacting to the text

Students may need some help with this very 'adult' theme, but should have plenty to say if prompted with ideas:

Against the writer's views:

- Such formal behaviour is stuffy, old-fashioned and unfriendly.
- It encourages an elitist attitude – especially among opera audiences.
- It is good for families to get involved in activities such as this – opening up 'high culture' to new audiences.
- The Fidget-Bottoms, it could be argued, are merely showing their enjoyment of each other and the music.

In favour of the writer's views:

- Most social occasions and meeting places have their own unwritten rules.
- Making high culture available to everyone popularizes it and reduces its value.
- Most of us have lost the ability to sit still and listen for long periods which was normal behaviour two generations ago.

Encourage students to talk about the 'dumbing down' effect of television and the Internet. For example, TV channels are more motivated now by viewing figures and profit than by quality and education (witness the rise in reality TV). Similarly, when TV tries to be educational, it reduces complicated subjects to a simple, superficial level. Students should give examples from their own countries.

Language focus: Inversion Page 144

1–2 Present on the board, eliciting answers from volunteers.

Answers

1 The order of subject and auxiliary verb is reversed. Where there is no auxiliary verb, as in a and d, *do*, *does* or *did* is inserted before the subject.
The writer is adding emphasis to these words by placing them at the beginning of the sentence.

2b We have no sooner settled .../As soon as we have settled ...
c You should on no account kiss .../You should not kiss your children on any account ...
d I do not whistle along to the music at weddings either.

Before students turn to the Grammar reference, see how much they know about inversion. Establish that:

- the words/phrases in bold, which require the grammatical inversion, are all connected – they all have a negative sense.
- there are other words/phrases which require this inversion. These include *not until*, *only when*, *on no account*, *under no circumstances*.

Practice

1–2 These could be done individually in writing. Remind students that where there is no auxiliary verb (as with exercise 1, question 1), they will need 'do' in the appropriate tense.

Answers

1 do we go to the cinema these days
2 have I seen such a terrible performance of Hamlet
3 must bags be left unattended
4 the very last page is the identity of the murderer revealed
5 someone complained at reception did they realize the painting had been hung upside down

2

1 Never again would he play in front of a live audience.
2 Hardly had she sat down to watch her favourite programme when the phone rang.
3 Under no circumstances will you be allowed to enter the auditorium once the play has started.
4 Not only did we go to the National Gallery, but we also saw a West End musical.
5 Not since Amy went to the circus as a child had she enjoyed herself so much.

3–4 These could also be done orally with a confident class.

Word formation: Nouns formed with *in, out, up, down, back* Page 144

1 Such nouns are an important part of advanced English – students will encounter them in the text-based papers. Note that the noun can be formed with the preposition before or after the original word (drawback = preposition after; background = preposition before).

Answers

a drawbacks **b** background **c** outburst

2 Such nouns might be tested directly in the word formation task in the Use of English exam. Exercise 2 provides direct practice of this.

This exercise is likely to prove challenging, so it could be done in groups of three.

Answers

1 downpour	6 outcome
2 upturn	7 setback/upset
3 income(s)	8 output
4 outbreak	9 upbringing
5 insight	10 breakdown

Check students have understood by asking the following:

Which one is similar in meaning to

- the amount of money you earn? (income)
- result (outcome)
- childhood (upbringing)
- the number of people who attended (turnout)
- shower of rain (downpour)
- increase (upturn)
- problem/obstacle (setback)

Extra activity

This could be written on the board. Do stress that this activity is reusing the words from exercise 2.

In a–d write a noun from exercise 2 which collocates with each of the words in the group.

Example:
high/poor/voter ___turnout___

a steady/sudden/torrential

____

b a middle-class/religious/sheltered

____

c manufacturing/agricultural/literary

____

d a valuable/rare/revealing

____

Answers

Answers to extra activity in Teacher's Book

a downpour	**c** output
b upbringing	**d** insight

Listening 2: Sentence completion

CAE Part 2

Page 145

Lead-in

Establish the meaning of *confession* in this context (= admitting something surprising).

Explain that you are going to play the recording until someone in the class comes up with the correct answer to the question 'What is Gaby's confession?' (= she did not go to university, which is surprising given her profession).

Give students a minute or so to read the sentences, and highlight those words in the sentences which tell them to listen out for the answer.

1 Now play the recording.

Answers

1 university libraries	**5** language
2 concentration	**6** family life
3 bad luck	**7** envy
4 arrogant	**8** debt

2 Allow the discussion to broaden out into other areas of university life, if the subject is proving interesting.

Listening script 2.20

(P = Presenter; G = Gaby)

P: Now, in our regular *Confessions* spot, we listen to award-winning writer Gaby Longfellow, who was recently described as 'the most versatile and prolific writer of her generation'. So what is Gaby's confession?

G: People assume that because I'm a writer, because I come from Oxford, and because I spend hours poring over books in university libraries doing research for my work, then I must have gone to university myself. And the plain truth of the matter is, of course, that I didn't. I don't have a degree.

During my school years I had a very full social life: I was in a theatre group, I sang in a choir, I had a boyfriend, I went rock climbing. Right through my teens concentration was never my specialist subject at school. I'd always be looking out of the window, thinking of the hundred and one other things I could be doing.

And so it was with my A-levels. Which I failed, quite spectacularly. I could have retaken them of course, but I was too worried the same thing might happen again. Failing once wasn't too bad – nearly everyone put it down to bad luck, as opposed to any lack of effort on my part. But if I'd failed again I would have been officially declared stupid. Or at least, that's how I saw it then.

But it never occurred to me that I was any less intelligent than my friends who did go to university. In fact, at the time I thought *I* was the clever one for not going, and I probably came across as being rather arrogant as a result. I went to live in London and had a wonderfully exciting time, experiencing many things that my undergraduate friends could not. It was a period that gave me ideas and inspiration for my writing. I also read voraciously and *always* seemed to have a book in my hand. My reading gave me a passion for language and all its various features; an aptly chosen word, a well-crafted phrase, a striking metaphor – these are all things I try to emulate in my own writing.

Do I have any regrets? No, none at all. Indeed, many of my friends agree that university was rather a waste of time. And some of them feel bitter because their degrees pushed them into the types of professions that are detrimental to family life, ones that keep them away from home. They always seem to be worried about losing their well-paid jobs and they have little time or energy to devote to the things, or rather the people, that really matter. I even detect a certain amount of envy from some quarters. A lawyer friend of mine is always asking if he can swap lives with me. I have a great deal of admiration and respect for lawyers, but not, I have to say, enough to want to become one.

But I wouldn't try to discourage young people today from going to university. It has its advantages as well as its drawbacks and people have to make up their own minds. But it doesn't help now that when graduates start work in their chosen profession, many of them are hopelessly in debt, simply because they have had to borrow huge sums in order to pay their way through university. The idea is that those with degrees will have well-paid jobs and can easily pay off loans in the future. There's no guarantee of that, of course, and besides, it tends to convert money and the prospect of higher earnings into the main incentive for university education. And that, I confess, is not something I agree with.

Vocabulary 2: *Read* and *write* Page 146

1 Ask this question to the whole class.

Answers

A 'prolific writer' is one who writes a lot.
To 'read voraciously' is to read a lot.

2 There are a number of useful collocations to do with reading and writing. Students work in pairs to complete them.

Answers

1 aloud	**3** good	**5** well	**7** plain
2 avid	**4** widely	**6** rough, neatly	

3 Direct students to the Additional material.

Reading and speaking: Gap year

Page 146

1 Ask a volunteer to read the explanation of gap years aloud. If appropriate to your students, ask how the UK situation compares with their own, and whether any of them have plans for gap years of their own. Then get them to answer the question in their Coursebooks.

2 Read the extract from the website together. Ask students whether they think universities and employers would be so enthusiastic in their country/ies.

Speaking 1: CAE Part 3 Collaborative task

Page 147

Before starting on the exam task, get students to cover the text for each picture and give them two minutes in pairs to talk about what each advert might say. Alternatively, this could be done as a whole-class activity.

When considering 'what you might learn', students can consider this both from a personal point of view and from the perspective of impressing future employers.

Students should hopefully have plenty to say on this topic, so regard this is as opportunity for fluency rather than as timed exam practice.

Remind students to interact with their partner – to listen and respond accordingly.

Speaking 2: CAE Part 4 Further discussion

Page 147

You might like to get students to change partners for this, so as to expose them to a maximum of different ideas.

Writing: CAE Part 1 Proposals Page 148

1 When students have finished reading the various input texts, establish that:

- the ideas on the notepad are your own (ie you the writer).
- the extracts on the right are from people you have contacted.

There are no right and wrong answers for the underlining activity – it is enough that students have done this, as it focuses their attention on the key information as they read the input. So there is no need to have a formal checking stage for this.

2 In order to answer this, students will need to think about how to combine the various bits of input information (which they are required to do with this task).

- Derek Turner's comment refers to Book Reviews.
- Audrey Perham's comment refers to Interviews, but also to Competitions, as she suggests using the tickets as a prize.
- Peter Tulleys' comment refers to Film Reviews.

There is also a note at the top of the notepad which says 'aim for variety'. So the above would seem to be a good combination.

Possible answer

Film review
Interview
Competition
Book review

In the above version, the two review sections are separated, for the sake of variety. Point out that other variations may be possible:

- One might, for example, combine the two review parts under one section – Reviews.
- One might also invent some details about Hadley Norris – it is fine to do this in the exam provided the invention is relevant and picks up on something in the input information.

Exam note:

- This is the first time the proposal has come up in the book. Proposals should be considered as very similar to reports, so students should be directed to Unit 3 to read the 'How to go about it' section.
- The difference with proposals is that whereas reports deal with past or present events, proposals focus on the future, in particular recommendations for action or discussion.
- Because of this recommending element, while reports are normally impersonal (typically the passive instead of 'I' and 'we'), in proposals 'I' or 'we' are needed.
- For a further example of a proposal see page 200 of the Ready for Writing section.

3 Focus students' attention on how the sample answer in exercise 3 organizes the ideas. Interestingly, the headings used are cleverly different from the ones used in the 'Possible ideas' input text. Then get them to comment on the first four bullet points and linking devices in the final bullet.

Answers

3

• the overall length of the answer
The answer contains nearly 400 words and is far too long. In the exam over-length answers are penalized if they include irrelevance and/or have a negative effect on the reader.

• the writer's selection and use of the input material
The writer has included all the input information rather than selecting what is relevant. As a result, the answer exceeds the word limit. It is not necessary to use all the input information for this task. In addition, he/she has lifted large sections of the input material instead of reworking it into original language. The writer has made only minimal attempts to expand on the input material and add his/her own ideas: eg *a good friend of mine* and *Why don't we include a review too?*

• the appropriacy and consistency of the register
Given the target reader – the secretary of the Arts club – any register would be appropriate as long as it is consistent. In this answer, the writer switches freely between formal and informal language: compare
an excess of art is not desirable
with
some stuff about local events and loads of different people

• the quality and range of the language
Rather simplistic throughout.

• the organization of ideas and use of linking devices
The proposal is organized into logical paragraphs with relevant headings. However, the answer is often rambling, and there is unnecessary repetition of the free tickets as prizes. The bracketed comments *(see below)* and *(I shall say more about that later)* are unnecessary. Linking is in evidence but limited to *and, so, but, also, too, because*, most of which are used more than once.

4 Students locate the bad grammar and correct it.

Answers

I suggest (that) you/we (should) include *or* I suggest including
I recommend you to inform *or* I recommend informing

5 Give this for homework.

Review 11 answers Pages 150 and 151

Use of English: Word formation
CAE Part 3

1 eventful	**5** considerable	**8** minorities
2 childhood	**6** inspiration	**9** output
3 freshness	**7** socially	**10** unequalled
4 literary		

Vocabulary

1 read	**5** suffered	**8** kept
2 taking	**6** catch	**9** turned/came
3 write	**7** came	**10** broke
4 Look		

Use of English: Open cloze
CAE Part 2

1 behind	**5** that	**9** would	**13** what
2 of	**6** like	**10** until	**14** instead
3 be	**7** which	**11** by	**15** while/whilst/although/though
4 both	**8** much	**12** is	

12 The world about us

Content overview

Themes

This unit is concerned with the natural world, the environment, global issues.

Exam-related activities

Paper 1	**Reading**
Part 3	Multiple choice (long)
Paper 2	**Writing**
Part 2	Articles
Paper 3	**Use of English**
Part 1	Multiple-choice cloze
Part 2	Open cloze (review)
Part 5	Key word transformations
Paper 4	**Listening**
Part 2	Sentence completion
Part 4	Multiple matching

Other

Vocabulary 1	Verbs with more than one use
Vocabulary 2	Attitude adverbials
Language focus 1	Conjunctions and linking adverbials
Language focus 2	Modal verbs 3

Listening 1: Sentence completion

CAE Part 2

Page 152

1 These questions may work best as a whole-class activity. A further line of questioning could be 'How do humans adjust their living habits to cope with extremely hot weather?' (= Avoid the midday sun, wear white clothing to reflect the sunlight, drink more water etc.) Then 'and what about desert animals?'

2 Now play the recording.

Answers

1 (white) salt	**5** (their) feathers
2 store/keep (rain) water	**6** large ears
3 fifty/50	**7** skin
4 (long) tail	**8** donkey

Listening script 2.21

Deserts cover about one seventh of the earth's land area. Rainfall is scarce and temperatures as high as 58 degrees celsius have been recorded there. Nevertheless, deserts are home to a rich variety of plants and animals, all of which have their own strategies for coping with the harsh conditions.

The desert holly, for example, draws up salt from the ground and releases it onto its leaves. The white mineral covers the leaves entirely and helps to reflect some of the daytime heat, in much the same way that white clothes do for humans.

The huge saguaro cactus, which grows in the Sonoran Desert of Arizona and Mexico, can live for more than 200 years. This is partly due to its ability to expand and store water. The cactus has ribs running along its length, which open out like an accordion, enabling the water which falls in the short wet season to be kept in its trunk. This allows the saguaro to flower every year, regardless of rainfall. A giant of the cactus world, the saguaro is a slow grower but it can reach heights of up to fifty feet and weigh as much as eight tons.

Like the plants, desert birds are also well equipped to deal with the conditions. The road runner, for example, uses its long tail as a parasol, bringing it forward over its head to create shade, thus enabling the bird to keep cool – a simple, yet effective strategy in an environment which offers little protection from the sun's rays. Birds, of course, also have their feathers to help them. In other, cooler parts of the world, these serve to keep body heat in. In the desert, though, their main function is to keep external heat out, and as a result many birds can spend long periods unharmed in the hot desert sun.

Mammals tend to avoid the sun, usually coming out only after night has fallen. The jack rabbit in America and the fennec fox in the Sahara, however, do venture out during the daytime. Their protection against the heat is a pair of extremely large ears. As well as enabling the animals to hear better, these contain blood vessels which are so close to the surface of the skin that any air blowing across them cools the blood that runs through them.

Those most archetypal of desert animals, camels, have a number of useful techniques and devices. Their nose is equipped with muscles, which enable them to close one or both of their nostrils and keep the sand out during sandstorms. Their feet have only two toes which are connected by skin. This spreads out as they walk on soft sand and keeps them from sinking into it. They can also retain vast quantities of water in their stomachs – not their humps as many people think. As a result they can go without drinking anything for four times longer than a donkey and ten times as long as a man.

So if it's not used for storing water, what purpose *does* the hump on a camel serve? Well, it may surprise you to hear that it's actually used by the camel to ...

Optional extra activity

This listening script is educational in a broad sense and full of interesting facts. Teachers could ask students to close their books and simply tell each other (in groups of three) what interesting facts they have learned. This can be an especially useful exercise in a foreign language.

Be sure to help them by supplying sentence stems such as:

I didn't realize that ...
I was surprised to learn that ...
It came as a surprise to me that ...
I had no idea that ...

3 Miss the final question if you have already used something similar in exercise 1.

Answers

The camel's hump is used for storing food reserves in the form of fat. Part of this can be converted into liquid if necessary.

Vocabulary 1: Words with more than one use Page 153

1 Ask students first to focus on the words in italics. See if they can remember the things referred to. If not they can consult the listening script at the back of their books.

Answers

it – the road runner's tail
their – feathers of desert birds
This – the skin which connects the camel's two toes

2 Now ask them to focus on the words in bold in exercise 1, and find the meaning of 'keep' in each phrase.

Answers

stay cool
make external heat stay out
prevents them from sinking into it

3 Students work in pairs to find the verb which fits in all three sentences.

Answers

1 know
2 welcome
3 pay
4 meet
5 wish

4 This exercise needs to be done carefully in writing and checked. Show how the examples work in replacing the expressions in bold in 0. Then give students in pairs fifteen minutes or so to do the same with numbers 1–5. This gives valuable practice in paraphrasing which is what students have to do in the key word transformations task (Use of English Part 5).

Answers

1 tell/inform her
become familiar/acquainted with
Are you familiar with/Can you name ...?

2 be happy to receive/grateful for your ideas/recommendations
very pleased to greet/have with us
something you are happy to see

3 It's not to your advantage if you
say something nice to me
take much notice of

4 be waiting for you on the station platform
be at all successful
do what is necessary to deal with the problem

5 intend to be impolite
hope she does well
given the possibility to make something happen (by magic)

5 Students discuss the questions in pairs.

Use of English 1: CAE Part 1 Multiple-choice cloze Page 154

1 If students need prompting, point out that while farm animals such as cows and sheep have traditionally been used for meat, there is now a growing international market for wild animals, such as crocodiles, snakes and sharks, to be farmed. Their meat is eaten and their skins go to make luxury items such as bags and shoes.

2 This exercise is aimed at getting students into the good habit of reading the whole text first before attempting any of the items.

Answers

Andy Johnson set up the farm to commercialize crocodile meat. His idea was to sell the meat more cheaply than illegal meat and so protect crocodiles from poaching.
Dr Clifford Warwick says that crocodiles are stressed in a captive environment.

You might also get students to close their books and ask volunteers to recall the key facts in the text.

3 Now students try the task.

Answers

1 A	4 C	7 A	10 C
2 A	5 B	8 D	11 A
3 D	6 C	9 B	12 B

Textual note
The name given to farming practice designed not to harm the environment is *sustainable farming*.

4 The following phrases may be useful when talking on this subject:

led to the extinction of
on/off the critical list
a protected species
an endangered species
a breeding programme

Well-known endangered species in the wider world are: Indian elephant, blue whale, American crocodile, Javan rhinoceros, Californian Condor.

5 This wordbuilding exercise focuses students on the other three options in each question, and how these words are used. In pairs students should choose any four of the 12 remaining questions, strike out the answer, and write a multiple-choice question using the three options.
One of these will be a new correct answer.
Be sure to monitor this for correctness.
The answer to the example sentence is C.

6 The pairs of students then move around the classroom and put their questions to as many people as possible.

Answers

Answers to Self-help section
Some 300,000 Australian saltwater crocodiles
has roughly tripled
a million or more animals
upwards of 90,000

Reading: CAE Part 3 — Multiple choice

Page 155

1 Stay in whole-class formation for this exercise. Ask a few volunteers the first question and brainstorm the likely qualities of a presenter. Explain that this will help with some of the multiple-choice questions which follow.

2 With the exam in mind, it is suggested that this would be a good time to try a timed reading. However, before beginning, do remind students of the instructions for how to tackle multiple-choice reading on page 7 of the Coursebook.

Answers

1 B 2 A 3 C 4 D 5 A 6 B 7 B

Spend some time on analysing where the answers came from in the text.

Answers

Answers to text location (Teacher's Book)

1. *the voice is like a piano played gently. You feel at home with this voice …*
2. This is the gist of the whole second paragraph, particularly lines 16–25.
3. The meaning is in the phrase itself, but the sentence *And we will be variously appalled …* (line 25) also helps.
4. This is the gist of the third paragraph, particularly lines 39–49.
5. This is the gist of the fourth paragraph particularly *he keeps out of the limelight*, lines 54–60 and lines 64–68.
6. This is the point of Attenborough's anecdote about the Cambridge academic (lines 72–83).
7. *He rocketed up through the ranks.*

This analysis should serve a useful purpose in terms of exam training. It shows how some questions in multiple-choice reading will look at details in the text and how others will focus on whole ideas developed over paragraphs.

Finally return to the list of qualities of a wildlife documentary presenter which was brainstormed in exercise 1. Give students two minutes only to scan the text and list what the text says on this subject. The question is: 'What qualities does Attenborough possess which make him a good presenter?'

Answers

According to the text:
he has a gentle familiar voice
he is modest
he has great energy
he doesn't like to be in the limelight
he enjoys being near animals
he likes travel and doesn't mind discomfort
he is both entertaining and educational
he is happy and optimistic

Reacting to the text
Students follow instructions.

Language focus 1: Conjunctions and linking adverbials Page 157

1–2 It is suggested that these exercises be done in class, as students will benefit from the extra resource of the teacher.

Answers

1A
a otherwise **b** so that **c** in case
1B
a even though **b** whereas **c** However

2A
a On the contrary **b** By contrast
c Despite this
2B
a In the meantime **b** By that time
c From that time on
2C
a As **b** On, of **c** For
2D
a In, to **b** As, as **c** from

3 This more productive task could be set as homework or done in class. Either way it needs careful checking if it is to be valuable.

Answers

Example answers

1 a we came home early.
b the rainwater leaked in through a hole in the tent.

2 a he would receive at least one present on his birthday.
b he gave her absolutely nothing.

3 a he'd had time to write emails to eight of his friends.
b she'd had to stay at work until 9.30 so as to get everything finished.

4 a you particularly enjoy sharing a beach with 3,000 other bathers.
b it's certainly worth spending a day there.

Optional extra activity
When looking at the Grammar reference section, draw students' attention to the other words listed under each category. Select any they find difficult and make short gapped sentences for them to complete.
Examples:
I impressed at the interview because I'd read up about the company ____________. (= beforehand)

My computer is being repaired and it's due back on Friday. ___________, you'll just have to phone me, as you can't reach me on email. (= Until then)

Listening 2: CAE Part 4 Multiple matching Page 158

Photocopiable vocabulary exercise on page 156.

1 Ask students to go into groups of three, and to outline the main issues involved. Give them the example of Child Labour as follows:

In many developing countries, children are forced to work in poorly paid jobs, sometimes in subhuman conditions. This is usually as a result of poverty, and in some cases because they have been orphaned by Aids. Some work in sweat shops, producing goods for Western markets. This leads to children missing out on an education and the perpetuation of poverty in the country.

The World Day against Child Labour is celebrated every year on June 12th.

Students produce similar ideas for the other five issues.

Answers

Possible answers/background information for teachers

Global warming: The build-up of carbon dioxide in the atmosphere, caused for example by high energy consumption, leads to a rise in the earth's temperature. This in turn can lead to a melting of glaciers and the polar ice caps, and a consequent rise in sea levels, flooding and destruction to coastal areas.

Whale hunting: This is still authorized by a small number of countries, despite an international moratorium and protests from environmentalists. It is justified either on scientific grounds or for commercial purposes and to prevent the whale population from growing too large and consuming huge stocks of fish.

Human rights: On December 10, 1948 the United Nations proclaimed the Universal Declaration of Human Rights. It included the following:

- All human beings are born free and equal in dignity and rights.
- No one shall be held in slavery or servitude.
- No one shall be subjected to torture or degrading treatment.

Violations of human rights occur throughout the World.

Women's rights: According to the Universal Declaration of Human Rights, women are entitled to the enjoyment of all human rights and to be treated equally to men in both economic and social life.

GM foods: Genetically modified foods, or GM foods, are grown from crops which have been altered through biotechnology to make them more resistant to insects and disease. The most common GM crops are soybeans, corn, cotton and sugar beet and are mainly used in processed foods or in animal feed.

Supporters of genetic modification say that it makes crops more productive and can also increase their nutritional value. Opponents point to the dangers of cross-pollination, whereby GM crops can spread their genes to other plants growing nearby. While producers say there are no health concerns associated with GM foods, opponents maintain that insufficient tests have been carried out and the long-term effects on health are unknown.

Since April 2004 strict regulations have been in force in the European Union concerning the labelling of foods which contain genetically modified produce.

Optional pre-listening activity

- Ask volunteers to describe what they can see in the three pictures at the top of the page.
- Write 'whale hunting', 'women's rights', and 'humanitarian work abroad' on the board.
- Students close their books and listen to the recording all the way through.

Ask them which speakers spoke about the pictures.

Answers

Answer to extra activity in Teacher's Book

Speaker 2 – voluntary humanitarian work abroad

Speaker 4 – whale hunting

Speaker 5 – women's rights

2 As students near the end of the book, they meet their most difficult multiple-matching listening to date. In view of this, break the task down as suggested in the following exploitation.

- Establish that each speaker is talking about action they have taken on a global issue.
- Play the first speaker only. Replay.
- Ask students to complete questions 1 and 6, ie the questions which deal with Speaker 1.
- Establish the answers, 1B and 6H.
- Play the first speaker again, and ask students to stop you when they hear the answers.
- The answer for 1 comes from *So there I was, the rich tourist in a developing country ... to blame.*
- The answer for 6 comes from *when I got back ... given more.*
- Now play the rest of the recording. Students try the rest of the task.

Answers

1 B **2** E **3** G **4** H **5** A **6** H
7 A **8** B **9** F **10** C

If the task has proved difficult, the listening script can be used for students to check their answers.

Listening script 2.22–2.26

Speaker 1

So there I was, the rich tourist in a developing country. Of course, you get people begging at home, but there, it was on every street corner. The poverty is so evident, so widespread, and I couldn't help feeling, as a wealthy Westerner, that I was in some way to blame. So I decided to do something to help, despite the attempts of my friend and travelling companion to persuade me otherwise. Every day we were there I put aside a certain amount of money to give to beggars. My friend told me I was being overgenerous, but when I got back home I couldn't help thinking I should have given more.

Speaker 2

A mate of mine often complained about all the suffering in the world – but he never did anything about it. He said it was difficult for individuals to change things. Well, I just couldn't accept that. I took it as a kind of challenge and applied for voluntary work overseas in a school for street children. I thought at first they might not accept me because of my age and inexperience, but I needn't have worried – I didn't need to have any special skills or anything. In fact, that was part of the trouble. Most people were as green as me so there was no real organization to talk of. Plus, I felt the government there could have done a lot more to help. A shame really, because I was so enthusiastic when I went out there.

Speaker 3

I did a concert last year to raise money for an international relief organization. My manager said it'd be good for my image – you know, to be seen to be caring about other people's suffering and so on. I'd love to be able to say that I did it because I admired the work they were doing and I was concerned about the issues they were fighting for. But that was more of an afterthought, really. I'm embarrassed to admit that my first instinct was to consider what was in it for me, what I stood to gain from it all. Sure, I did the concert for free and helped to raise lots of money for charity, but it's not something I boast about. I'm not at all proud of myself.

Speaker 4

I saw this photograph of activists in a small rubber dinghy moving up alongside one of those huge whaling boats. It was a striking image, and it made me think that if they can risk their lives in this way to stop the suffering of an animal, then I can surely risk some of my money to help them. The trouble was, though, I chose the wrong moment to be generous – I didn't realize just how little money there was in my account when I sent off the cheque. It left me with next to nothing and I couldn't afford to go away on the weekend trip I'd planned with my friends. I wished afterwards that I hadn't been quite so willing to help out.

Speaker 5

Back in the Sixties, of course, women's rights still wasn't much of an issue. People just seemed to accept that we got paid a lot less than men, even though we had to do exactly the same work. Amazing, really. I mean, if I'd been a man, I'd have felt so guilty about it all. I wanted to help put that right, to challenge existing perceptions. So I got all the girls on the shop floor to go on a protest march through the town – there must have been about 500 of us altogether. We should have done it years before. They couldn't sack us, of course – there were too many of us – and when I realized that, it spurred me on. In fact, that's what made me go into politics, so I could continue the struggle.

3 This speaking point is likely to work best as a whole-class activity rather than pairwork. Point out that there are many little things we can do as individuals: giving money, taking part in protests, refusing to buy certain products, making an effort to restrict car use etc.

Language focus 2: Modal verbs 3

Page 159

It is likely that exercises 1–5 will need to be presented to the whole class, and pairwork can be reserved for the practice stage.

1 Some students may notice that A1 and B2 are not actually modal verbs – this point will be dealt with in exercise 3.

Answers

A Speaker 5 (women's rights)
B Speaker 2 (voluntary work abroad)

2 Make sure students have got the difference between *didn't need to* and *needn't have*. *Needn't have* is used when you did something unnecessarily.

Answers

A
past obligation: we were obliged to
speculation about the past: there were probably
past regret: it would have been better if we'd done

B
I worried but it wasn't necessary
It wasn't necessary to have any special skills and I didn't have any.

3 The question of what is and what isn't a modal becomes important in advanced grammatical distinctions, especially with 'need'. Sometimes it is modal (I needn't have), sometimes not.

Answers

had to and *didn't need to* are not modal verbs. Modal verbs go with a main verb (*I can go*; can = modal, go = main)
Modal verbs express the mood or attitude of the speaker and are followed by the infinitive without *to* (with the exception of *ought to*). In addition, an auxiliary verb is not used to form the negative of a modal verb (*I must not*, *I shouldn't* etc).

'*We should have done it years before*' could also be written as '*We ought to have done it years before*'.

4 Elicit each one and write it on the board.

Answers

a must – internal obligation: I think it is necessary to go
should – expectation: my son is expected to be home
have to – external obligation: I am required to take him

b shouldn't – recommendation: it is not good/advisable to tell lies
don't have to – no obligation: it is not necessary to tell him the whole truth
mustn't – prohibition: I don't want you to let him know

5 In the negative form of the present tense the distinction with *need* becomes even more subtle.

Answers

The modal form of *need* is not used in positive sentences, so the non-modal form is required in both cases.
You need to do it now – we're in a hurry.
You need to be tall to be a good basketball player.

Practice
1 This should be done in pairs.

Answers

1 needn't/shouldn't
2 must/should
3 have/need
4 should
5 needn't/don't need to/don't have to
6 ought to/must/should
7 needed to study/ought to have studied
8 should

2 Put the following example on the board:

Example:
Student A I cleaned the flat specially for tonight, but I shouldn't have bothered.
Student B Why? Have they phoned to say they can't come?
Student A No. It's just that there are muddy footprints everywhere.
Student B Well, you should have taken your shoes off before you came in.
Student A They're not *my* muddy footprints!

Vocabulary 2: Attitude adverbials

Page 159

Point out the importance of this in the exam.

- Questions in the reading paper, especially on the multiple-choice task, often test the attitude or opinion of the writer.
- Attitude adverbials are commonly used as linkers in writing. The writing section later in this unit is an article (refer students to page 161), which requires opinions to be expressed. Students will need to use attitude adverbials when writing their article.

Answers

1 rightly
2 Strangely
3 Disappointingly
4 predictably
5 understandably

Use of English 2: CAE Part 5 — Key word transformations

Page 160

Here is some help for some of the more difficult questions.

2 The first part of the answer (make it to) is an informal way of saying 'attend'.
3 The first part of the answer (in case) is paraphrasing 'There's a chance that'. The main verb which goes with 'across' to make a phrasal verb is paraphrasing 'find'. The key word is being used with a preposition to mean 'find'.
4 The key word is used in a phrase which means 'while we're waiting'. 'I suggest you' in the first sentence must be paraphrased to produce a similar verb using 'to'.
5 The key word is used in a single long phrase which means 'because'.
7 The key word is used as part of a phrasal verb meaning 'refuse'.

Answers

1 have paid/given careful attention to
2 it to the meeting apart
3 case you happen to come
4 in the meantime try/I advise you/I recommend you/you ought
5 on account of the fact (that)
6 (an obligation) to add my name/signature
7 have been tough/difficult/hard to turn down
8 have taken part in

The exercise produces very useful chunks of language for students to record in their notebooks:
pay (careful) attention to
make it to the meeting
in case you happen to
in the meantime = meanwhile
on account of the fact that = because

Ask individual students to use some of these spontaneously in different situations, eg 'I'm afraid I can't make it to the party'.

Writing: CAE Part 2 — Articles

Page 161

1 Students should not need any prompting of ideas, but possible suggestions might include: drugs, bullying, lack of amenities, Internet chat rooms, peer pressure, parental expectation, finding employment. Any of these might be discussed.

2 Students relate the information to the situation in their own country/ies.

3 In pairs, students analyse the model answer, making notes on each of the categories.

Answers

3

a Yes

b Yes. There are four paragraphs of similar length, each performing a separate function:
Paragraph 1: Example situation
Paragraph 2: Explanation of problem and further examples
Paragraph 3: Current trends and main causes of problem
Paragraph 4: Suggested action
The article has also been given a relevant heading.

c Yes. A range of linking devices has been used, including several attitude adverbials.
Attitude Adverbials: *Sadly*, *Worryingly*, *Ideally*, *Unfortunately*

d Yes. There are numerous examples, including: *a torrential downpour, a more sheltered sleeping spot, they struggle to make ends meet.*
Several phrasal verbs are used.

e Yes. There is a slight mix of registers, but this is entirely appropriate, given the aim of the first paragraph, to engage the reader and provide an illustration of life on the streets. Paragraphs 2 to 4 are a little more formal and appropriate to the aim of explanation and giving an opinion on a serious issue.

f The first paragraph involves readers and engages their interest by asking them to imagine themselves in the situation of a street child. Note the direct address and repeated use of *you*. The final paragraph includes rhetorical questions, the second of which gives the reader food for thought.

4 At some stage students should be starting to get accustomed to doing timed essays in class.

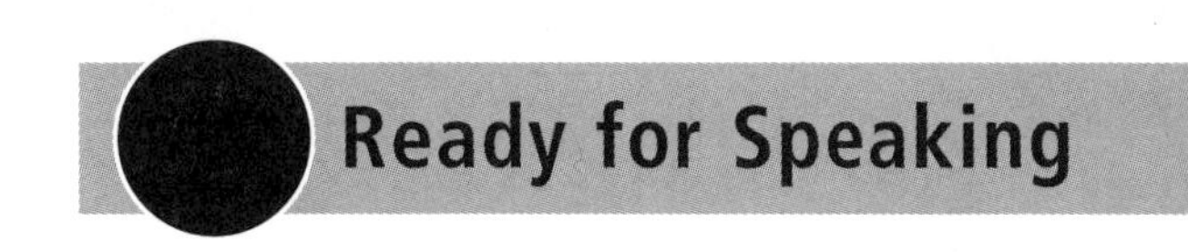

Review 12 answers Pages 162 and 163

Use of English: CAE Part 2 Open cloze

1 at
2 a
3 be
4 or
5 this/that
6 In
7 towards/*toward
8 with
9 to
10 while/whilst/when
11 and
12 nearly
13 over
14 for
15 not

*more common in American English

Modal verbs

1 could
2 would
3 might
4 needn't
5 shouldn't
6 shall
7 won't
8 must

Collocation revision: Units 1–12

1 challenge
2 changes
3 smell
4 time
5 relationship
6 sleep
7 ankle/wrist
8 decision
9 views
10 voice
11 sight
12 meet

CAE Paper 5

Speaking

Part 1 Social interaction
Part 2 Long turn
Part 3 Collaborative task
Part 4 Further discussion

In this unit, students go through the various stages of the speaking test, finding out exactly what happens at each stage, how long each stage lasts and looking at useful strategies and language they can employ.
For guidance on the teacher's likely role during speaking activities, see Teacher's Book Units 1 and 2.

Introduction Page 164

Explain that students are going to read a summary of good advice to candidates in the exam. This has been made into a gap-fill activity. Ask them to complete this individually.

Answers

1 ideas
2 silences
3 vocabulary
4 attention
5 repetition
6 pictures
7 element
8 discussion
9 opportunity
10 opinion

Go through the advice and make the following points:

Demonstrating your abilities
Second bullet – Obviously native speakers pause, hesitate and repeat themselves. A certain amount of this can actually make you sound authentic – but constant pausing to think of words is not going to impress the examiner.

Following instructions
Second bullet – Candidates often think they will be penalized for asking for repetition. Clearly if they do this all the time they will create a bad impression, but in real life native speakers ask for clarification often enough! The important thing is to ask for clarification in an impressive way. 'I don't understand – please repeat' is KET level language,

but 'Sorry I've missed the point', 'Sorry, I'm not 100% clear what I have to do', or 'Sorry would you mind saying that again' are much better.

Taking turns

You are assessed on your interactive communication, so an excellent candidate who does all the talking and does not listen to his/her partner is not going to do well. It is important to listen hard and respond spontaneously and appropriately to what your partner says. Don't interrupt your partner, but it is ok to make 'listening noises' to encourage the speaker, as in English it is rare to remain completely silent when someone is speaking to you. These may be things like smiling, nodding your head, and saying 'Yes', 'Mmmm', 'Really?', 'Absolutely' in the right places.

Part 1: Social interaction Page 164

1 Students follow the instructions. If you wish to do this as exam practice, under exam conditions, note that the total time for the task is three minutes. In the exam, students do not see these questions, so remind them that they can ask for clarification.

When students have finished, they change roles. This can be done three times, so that each student gets a go at being the interlocutor. There are enough questions for this, and questions can always be repeated if necessary.

2 In the Ready for Speaking section there are recordings of two students taking each part of the test. Students listen to Part 1 and then speak in pairs about the two bullet points.

Answers

Comments

Ana's contributions are of reasonable length, though they could certainly be developed more. She is clearly hindered by the level of her language: she uses a limited range of vocabulary and her responses are rather inaccurate.

Janusz is clearly a stronger student. He develops his responses well, uses a much wider range of language, and in this part of the test at least, there are no inaccuracies.

Note: The listening scripts for Ready for Speaking do not appear in the Coursebook.

Listening script 2.27

(I = Interlocutor; J = Janusz from Poland; A = Ana from Spain)

Part 1

I: Good morning. My name is Andrew Milton and this is my colleague Susan Meredith. And your names are?

A: I'm Ana.

J: And my name is Janusz.

I: Can I have your mark sheets, please? Thank you. First of all, we'd like to know something about you. Janusz, what are your main reasons for learning English?

J: Erm, because it's er, it's very useful, very necessary for me. I began to work with international projects and I felt that I needed to improve my English. I hadn't studied any English since I left school and I was getting a little bit rusty, so that's why I signed up for a course.

I: Ana, what do you need to do to help you pass the CAE exam?

A: Erm, I think I must to do a lot of exercises, practical exercises for grammar and writing. Yes, and maybe practical exercises for, for speaking, too.

I: What do you enjoy doing in your free time?

A: In my free time? Er, I like to read. Er, I like very much reading books about adventures, novels, these kinds of books. And I like go to the cinema. I go once a month, twice a month sometimes. But I would like to go there more frequently.

I: And how about you, Janusz?

J: Well, er, you know I think Ana and I share more or less the same interests. I read a great deal, and I'm a regular cinema-goer. I particularly enjoy getting together with friends, though. It doesn't matter what we do – I just like being in the company of people I get on with. I'm not one of those people who can be on their own for very long.

I: What have been some of the happiest moments in your life recently, Ana?

A: Well, my wedding! It was a perfect day, it was in last September. I enjoyed a lot, I wasn't nervous, I feel very quiet and I could see all my friends and my family, and everybody was happy. It was perfect.

I: Janusz?

J: Well, *my* happiest moment is more related with work. I gained promotion last year in my company, and that's something I really wanted to achieve. It's given me a lot more financial, er, a lot more, er, yes, stability, and it means I have the opportunity to travel as well. As I said before, that's why I've been studying English again.

I: Ana, do you prefer going on holiday with your friends or family?

A: Er, I prefer go with my friends. It's more funny for me. I like my family, I don't have any problems with them, but, er, if I'm looking for funny, for something funny, it's better to go with my friends.

I: If you could afford your ideal home, Janusz, what would it be like?

J: Probably not the one I have! I like my house, it's very spacious, very light and airy, but it's in a small village, and that's a big drawback for me. I like city life very much, I need to be in the centre of things, not stuck out in the middle of nowhere. So my ideal home would be much the same as the one I've got at the moment, but in the middle of a big city.

Part 2: Long turn Page 165

Note that the aim in Parts 2 and 3 is to bring in topics from the Coursebook which have not previously appeared in exam task format. This means you can refer them back to concrete vocabulary they have studied (see word lists and vocabulary focus in units of coursebook; for Part 2 Task One, see Unit 4 (Time); for Task Two see Unit 11 (Read and write)).

Task One

1 Read the task together and the first bullet point of the 'What to expect' box. Note that

- the two related questions for Student A are always shown on the page.
- Student A chooses two of the three pictures.
- Student B's question is different – it will involve looking at all three pictures, choosing one of them and justifying this choice.
- although Student B is expected to remain silent during Student A's long turn, Student B should still listen carefully to what Student A is saying. This is for two reasons. First it is much easier for Student B to comment on the pictures if (s)he has already heard another person talking about them, and second Student B might want to refer to something Student A has said.

Encourage students to use past modals, eg what might have happened to make her so pressed for time?

2 Before students do the task, refer them to page 166. In pairs they comment on the three candidates' extracts.

Answers

Comments

a No attempt is made to compare the pictures. The contribution is limited to a description of the two pictures with a single, short comment on why they might be checking the time. This candidate will probably find it difficult to continue talking for one minute, as he/she is likely to run out of things to say. Linking of ideas is limited to the use of '*because*'.

b Candidates often waste time identifying the pictures they are going to talk about, rather than getting on with the task. Students should be made aware that they will only ever have to compare two of the three pictures. They should not, as this candidate seems to want to do, attempt to talk about all three. Candidates should also avoid merely repeating information given in the instructions (*'all three pictures show women checking the time'*) or stating the obvious (*'This woman is an athlete'*).

c This candidate begins comparing the pictures immediately, rather than merely describing them. Ideas are linked well (*'both convey'*, *'the athlete, on the other hand'*, and *'suggesting something unexpected has happened'*) and there is an attempt to use a range of grammar and vocabulary.

3 Now students do task one.

Task Two

1 When they have finished task one, change roles as instructed, referring to the Additional material section of the coursebook.

Now students do task two.

2 Students listen again to the CD and answer the questions in their books.

Answers

Comments

Janusz's language is very varied, particularly when speculating. He uses a range of modal verbs and other structures for this purpose: *She might have realized, she may be phoning, she could also be phoning, she's most probably learning, she doesn't seem to be, the little girl looks as if she's watching.*

However, he fails to address the part of the task which asks him to say 'how much influence time might have in their daily lives'. He seems to have

forgotten this and the fact that the questions are printed on the visuals page, and he struggles to find more things to say.
Ana, on the other hand, completes her task satisfactorily, though once more her language is not very varied. She opens with *in this picture* each time and her language of speculation is limited to the use of *I think* and *maybe/perhaps* with present simple or present continuous, or else *seem(s) to be*. She searches for words, repeats *or something (like that)* and uses language incorrectly eg *it's probable this is the mother, put her a new washing machine, he seems to be concentrated*.

Listening script 2.28

(I = Interlocuter; J = Janusz; A = Ana)

I: In this part of the test, I'm going to give each of you three pictures. I'd like you to talk about them on your own for about a minute, and also to answer a question briefly about your partner's pictures. Janusz, it's your turn first. Here are your pictures. They show people who are checking the time. I'd like you to compare two of the pictures, and say why the people might be checking the time and how much influence time might have in their daily lives. All right?

J: OK, the woman with the phone and this child here are checking the time for very different reasons. I would say that this woman is looking at her watch probably because she's busy, she's late, er, she has an appointment to get to and she has a little girl to take care of as well. She might have realized she's late for her appointment and she may be phoning her work to make some kind of alternative arrangement. She could also be phoning her daughter's school to let them know the girl is going to be a bit late. On the other hand, in this one, the girl and the adult are having fun, they are comparing the times in their watches. She's most probably learning how to tell the time, and she doesn't seem to be in any kind of a hurry. So this is a difference – that woman's very stressed about the time, and this little girl isn't worried at all. Er, what more can I say? Well, the little girl in the first picture looks as if she's watching television, and she's very calm, which is in contrast to her mother, who is very stressed, as I said. And, er …

I: Thank you. Ana, for which person do you think time has the greatest influence in their daily life?

A: I think for this woman with the phone, the time is one of the more important subjects in her life, because she seems to be a working woman, a mother, so the time is very important for her. She has to do a lot of things, both at home and at the work, and she is probably always running to do things, er, looking at her watch all the time.

I: Thank you.

Now, Ana, here are your pictures. They show people reading. I'd like you to compare two of the pictures and say what and why these people are reading, and how they might be feeling. All right?

A: OK, er, in these two pictures there are two people who are in the home, but in this picture they are in the kitchen, whereas in this one they are in the living room, or, or, or something like that. It's probable this is the mother because she has her arm on the boy, and the boy seems to be reading to her, maybe because she … because he has to do it for homework. I think it is in the morning before he goes to school, because his hair is very, er, very … very tidy. He seems to be concentrated, and I think she is very … mmm … proud. We can see she is smiling. In this picture she is also very concentrated. I don't know what she is reading. Maybe it's a … a bill or something, because perhaps the man is putting her a new washing machine or something like that and she has to pay. Ah, or, yes, maybe, maybe he is her husband or boyfriend and she is reading the instructions to see how to put it … the new washing machine.

I: Thank you. Janusz, which person is most interested in finding out what is written?

J: Erm, well, I suppose the most obvious thing to say would be the man reading the medicine bottle, because it affects his health, but perhaps he's a little worried and nervous and doesn't want to hear what the doctor is saying to him. So I'd say this lady here is more keen to know what is written – she has a new machine for her kitchen and she wants to know exactly how much she has to pay, or, or what the conditions of the guarantee are.

Part 3: Collaborative task Page 166

1 Go through the task together and refer students to the 'How to go about it' box. In Part 3, describing the pictures is absolutely not what is required. The problem-solving task, not a description of the pictures, should be the basis for the discussion.

Remind students there are two clear elements in this task. The collaborative task requires some sort of 'working towards a conclusion', often a ranking activity. This means that, ideally:

EITHER students need to signal a change in their discussion with something like: 'Now, we need to make a decision on which two are most rewarding,'

OR at the very least they need to refer to the second element (working towards a conclusion) as they are doing the first element. For example, when discussing the tour guide picture, they should be saying things like: 'I think this would be high on my list because of the travelling aspect and the fact that you're always meeting new people.' Or 'personally I wouldn't go for that picture, but we can make a decision in a minute.'

This part of the test is looking at students' abilities to interact and negotiate. Students should beware of overusing 'Do you agree'? and 'What do you think?'. There are plenty of variations on these questions (put these on the board):

Don't you agree?
Wouldn't you agree?
Don't you think?
How about you?

Now students do the task.

2 As before, students listen and respond in pairs.

Answers

Comments
Ana chooses the musician and the cabinet maker; Janusz chooses the musician and the politician or journalist. Note that students do not have to agree in their conclusions.

They tentatively make their first choice after discussion of the third photo, and move towards making their second choice near the end of the three minutes. This is a good technique: students who decide too soon often struggle to talk for the full three minutes. In addressing the second part of the task 'as they go', they are making it clear to the examiners that they are working towards a conclusion.

Interaction in this part of the test is very good. They respond to what each other says, sometimes inviting their partner to comment with a question: *Don't you agree? What do you think? Really?*

Listening script 2.29

(I = Interlocuter; J = Janusz; A = Ana)

I: Thank you. Now I'd like you to talk about something together for about three minutes. Here are some pictures showing different jobs. First, talk to each other about the most and least satisfying aspects of these jobs. Then decide which two jobs are the most rewarding. All right?

J: Erm, well, let's start with the dentist. I imagine the best thing about being a dentist is that they earn very good money! Don't you agree?

A: That's right – I don't think there are many poor dentists in my country. Also, it's very good for them to be aware of the health of the people. It's something that is important for a dentist. A dentist is working for another person, doing something good for them. And something negative? What do you think?

J: Well, personally I wouldn't feel like working with somebody's teeth all day long. This isn't a very exciting prospect. On the other hand, it's a secret ambition of mine to be a politician. As a politician you have the chance to make decisions which can solve people's problems, to help them overcome their difficulties. And that would make me feel very satisfied. How about you? What do you think?

A: Yes, it's an important thing. Like the dentists, they are working for other people. But in contrast, they have to support the criticisms of the opposition and at the end I think it's not something good for them to be all the day listening something negative about you. Erm, the singer too is famous but I'm sure she's earning a lot of money, more than the dentist or the politician.

J: Yes, and probably she likes her profession. It must be extremely satisfying to be able to compose your own songs, your own music and then to perform them in front of an audience of people, of fans who admire you, who look up to you. Then again, I'm sure she has to spend lots of time away from home, which might not be so attractive.

A: That's true. I think another disadvantage is that it's a very instable profession – one minute you are on the top, another minute you are absolutely down.

J: But if you're a serious musician, and you enjoy continued success, I imagine it must be one of the most rewarding jobs there is.

A: I agree. So let's maybe have that as one of our two most rewarding jobs.

J: Right, OK. Let's move on to this one now, the journalist. I think I'd have either that or the politician as my other choice.

A: Why do you say that?

J: Because as a journalist you're always close to the facts, to the news, close to what is happening in the world. Like the politician it's a job where what you say can have a significant effect on things, and that for me is what can determine whether a job is rewarding or not. What might be your other choice?

A: Well, I think this one, the cabinet maker.

J: Really?

A: Yes. Working with your hands is very interesting. And it's a bit like the musician – you are creating something which other people will enjoy, will appreciate.

J: But I imagine you'd need to be a very special type of person to be able to spend all day in a workshop, without talking to anyone. Personally, I wouldn't find that very fulfilling – it would probably drive me a little mad. I would need to have contact with people, like the journalist, the politician, or even the tourist guide.

A: I think to be a tourist guide is a little boring, just repeating the same things again and again to different people.

J: Maybe, but at least you can …

I: Thank you.

Part 4: Further discussion Page 167

See teacher's notes in Unit 5 of the Teacher's Book (page 58) for further description of what is required of candidates in Part 4 of the test.

The main point to reiterate is that although the interlocutor is theoretically in control of the interaction, candidates are expected to take the initiative and develop the discussion. They should not merely respond to the examiner's questions with short answers. The speaking sections throughout the book have encouraged students to do this. The focus of the next listening is on this.

1 Students do the task.

2 Students listen to the CD.

Answers

Comments

In contrast to Part 3, in this part Janusz and Ana have not understood that they can and should interact with each other. The interlocutor continually has to prompt them to respond to each other's comments, sometimes leaving a pause, which they fail to pick up on. At one point, Ana tentatively asks, *Can I say something more?*, showing that she is unaware that this is a discussion rather than a simple question and answer session. In her last turn, she does respond to a point made by Janusz (*I agree with you*) but then limits herself to repeating the same ideas that he has just expressed.

Listening script 2.30

(I = Interlocuter; J = Janusz; A = Ana)

I: Janusz, which would you prefer to have: a job which is well paid but monotonous or one which is poorly paid but fulfilling, and why?

J: I would choose one which is not so well paid, but which is fulfilling. I think it's important to have motivation, otherwise your daily life can be very dull, very tedious. But I have to confess that in some periods of my life, if somebody gave me the opportunity, I might well choose a well-paid but boring job.

I: Why?

J: Erm, well, if I have money problems, or for example if I felt a real desire to travel – for pleasure, not for work – then I would maybe think more about the salary than the, than the, er, than how fulfilling is the job.

I: Ana?

A: I prefer a good paid job, even if it isn't so fulfilling, because, well, I can fulfil my ambition in other subjects that it's not job. I can have enough time to be with my husband, for example.

I: Janusz, Ana, do you think that school prepares young people adequately for the world of work?

A: Well, in my case I think my training was good for the job I do, but I think nowadays childen are not receiving a good training for work. They have less knowledge than before.

I: Janusz?

J: Well, I think it depends on what job we are talking about. School trains students to do a very specific type of work. It trains you to be a good employee, that's all. There's no help or guidance if you want to be an artist, for example, or, or a leader.

A: Can I say something more?

I: Yes, of course!

A: I agree with Janusz. I think school doesn't give enough importance to creative skills, to being creative. This is another problem of the school nowadays.

J: Yes, it's not creative enough.

I: What do you think is the ideal age to retire?

A: As soon as possible! No, I think for example 50 years old is a good age because you are still young enough to do a lot of things, and you have worked enough to have the money to do those things.

I: Do you agree, Janusz?

J: Er, well, I think it's a pity to retire so young. At the age of 50 you have the experience, you have the training, you know more about the work you do. I think this is a good age to do really good things at work. When you are young, you are not very expert, but later in life you can contribute a lot more. It's also a good age to pass on your skills and your wisdom to other people, to younger people. So no, I think 60 or 65 is a good enough retirement age.

I: Ana?

A: Well, I think the age for retiring will always be the same as it is now, so 60 or 65, but I would like that we can retire earlier. Everybody spend all their time working, working, working all the time and life is very short. So I don't think we should work all our life like this.

J: Well, I don't agree.

I: Do you think people who earn large amounts of money have a moral obligation to donate money to charity?

J: Yes, I agree with that. The world is not very just and I think there is a moral obligation for rich people to redistribute their money, their wealth. I don't think it's right for example that footballers earn vast amounts of money, and then spend it all on fast cars, and big houses and so on. Poorer people, people in developing countries could use the money more, more, er, with more wisdom.

A: I agree with you, because the world is not very just and some people have too much money which they spend on silly things, on things which are not useful and people in poor countries, like the developing countries don't have anything. It must to be redistributed better.

J: That's right.

I: Thank you. That is the end of the test.

13 Food for thought

Content overview

Themes

This unit is concerned with eating and drinking, food and diet.

Exam-related activities

Paper 1	**Reading**
Part 1	Multiple choice (short)
Paper 2	**Writing**
Part 2	Informal letters
Part 2	Reports
Paper 3	**Use of English**
Part 3	Word formation
Part 5	Key word transformations (review)
Paper 4	**Listening**
Part 1	Multiple choice (short)
Paper 5	**Speaking**
Part 2	Long turn

Other

Vocabulary 1	Eating and drinking
Vocabulary 2	Deception
Language focus 1	Comparisons
Language focus 2	Adverbs of degree

Vocabulary 1: Eating and drinking

Page 168

1 There are many useful collocations and longer fixed phrases to do with eating and drinking. Students complete the gaps in pairs, and help each other with any meanings they are unsure of.

Answers

1 thirst	**5** appetite
2 hunger	**6** eater
3 food	**7** stomach
4 drink	**8** meal

2 Either before or after exercise 2, check the meanings with the following questions:
Which verb here describes what a fussy eater does? (*picks at his food*)
Which one would you do if you object to alcohol? (*have a soft drink*)
Which one describes eating very fast? (*gulp down your food*)

Which one means that your body desperately needs food? (*feel faint with hunger*)
Which one describes someone who always eats a lot? (*a big eater*)
Which one means a large and satisfying meal? (*a square meal*)

3–4 The words selected are all common and useful, and students should be able to use them to talk about their own eating habits.

Speaking: CAE Part 2 Long turn Page 169

1–2 Emphasize the importance of sticking to the point, given that time is limited in the exam. Student A is to talk about:

- considerations when planning the meal
- enjoyment.

Relate some of the factors in the 'How to go about it' box to some of the pictures: obviously time was an issue for the young man who is studying, health was an issue when preparing for the children. This will draw students' attention to these things and also give them ideas for how to begin the task.

Finally, encourage use of:
might have been/verb would have been/verb
must have been/verb

You might also get the listening student (initially Student B) to comment afterwards on how well the speaking student did the specific task set.

As discussed in earlier units of the Teacher's Book, give selected students some feedback, either on their mistakes, on their ideas, or on their performance of the task.

Use of English: CAE Part 3 Word formation Page 170

Divide the class into ten groups. Give one of the words in capital letters to each group. They must write down the various grammatical forms that their word can take, including any negative forms. They can use a dictionary, but only after they have tried it for themselves.

Gather information from each group and write the results on the board. You may need to prompt students.

Answers

Likely answers to task in Teacher's Book

SET	setting, outset, setback
DINE	dining, diner = restaurant, diner = person
RESIDE	residence, resident, residential
REVEAL	revealing, revelation
WELCOME	unwelcome, welcoming
FIND	finder, finding (n)
RATE	overrated, underrated
ENJOY	enjoyment, enjoyable
APPEAR	disappear, (dis)appearing (dis)appearance, apparent(ly)
TRAIN	trainer, training, trainee

Select any words that your class may find difficult and elicit/exemplify in short phrases or sentences.

1 With the words on the board as a reference, students try the exam task. They know that the answer for each gap will be among those on the board. This is 'Multiple-choice word formation'!

Answer

1 setting	**5** unwelcome	**8** enjoyable
2 diners	**6** findings	**9** appearance
3 residential	**7** overrated	**10** training
4 revelations		

2 Students discuss in pairs.
Here are some additional speaking points on the topic of food. They could also be slotted in at other points in the unit if you prefer not to use them here.
Have your tastes in food changed as you got older?
What is your favourite dish? How is it prepared?
What are the basic characteristics of your country's cuisine?
What things can put people off food?
Are you adventurous or conservative about your food?
How has climate influenced your country's cuisine?
Talk about any new diets, food combinations, wonder foods etc that you have read about in magazines.

Writing 1: CAE Part 2 Informal letters Page 170

1 Students read the task and sample answer to themselves.

2 Do this part of the analysis together as a whole class.

Answer

No. The writer has not made any attempt to reassure her friend. On the contrary, comments such as *'I'm not surprised you're a bit daunted by it all'*, *'my own bitter experience'* and *'even if it leaves you utterly exhausted'* will only serve to make him more nervous.

3–4 Students analyse the sample answer as instructed. This might be done in groups of three. Student A looks for expressions of advice, Student B for wide range of language, and Student C for ways in which the writer shows interest and refers to her own experience.

Answers

3 The following expressions introduce advice:
don't make the same mistake as I did and lay on
there's no point preparing
You'd be much better off filling
That's not to say you shouldn't put out
it's not worth going
I wouldn't spend hours making one if I were you
whatever you do, make sure you don't let
... is not to be recommended
Other evidence of a wide range of language includes:
you're a bit daunted by it all
pass on a few tips
my own bitter experience
lay on a huge spread

4 Showing interest in the event
It's hard to believe that Luke's about to celebrate his fifth birthday.
I'm sure Luke and his friends will have a great time
Let me know how it all goes, won't you?

Referring to her own experience
a few tips that I learnt from my own bitter experience in September
don't make the same mistake as I did
they were the first things to disappear at Lara's party
Lara's friends hardly touched hers

5 This task should be relatively straightforward once students have enough ideas. The gathering and sharing of ideas can be a highly useful fluency activity as well as supplying ideas to those students who might write well but have difficulty in thinking of what to write about.

- Focus on the first bullet point in the 'How to go about it' box.
- Put students in groups of three.
- Each group selects any two (but make sure all six of the situations are covered by at least one group in the class). If they need help with ideas, they might consider the following aspects: cost, quantity, type and range of food, preparation, special dishes or equipment, location, what to do in the event of rain etc.
- Feed back thoroughly, and be prepared to input your own ideas where necessary.

Sample answer

Hi Berti
Yes I can certainly give you some advises about preparing a barbecue for your football club's dinner. I've gone to lots of these parties for end of season.

The first thing to think is when you want to serve the food. Obviously is the barbecue difficult to take to the venue, and it takes time to set up all the tables etc and take all the food from your car. If you serve the food too early some people may not arrive yet. If too late and the children may get so hungry, they start getting tired and silly. So I would recommend to tell people you will serve the food at, for example, 8 o'clock.

Of course, for a barbecue, even in summer, you'll need a plan for if it rains. When I prepared it we hired a small tent. In the end we needn't have it, but better safe than sorry.

Third thing, you need to know how many people are coming and if there are vegetarians. You can get 'veggie burgers' for them. But don't go crazy with the salads – it always seems the salad that gets thrown away. It's so difficult to eat lettuce from a paper plate with a plastic fork – most people don't bother.

> Anyway, that's all I can think of now, but give me a ring if you need anything. Just relax yourself and prepare it in detail – then you'll be absolutely fine and it will too!
>
> Dietmar

Examiner's comment

Content: The writing is slightly under length and although the letter adequately covers the first two points (detailing your previous experience and giving advice), more attention to the reassurance section would enhance the completion of the task. Simply to say *'relax yourself and prepare it in detail ... .'* is not very reassuring.

Organization and cohesion: The organization is appropriate and logical for an informal letter. The paragraphing nicely reflects three different points the writer considers important (timing of food, a bad weather plan, preparing salad). However, a number of sentences are confusing or difficult to follow, eg *'If you serve the food too early some people may not arrive yet.'*, *'In the end we needn't have it ... .'*

Accuracy: The writing is mostly accurate despite some confusing sentences. The use of language is sometimes rather vague (*'When I prepared it ... '* *'and it will too!'*) and the use of the word *'advises'* in the second line.

Range: The range of language used is sufficient yet unambitious (*'you'll need a plan for if it rains'*, *'Third thing you need to know ...'*).

Register: The register is appropriate for an informal letter.

Target reader: The reader would be partially informed, if not very reassured.

Mark: Band 3

Multiple choice

Pages 172 and 173

Photocopiable vocabulary exercise on page 157.

1 You might supplement these questions with others, such as 'If you get ill in this way, what can you do about it? Do you pay any attention to the sell-by date? Is this information more relevant with certain foods than others?'

We might read the information on tins and packets to find out:

- whether it is organic – grown and produced without the use of pesticides or other chemicals
- whether there are added preservatives, flavours, salt and sugar and 'E's'
- whether it is made from natural ingredients
- the nutritional value
- the number of calories.

2 Students look at the first text and try questions 1 and 2 individually.

Answers

1 C **2** B

Draw attention to the 'reference' focus of question 1, which is something candidates can expect to meet in the exam. Here 'they' refers back to the subject of the sentence – 'a number of people' seven lines previously. In the question this is paraphrased as 'affected consumers'.

Then look at the second extract. Point out that in the exam one of the three Part 1 tasks may be a piece of fiction. This time students might try the questions in pairs or threes.

Answers

3 C **4** B

You might take the third extract together, in whole-class mode, in order to vary the interaction pattern. Before attempting the task, explain that there are various kinds of 'food inspector'. Ask students to tell you what kind of work they do (= some visit restaurants and other eating places to ensure that they are meeting the required standards of hygiene, some eat in restaurants and write reports about the quality of the food which are later published in books, others visit shops to look for packaging material which makes false claims or is misleading). Ask students to read the first paragraph of the third extract, and elicit from them that this text concerns the last type of inspector.

Answers

5 A **6** D

Reacting to the text

You might also ask why processed food is not good for people.

Language focus 1: Comparisons

Page 174

Sections A–E could be given as homework, while the Practice section which follows should be done in class.

Answers

A Comparisons
Where alternative answers are given, the first answer is that which appears in the reading text.

1 **a** much, as **b** The, the **c** likened/compared **d** more **e** later **f** now/currently/nowadays, before

B Qualifying comparisons
a a great deal **b** far **c** just **d** slightly **e** much

C *Like* and *as*
a like **b** as **c** as

D **1a** such **b** so **c** so
2 *so* is followed by adjectives and *such* is followed by an indefinite article in the examples given in the Coursebook.

E **1** better **2** like, near **3** as **4** much **5** long **6** close

Optional extra activity
Refer students back to exercise B. Look again at the answers for a and c. Write the two sentences on the board with gaps, ie
Food is often ______ less important than the environment in which it is eaten.
It claims to be a health cereal but it contains _______ as much salt as ordinary cereals.
Ask them to complete the gaps in as many ways as possible.

Answers

a much, far, a lot, an awful lot, significantly, considerably
c almost, about, nearly, twice, three times

Vocabulary 2: Deception Page 175

1–4 Check the answers exercise by exercise. In particular the table in 1 needs to be completed correctly before students can proceed.

Answers

Noun	Verb	Adjective	Adverb
------	mislead	misleading	misleadingly
fraud	defraud	fraudulent	fraudulently
deception	deceive	deceptive	deceptively

2 **1 a** misleadingly **b** misleading
2 a deceptively **b** deceiving
3 a fraud **b** fraudulently

3 **1** out **2** in **3** into **4** for **5** through **6** for

4 a bogus financial adviser
the smooth-talking confidence trickster
the conman's trickery
his false promises
I feel a bit of a mug (informal)

5 Students follow instructions.

Listening: Multiple choice

CAE Part 1

Page 176

1 Stay in whole-class mode and ask these questions of a few students.

2 Students try the task individually.

Note: Farmers' markets are common in British towns. Typically on a Saturday morning, local farmers bring fresh produce to sell. They are very popular as people are becoming more and more aware of the problems associated with eating processed supermarket food.

Answers

1 B **2** C **3** B **4** A **5** A **6** C

3 Students go into pairs to answer the questions, and to react to any other points of interest to them in the listenings.

Encourage students to analyse the listening script (page 238 of the Students' Book) for useful lexical combinations. Examples:
by the time they get here
that's how they're supposed to look
they keep coming back for more
miss the point
it's hard to say no (when temptation is right in front of you)
not to mention

that kind of thing
pigged out on chocolate
I couldn't have done it without him.

Note: Remind students that here, in order to fit in with the topic of the unit, the three extracts are thematically related, but that in the exam this will not be the case.

Listening script 2.31–2.33

(I = Interviewer; M = Market Stall holder; S = Shelley)

Extract one

I: Good morning sir. Jane Marsh from Devonport Community Radio. Is all your produce organic?

M: Yes, from the carrots to the cauliflower. And what you get here actually tastes of something – I mean the flavour is really superb. Here – and see – the carrots crunch the way they're supposed to. Not like those bland, cardboard things you find in the supermarket. The fruit and vegetables there may have come all the way from some exotic place but they're all dried up by the time they get here. We're charging a little bit more for our stuff – but when you try it – you'll see why.

I: And I suppose you're also having to persuade people that a few marks on an apple or a cucumber that's a bit bent – well that's how they're supposed to look. People can be a bit fussy like that, can't they?

M: Well the first thing to say of course is that we don't use pesticides or anything that isn't natural. That explains why the fruit and veg looks the way it does and what attracts regular customers to the market. And they know it's extremely fresh. Straight from the field to here. But yes, you're right, first-time customers – you can see they're a bit anxious because a pear or a potato isn't perfect on the outside. But as I say, once they've tried it, they keep coming back for more. And it makes me laugh how they bring along their old plastic bags from the supermarket. It's good to see some recycling – although I'd prefer my name on the bag!

Extract two

Man: Good morning Tricia – we've had a lot of messages from listeners this morning about the government's new policy about the kind of food eaten in schools. There seems to be some misunderstanding about what the policy actually means.

Tricia: Yes, some people have missed the point. We're not saying what pupils can and can't bring to school. If they want to eat a chocolate bar at break time, or have a fizzy drink before class, we won't be asking teachers to go out there and confiscate them. But we do say that schools must now be responsible for what they provide. So rather than having pies and chips on the menu five days a week, well, they'll be serving up things like pasta, wholegrain sandwiches, fresh fruit and so on.

Man: I see. But isn't the childhood obesity problem in this country more the responsibility of the parents? Shouldn't they be keeping an eye on their kids' consumption?

Tricia: I believe that most do. At least when they can – but there's all that time when their children are out of their sight. Even though we've had a great many campaigns on the obesity issue – I mean, today's children do know about what's good for them and what's not – it's hard to say no when temptation is right in front of you. Junk food at school is just part of a wider junk food culture. It's in the corner shop, in the petrol station – not to mention all the fast food outlets. We just want to exclude school as an outlet.

Extract three

I: Shelley – you've just been voted SlimRight Winner of the Year. You look absolutely marvellous but how do you feel about winning?

S: Oh, thrilled, and so are my kids. I mean, they never said anything about my weight but I suspect they were very scared. They probably knew more about the health risks than I did. I suppose that's why I never made an effort before – I didn't feel particularly ill, and my appearance had never really bothered me. It's never stopped me socializing. But one day I overheard someone say that once you get to my size – my old size – there's nothing you can do. And I thought that's ridiculous, and it sort of motivated me to set myself a challenge. Being a SlimRight winner is a bonus – but it was more about my own goal.

I: And how did you actually go about losing the weight? I'm sure many people would love to know your secret.

S: Well – you need a nutritionist. Mine put together a whole series of menus that were balanced and healthy. Some things were new to me like lentils and beans, nuts – that kind of thing – but it was all pretty tasty and fairly easy to cook. Having someone really take a personal interest in your well-being – it reminded me of the lovely priest in the church I used to go to as a child. Even when I admitted one time that I'd given in and pigged out on chocolate, he just gave me a recipe for home-made muesli bars and said 'Here, try these instead.' I had that kind of patient encouragement all the way – I couldn't have done it without him.

Language focus 2: Adverbs of degree

Page 177

1–2 Go through exercises 1 and 2 in whole-class mode.

Answers

Absolutely is used with non-gradable adjectives such as *marvellous, fascinating* or *freezing*. *Very, fairly* and *a bit* are used with gradable adjectives such as those in a, c and d. We do not normally say *very marvellous, fairly fascinating* or *a bit freezing*. Nor do we say *absolutely anxious* or *absolutely easy*.

Examples of other modifiers which can be used with gradable adjectives are:
a little, slightly, rather, quite, somewhat, relatively, moderately, reasonably, pretty, extremely, really

2
Gradable: *frightened, pleased, dirty, tired*
Non-gradable: *furious, ridiculous, huge, incredible*

3 Note that there is a subtle difference in pronunciation: (a) must be said tentatively (there is a lot of emphasis on the word 'quite' and the voice does not go down fully at the end of the sentence) and (b) with certainty (the voice goes up with 'quite' and down at the end of the sentence).

Answers

a fairly **b** absolutely

4 Point out that many of these collocations are revision, as they have occurred in previous units.

Notes:

- The most common collocations of *wholly* seem to be negative.
- Whilst *entirely old* is not a collocation, *entirely new* is.
- Note that *utterly* is usually used with negatives (eg *impossible*, *miserable*, *exhausted*, *ruthless*).
- Other common intensifying adverbs are: *seriously, deeply, desperately, acutely, bitterly, thoroughly, enormously, hugely*

Answers

4

1 clever	**4** old
2 worried	**5** qualified
3 informed	**6** intelligent

5 Students follow instructions.

Writing 2: CAE Part 2 — Reports Page 177

Spend some time discussing the first bullet point in the 'How to go about it' box with students. They might also consider whether more time/income is now being devoted to eating out.

Draw attention to the two possible paragraph plans. Notice that paragraph plans can often simply follow the bullets in the task, but there is also often a 'cleverer' way of doing it. In B the paragraphs use the information but in a different way.

Review 13 answers Pages 178 and 179

Vocabulary

1 A	**4** C	**7** A	**10** A
2 D	**5** C	**8** C	**11** B
3 B	**6** B	**9** D	**12** A

Comparisons

1 near as
2 much a
3 same as
4 the more
5 far the
6 such a
7 much the
8 did his

Use of English: CAE Part 5 — Key word transformations

1 likes junk food just as
2 is deceptively simple in (its)
3 interest in eating/my appetite as soon as
4 far the most imaginative (recipe/one)
5 from more stress/stress more than ever (before), *or* more than ever (before) from stress/from more stress ever since
6 near as bad as
7 close second to the
8 a great deal more

14 Money matters

Content overview

Themes

This unit is concerned with money, shopping, consumerism.

Exam-related activities

Paper 1	**Reading**
Part 4	Multiple matching
Paper 2	**Writing**
Part 2	Contributions: guidebook entry
Part 2	Set books
Paper 3	**Use of English**
Part 3	Word formation
Part 4	Gapped sentences (review)
Paper 4	**Listening**
Part 2	Sentence completion
Part 3	Multiple choice (long)
Paper 5	**Speaking**
Part 3	Collaborative task

Other

Vocabulary 1	Money
Vocabulary 2	Quantifying nouns
Language focus	Noun phrases

Speaking: CAE Part 3 Collaborative task

Page 180

You may wish to do the task under exam timing conditions. However, the topic provides an opportunity for really engaging with many of the big issues in society today. The extensive notes which follow should provide plenty of ideas for discussion. It is recommended that some time be spent on this. Inevitably not all of these ideas will suit all countries, and may need to be adapted.

Sport – money has brought professionalism and sport has become big business. With it has come drug abuse, loss of the amateur spirit of playing fair and trying your hardest, the need to win at all costs, bad behaviour, young superstars who go to the dogs because they do not know how to cope with suddenly having loads of money.

Education – In some countries private education is an option for those who can afford it. Money enables schools to look like pleasant, welcoming places where children can feel safe and happy. Money is essential to enable schools to function properly, with well-stocked libraries and up-to-date computer facilities.

Health – Public/state money provides free health for all in many countries, but with an ageing population this is proving increasingly difficult. Again money is essential for hospitals to function properly. The nursing (and teaching) profession is notoriously underpaid in some countries, with the result that it is difficult to attract new recruits. In some countries the health service is losing a lot of money because of individuals sueing (if for example doctors make a misdiagnosis or an operation goes wrong). Another big debate at the moment concerns certain people who cost the state a lot of money in health care, (eg people with liver disease through alcohol abuse, people with lung cancer from smoking). Should such people be entitled to free health care when they have ignored government health warnings and failed to take care of their bodies?

Culture – In many countries, government money subsidizes the arts; and museums, galleries, exhibitions etc could not function without it. Is it right for governments to spend money on this – bringing the arts to the people and encouraging a wide cultural education? Also is it right for the huge costs of making blockbuster films to be passed on to the cinema-goer?

Relationships – True love should be above such things as money, but the fact remains that having some money, nice clothes, a car etc can help young people attract each other and feel confident in themselves!

Housing – High house prices mean that young people often have to stay in the parental home longer than they would wish. Money enables them to be more independent.

Vocabulary 1: Money

Page 180

1 This matching exercise could be done in pairs.

Answers

1 a – 3, b – 4, c – 1, d – 2
2 a – 3, b – 4, c – 2, d – 1

2 These questions should stimulate some interesting speaking points as well, particularly when explaining or clarifying. Be sure to exploit this with other questions such as 'Do you approve of buying things on credit?' 'Have you met other ways of paying for things when travelling abroad?'

Answers

Possible answers (this may vary from country to country!)
People usually pay in advance for using services and facilities (cinema, theatre, museums, sports matches, public transport).
People usually pay in arrears for professional fees (dentist, plumber, mechanic), also for bills (rent on house, electricity etc).
People usually pay in instalments for material goods that are too expensive for them to pay in full (car, TV, electrical goods, settee).

Verb + adverb collocations

1 This could be done quickly as a whole-class activity.

Answers

a generously **b** freely **c** hard **d** heavily

2 Students follow instructions.

Sentence completion

Page 181

1 Students answer question in Coursebook.

2 Now students do the task.

Answers

1 Student Loans Company
2 term
3 budget planner
4 overdraft
5 two evenings
6 (course) tutor
7 (faculty) noticeboard(s)
8 (student) travel

Listening script 2.34

Hello, I'm John Lister from the Student Financial Advice Centre here on the university campus. My main aim today is to give you one or two bits of advice on money matters before you get down to the main task of studying next week.

As you may know, not so long ago you might have received a student maintenance grant from the Local Education Authority to pay for all your living expenses. Now, of course, these grants don't exist and you have to borrow that money from the Student Loans Company. If you haven't applied for your loan already, make sure you do it soon, otherwise you may have to wait several months for your first payment. If you have, then you can expect to receive the money once a term; in other words, in three equal instalments over the course of the year.

And that's the first problem, really. Many students find that their money disappears almost as soon as they get it – and it's often because they fail to plan their finances carefully. To prevent the same thing happening to you, you can download your very own budget planner from the university website. It'll help you record your expected income and expenses for the year and then calculate how much you've got left over for yourself each month. It's worth having a look.

Even then, you may still find that you need a bit of extra financial help, particularly in the first term, when your outgoings will probably be quite high. So if you haven't already opened a bank account, bear in mind that some banks offer better overdraft facilities than others. Shop around a bit – find out how much you can go overdrawn without asking for permission from the bank and without paying any extra interest.

You can, of course, supplement your income by working part time, but you have to make sure you strike a balance between work and study. Some students here work over 20 hours a week in part-time jobs, but I personally wouldn't recommend any more than two evenings a week. That's for you to decide of course, but I'd certainly wait a few days before applying for jobs, at least until you've got your timetable.

Now it's clear that a major expense each year is going to be books. For that reason, it's well worth having a word with your course tutor before you rush out and buy everything on your reading list. He or she can advise you on which books are the most important to have. You might also find that you can buy some secondhand from students in higher years who don't need them any more. Keep an eye on the noticeboard in your faculty building for that.

And when you pay for things, always make a point of asking for student discounts. Don't just assume the shop assistant knows you're a student – not even in the university bookshop. Get the most out of your student travel card and be very careful how you use your credit card. Every year dozens of students come to us at the Advice Centre with huge debts they can't pay off – and in most cases, it's all down to their credit card.

If you have students in the class who have already been to university, get them to react to the text, eg Outline the system in your country for applying and paying for your university education. Did most of your friends manage to support themselves? Did you obtain a part-time job to help finance your studies?

3 This could be done briefly in pairs with a whole-class feedback.

Writing 1: CAE Part 2 Contributions: guidebook entry

Page 182

Go through the question and 'How to go about it' box. Explain that a guidebook has entries for different areas all in the same format, so this piece of writing does not require a separate introductory and concluding paragraph. It needs an introductory sentence which will lead in to the first paragraph, such as:

Visitors to X will be delighted by the huge range of reasonably priced hotels and restaurants on offer, although it must be said that the public transport is relatively expensive compared to most capital cities.

Students will need to be selective about the information in the 'How to go about it' box. Planning to write four paragraphs on general information and advice (on accommodation, food, transport and shopping) plus two on places to visit and things to do is likely to lead to an answer which is much too long.

Answers

Answers to Useful language section

a saving **b** money **c** discounts **d** ticket **e** bargains **f** costs

Sample answer

Japan

Everybody says Japan is expensive. Do not believe it. There is a way you can spend only a little and go cheap. My advice is 'go countryside, not stay only in big cities'.

Accommodation:
Accommodation is generally expensive in Japan, but if you want to stay at traditional Japanese style B&B. called 'Ryokan' it would be cheaper than European style hotels. Also, if you travel countryside, the Ryokan usually has its own hotsprings facilities. In addition, local people are so nice in countryside, they wish t offer you a free accommodation and dinner, even they can not speak any of your language!

Transport:
Japanese public transport system is fantastic. it is not cheap. though. I advise you to buy a rail travel card in your country before you leave. It will save you a lot. The fastest train called 'Shinkansen' is the best way to go to countryside. When you arrived at station, then you can not find any bus service or taxies, ask local people. They will give you a lift happily.

Food:
Japan is a seafood lover's heaven. They sashimi or sushi. These are made of raw fish. Unfortunately, Japan is not a vegetarian friendly country because we use fish soup in any food. basically.

Shopping:
You can find good handmade souvenirs in any local souvenir shops. Traditional food would be an ideal souvenirs because you will be able to -share the taste with your friends when you goe back to your country.

By Etsuko Morita

Examiner's comment

Content: The content is appropriate and each point is adequately developed.

Organization and cohesion: The contribution for the brochure is well organized, and good use is made of headings. It would have been improved by the inclusion of a concluding paragraph. The sentences are often too short and would benefit from linking.

Accuracy: There are many errors, though these do not impede communication – (*'not stay only in big cities …', 'even they can not speak any of your language!', 'when you arrived at station'*). Punctuation and spelling are sometimes also at fault.

Range: The range of structures used is too limited for CAE level, but the vocabulary is adequate and there is some good phrasing – (*'traditional Japanese style B&B', 'good handmade souvenirs', 'share the taste with your friends'*).

Register: The register is consistent and wholly appropriate.

Target reader: The target reader would be informed, but distracted by the errors.

Mark: Band 2

Use of English: CAE Part 3 — Word formation

Page 183

1 Ask in what circumstances students might 'come into money'. Elicit the words 'inherit' and 'left me something in her/his will'.

2 Before students attempt the exam task, write the following parts of speech on the board:
noun noun noun noun noun adjective
plural noun adverb adverb adverb

Ask students to agree in pairs on what part of speech the gap requires.

Answers

Answers to activity in Teacher's Book

1	adverb	**6**	noun
2	noun	**7**	adjective
3	adverb	**8**	adverb
4	plural noun	**9**	noun
5	noun	**10**	noun

Now students complete the gaps.

Answers

1	conclusively	**6**	outlook
2	assumption	**7**	dissatisfied
3	surprisingly	**8**	considerably
4	responses	**9**	pleasure
5	inheritance	**10**	contentment/ contentedness

3 Some ideas if none are forthcoming: happiness comes from being busy, from a sense of stability, from striving for better things, from having to struggle a bit in life. Once you have everything, you get bored.

Reading: CAE Part 4 — Multiple matching

Page 184

1 Other possible lines of questioning: do you like to wear out the clothes you have before you buy new ones? Do you believe in keeping up with fashion? If you have unfashionable things in your wardrobe, what do you do with them?

2 Now students do the task.

Answers

1 C Knowing how to sew helps
2 A I wait until things are falling apart before I buy something new
3 B I grew up this way; when I was little, frugality was a way of life
4 B a costume to wear when I'm on stage
5 D a pile of my clothes got chucked out because my flatmate thought they were rubbish
6 A I would often go on huge shopping sprees
7 C I've seen people driven to debt by their need for the latest Fendi bag
8 D there is too much importance placed on clothes and appearance ... attracts attention.
9 B I try not to buy anything ... code of practice.
10 C I've been to parties where ... confused them.
11 C I'm aware that most people are not like me.
12 D I don't feel strongly enough to object politically
13 A I simply don't feel the pull of boutiques any more
14 B I'm a voracious clothes shopper
15 A The fact that I was living ... I was doing

Reacting to the text
Try to pull useful language out of the conversation, or work the following expressions into the conversation:

My clothes were all **handed down to me** from my big sisters.
I'm not **materialistic** at all – I don't want lots of nice new things all the time.
Shopping is **a waste of time and energy**.
Too much importance is placed on/attached to physical appearance.
We live in **a throwaway society**.

Vocabulary 2: Quantifying nouns

Page 186

1 Write the four quantifiers on the board with a question mark after each one. First ask if anyone remembers (from the reading text) which nouns go with the quantifiers. Then students search in the text.

Answers

Clothes is used after all of them.
tons of clothes (line 13)
heaps of clothes (line 24)
bags of clothes (line 35)
a pile of my clothes (line 94)

2 Point out that there is a wide range of quantifying expressions in English, commonly used by native speakers both in speech and in writing (*of* is the second most common word in English, second only to *the*). While such expressions are most likely to be tested directly in the Use of English paper, they might also appear in any other paper.

2–4 These exercises are suitable for pairwork.

Answers

2

a salt	**e** champagne
b water	**f** youths
c flames	**g** furniture
d homework	**h** biscuits

3

1 children	**6** furniture
2 news	**7** holiday
3 words	**8** milk
4 bees	**9** wool
5 progress	**10** sadness

Optional extra activity
Students use English–English dictionaries to find other useful collocations for each quantifying noun and record them in their notebooks.

Multiple choice

Page 187

Photocopiable vocabulary exercise on page 157.

1 Link the topic of this listening with the reading text on women who rejected consumerism. Ask if anyone in the class has heard of a Buy Nothing Day in their country. What are its aims and how does it work?

Now students do the task.

Answers

1 B **2** A **3** D **4** B **5** C **6** D

2 Many British people would probably answer that they sympathize with the views and aims of the organizers and get fed up with aspects of consumerism such as the commercialization of Christmas. Nevertheless, they reserve the right to buy presents for their family and friends, and indeed it is expected that they should do this. So many British people would probably find the actions of the organizers rather puerile.

Listening script 2.35

(I = Interviewer; C = Chris)

I: When was the last time you spent the whole day without buying anything? With us today on *Local Lookout* is Chris Dawson, a committed anti-consumerist who will be taking an active part in next week's Buy Nothing Day. Chris, apart from buying nothing, what exactly is the aim of Buy Nothing Day?

C: Firstly, let me say that it is anything but a day of militant action with angry anti-government slogans and boarded up shops closed for business. We're much more into persuasion than provocation as a means of bringing about change. We want to make shoppers question the need to consume and get them doing other things, like spending time with people, as opposed to spending money on them.

I: The obvious question here is 'Why?' What's wrong with shopping?

C: We're not saying people are bad because they go shopping. But they do need to think more about the products they buy. Whether, for example, their new trainers were produced using cheap labour in countries where workers' rights are virtually non-existent. What materials and production methods went into producing them, and the effect this might have on the planet. It's all very well for shopping malls to offer a wealth of choice but this should not be at the expense of the environment or developing countries.

I: Indeed. But if people buy nothing on just one day, is it really going to change all that?

C: Well, for quite a few, Buy Nothing Day will indeed be a life-changing experience, not just a one-off thing.

In previous years a lot of people have made long-term commitments to consuming less and recycling more. And that can only be a good thing.

I: So it's an annual event, then?

C: Yes, it is. In Europe it's always the last Saturday in November, while in the States they always have theirs on the day after Thanksgiving, at the start of the Christmas shopping season.

I: Presumably then, Chris, you're against Christmas shopping, too.

C: Good question! I'm afraid to say my family would never forgive me if I didn't get them anything, though they know how I feel about the whole thing. I just get so annoyed at the whole run-up to Christmas – already in October the shops have got their Christmas stock in, and the January sales start before you've even had a chance to finish your turkey. So it's handkerchieves and socks if they're lucky, and maybe something special for my girlfriend.

I: Let's come back in time if we may, Chris, to next Saturday. What exactly will you be doing then, apart from not buying anything, that is?

C: Ah well, er, I'm not so sure I can tell you that, I'm afraid. Don't want to give the game away. Of course, there'll be the usual handing out of leaflets and putting up of posters and so on. But as for the rest, I can't say. You'll have to wait and see.

I: Last year, then. Tell us about that.

C: Last year was all a bit surreal, really. A group of us – fifteen altogether – all dressed up as sheep and went from shop to shop making loud sheep noises. And behind us we had a shepherd with a sign saying 'Don't follow them, follow your conscience'.

I: And what were people's reactions to it all?

C: Well, the shopkeepers were generally quite hostile, though we were expecting that. I suppose they saw us as a threat to business, and most of them moved us on. Quite a few of the customers saw the funny side of things and had a little chuckle – one or two even joined in – but on the whole they couldn't quite believe that someone was questioning the ethics of shopping. It certainly made them think – which is what we wanted, of course.

I: Is interest in Buy Nothing Day growing? How do you advertise yourselves?

C: It's getting bigger every year. Yes, we have our leaflets and posters – which you can download from the Internet, by the way – but up until now, at least, it's mostly been down to word of mouth. That may change, of course, as we get bigger and better organized. At the moment it's celebrated by about a million people in nearly 50 countries – and that's without the support of TV. In the US, for example, none of the major channels wanted to run the Buy Nothing Day commercial, because they said it went against the country's economic policy.

I: Yes, indeed. So, Chris, if we want to get involved in all this, how do we go about it? Who organizes it all?

C: That's the beauty of it all, really – you do. You just go to the Buy Nothing Day website – buynothingday dot co dot uk – and they give you ideas for what to do. You might want to dress up as something, set up a swap shop ...

Language focus: Noun phrases

Page 188

Note: This is a difficult point of advanced grammar and the descriptions of use (see Grammar reference) are highly complicated. The rules are there for reference, but it may be more helpful to ignore the rules and simply learn each noun phrase as an item of vocabulary. In any case, if students have reached advanced level they will probably have acquired an instinct for what is correct without necessarily being able to explain why!

1 Certain semi-formal texts at advanced level are likely to contain plenty of noun phrases (like this text on consumerism). The seven featured here all appeared in the text.

Answers

noun + noun: production methods, the January sales, shopping malls
noun 's/s'+ noun: next week's Buy Nothing Day, workers' rights, people's reactions
noun + preposition + noun:
a wealth of choice, a threat to business, the ethics of shopping, at the expense of the environment

2 Students work together to find and correct the wrong option. At this stage they should not attempt to explain why.

Answers

1 **b** wine glasses
2 **a** chicken soup
3 **b** the roof of our house
4 **b** a Sunday newspaper
5 **b** a three-day course
6 **a** that shop window/the window of that shop
7 **b** top of the page
8 **a** the dismissal of a member of staff from the catering department
9 **b** a man of average height
10 **b** new children's clothes

After reading the Grammar reference, students look again at their answers and see if they would change any of their decisions.

3 Having read the Grammar reference, students give explanations for each of the noun phrases in exercise 2. (A very good class which has not made mistakes in exercise 2 can miss this stage.)

Answers

1 'Noun of noun' (*glasses of wine*) is used to refer to the drink.
'Noun + noun' (*wine glasses*) is used to refer to the container.

2 The 's genitive (*lamb's wool*) is used for products from living animals.
'Noun + noun' (*chicken soup*) is used for products from dead animals.

3 *door handle* is an accepted compound noun: *house roof* is not, so an *of* structure is required. The 's genitive (*house's roof*) is not likely since house is an inanimate object.

4 The 's genitive (*last Sunday's newspaper*) with a time expression is used to refer to specific moments or events.
'Noun + noun' (*a Sunday newspaper*) is used to refer to things that occur or appear regularly.

5 The 's genitive is used with time expressions to refer to duration (*four weeks' holiday*).
When the head noun (*course*) is countable, the modifying noun (*three-day*) is normally in the singular and hyphenated. Since the modifying noun functions as an adjective, no plural *s* is added.

6 *Shop window* is a recognized compound noun and normally found in that form. Note the position of the demonstrative in the *of* structure.
Whilst the *source of his inspiration* is also correct, *source of inspiration* is a collocation and generally found in that form.

7 Nouns such as *top, bottom, middle, side, edge, back, front, beginning* and *end*, which refer to a part or something, are normally used in an *of* structure. Mountain top, roadside, seaside are exceptions.

8 When the head noun (*dismissal*) is modified by a long and/or complex phrase (a member of staff from the catering department) the *of* structure is preferred.
Note that the 's genitive can be used for an action done by or to a person.
eg *Mr Smith's resignation, the President's murder*

9 'Noun + noun' (*brick construction*) can be used when talking about what something is made of. In other cases, when describing the characteristics of a person or thing, the 'Noun of noun' structure is used.

10 a (*children's new clothes*) is a 'specifying genitive' here: it refers to specific clothes worn by specific children. In this case the adjective describing the clothes can be placed between the two nouns.

b (*new children's clothes*) is a 'classifying genitive' here: it refers to clothes worn by children in general. In this case the two nouns cannot be separated.

4 Students could work individually on this. When they have finished they should record any of the collocations which are new to them.

Answers

2 e **3** a **4** c **5** g **6** b **7** h **8** f

5 Students follow the instructions in their books. Point out that the phrases they will be working with are also very common and useful.

6 This exercise provides an opportunity to vary the lesson and allow for a fluency task. This could be missed out if you wish to concentrate solely on the language point.

Self help:
This would be very suitable as a homework task.

Encourage students to set out the noun phrases in groups (eg sense of achievement/relief/smell), leaving room for the addition of other items to each group, with example sentences.

Answers

Noun + noun: go on huge shopping sprees (A), charity shops (A and B), a voracious clothes shopper (B), swap parties (B), a fabric flower (C), the latest Fendi bag (C)
Noun of noun: (this list does not include those quantifying nouns which have been focused on in the Vocabulary section) a way of life (B), an ethically sound code of practice (B), the issue of excessive consumption (C), the centre of attention (D), the act of shopping (D), a waste of time and energy (D)
Other *of* structures: the pull of boutiques (A), the middle of the floor (B)

Writing 2: CAE Part 2 Set books Page 189

For advice on how to deal with each task type refer to the Ready for Writing section and also to the following pages:

Review – Unit 6 Student's Book page 76 Teacher's Book page 65
Essay – Unit 5 Student's Book page 68 Teacher's Book page 60
Article – Unit 12 Student's Book page 161 Teacher's Book page 124
Report – Unit 3 Student's Book page 34 Teacher's Book page 34

1 Students follow the instruction in their books.

2 Hopefully students will, in giving reasons for their choice, share useful ideas about likely content of various tasks. Tell them to relate their discussion to the set book they have read. They are coming up with spontaneous ideas; they should not sit and plan together at this stage.

3 Students could try to reach agreement first with their partner, before being given the answer.

Answer

b

4 Now students will need to analyse in more detail. Allow ten minutes or so for this. The best approach here might be for them to work individually, making brief notes, and then compare with a partner.

Answers

Relevance: The writer explains how the structure of the novel and the diversity of characters both teach and entertain the reader.
Overall structure: The answer is well structured with an introduction, clear development and an appropriate conclusion.
Sophisticated language: The answer contains many instances of advanced level vocabulary including *gain an insight into, makes for a fast-moving pace, learn the tricks of the trade, maintain our interest, print the truth*
Linking devices: Cohesive devices are used appropriately throughout, both within (eg *Certainly* and *Of more interest, though*) and between paragraphs (*Similarly* and *Indeed*).
Quotations: These are used appropriately in paragraphs 1, 3 and 4.

5 Students write their answers for homework.

Review 14 answers Pages 190 and 191

Noun phrases

1 state of shock, the announcement of his resignation/his resignation announcement
2 car keys/keys to the car, back of the drawer
3 mug of cocoa, cow's milk, caravan site
4 seven-hour delay/delay of seven hours, airport departure lounge/departure lounge of the airport
5 youth of average build, yesterday's robbery
6 gold neck chain/gold chain around his neck, diamond nose stud/diamond stud in his nose, matter of personal taste, idea of fashion
7 two months' work, day's rest
8 series of talks, number of topics, protection of the environment

Vocabulary

1 C 2 B 3 D 4 D 5 B 6 A 7 B 8 C 9 C 10 D

Use of English: CAE Part 4 Gapped sentences

1 set 2 sense 3 hard 4 pick 5 price

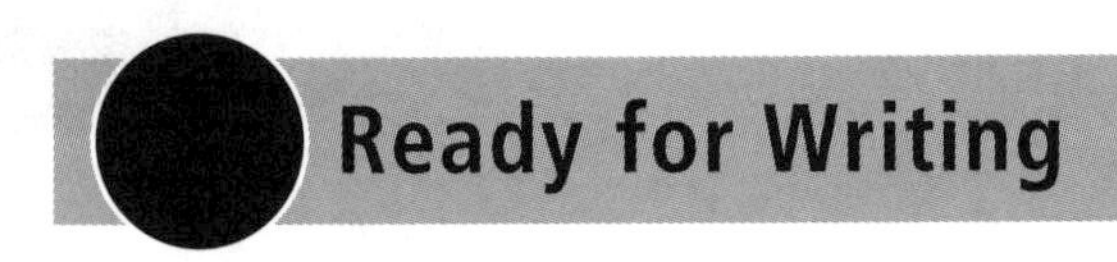

Ready for Writing

CAE Paper 2

Writing Part 1

Part 1 Compulsory task
Part 2 Choice of tasks

Starting with an introduction on marking, planning and register, the unit then proceeds to give models and useful language for most of the possible task types in the paper.

Introduction Page 192

The '150 words of input' refers to what candidates have to read on the question paper, and should not be confused with the 180–220 words that they have to actually write in their answers.

Marking Page 192

It is very important for students to know that these are the assessment criteria. Some students are surprised to learn that their writing is judged so widely, and that assessment is not just a case of looking for errors. This activity could be done as pairwork.

Answers

2 Content
3 Organization and cohesion
4 Target reader
5 Accuracy

Notes:

- The point in 2 is that while it is important to address all the content points, common sense tells you that you don't have to pick up on absolutely every detail in every note.
- All the criteria here are important, but the one overriding thing is the effect the piece has on the target reader. If the piece does not have the intended effect (eg in a letter of complaint, if it is not clear that the writer is dissatisfied and is asking for compensation) then it will not get a 'pass' mark, no matter how well written it is.

Planning and checking Page 193

Given these marking issues, it follows that there are important things to consider at the planning and checking stage. Students do the matching exercise in pairs.

Answers

2 d **3** g **4** h **5** e **6** f **7** a **8** b **9** i

Register Page 193

1 Draw students' attention to g) in the marking exercise they have just done. This might sound difficult and intimidating for them, and they may need some reassurance over this. It is not the case that each task type has its own register which has to be kept to. It is rather a common sense matter – clearly a report or proposal to a manager should not be too colloquial or informal, because that would create a bad impression. The important thing is for students to recognize from the situation in the task whether to write in a formal or informal style, and to keep to it. It is very important to be consistent in this respect.

Students complete the task as instructed.

Answers

1 success
2 obtaining/achieving/attaining
3 expressed/showed/ (or in present tense express/show)
4 position/post
5 employment
6 owing/due
7 unable
8 improvement
9 contact
10 meantime

2 Elicit the answers in whole class mode, and ask for examples for each category. Write these on the board.

Answers

Suggested answers

Informal letter	Formal letter
• the use of *get* in informal register	
get a grade	*obtain/achieve a grade*
try to get a job	*apply for position/post*
get better	*an improvement*
• use of phrasal verbs in informal register	
take you on	*offer you employment*
• greater use of nouns in formal register	
passing your exams	*your recent success in your examinations*
you said you'd be interested	*you expressed an interest*

the way the economy's been recently	*the current economic climate*

- use of abbreviations in informal register

exams	*examinations*

- linking words

But	*However*

- informal punctuation
  dashes and exclamation marks
- other differences

Believe me	*I assure you*
we'll be in touch	*we shall contact you*
as soon as they do	*When this occurs*
Dear Jilly/All the best	*Dear Ms Holden/Yours sincerely*

Models and tasks Page 194

In the pages that follow there are models with comments on useful language, and a new task for students to do for:

Part 1 Formal letter
Part 2 Article
Part 2 Essay
Part 2 Information sheet
Part 2 Contributions: brochure and guidebook entries
Part 2 Proposal
Part 2 Report
Part 2 Informal letter
Part 2 Review
Part 2 Character reference
Part 2 Application letter

Of course, although exemplified here as Part 2s, some of these task types might also be in Part 1 (letters, proposals, reports and articles). If so, they would still have the same format.

Note on word length

- Word length is not a specific issue. It is covered by other marking categories. Students should not worry if they write a little less or a little more than the number of words specified.
- If they are significantly under the word limit, it is likely that they will have underachieved on content and task completion.
- Weaker students who write too much are usually straying from the point. The irrelevance would affect **organization** and **content**.
- Strong students who write too much may have lots to say and be struggling to say it in 260 words. So clearly, they would not be penalized.
- However, such students are in a sense penalizing themselves by writing over length, as they have probably already got their 5 mark from their 260 words, and writing over length may mean they are short of time for their other piece.

Part 1: Formal letter Page 194

Ask students to read the information on page 194 only (ie not the model answer).

Address the following questions to the whole class, books closed if you wish:

- Where is the extract 'Host families in the dark taken from? (a local newspaper)
- What is it saying? (That language students in the town have little contact with local people, and that their schools seem to do nothing for them.)
- Who is Gwyneth Jones? (a local resident and 'host mother' to language students)
- What does the Social Secretary have to write? (a letter to the newspaper editor)
- What information should the letter contain? (It should complain mildly about the letter in the newspaper, it should correct the information in it, it should publicize the school by informing people about the Open Day.)
- Who are the target readers of the letter you will write? (both the editor of the newspaper and the newspaper's readers)
- What effect should it have on the target readers? (They should be convinced that the original newspaper article was misinformed and they should be informed about the school's activities.)
- What register should the letter be written in? (fairly formal)

Now students may read the model answer on page 194. Ask them to check:
1 that the piece is written in a fairly formal register.
2 that it has the desired effect on the target reader.
(Answer = yes in both cases.)

Remind students that the models in the Ready for Writing unit are **all** good models.

As students are reading, draw attention to any points that you wish to emphasize. Be sure to talk about the clever rephrasing of language in paragraphs 2 and 3 of the letter.

Useful language
Go through this together. These are all phrases that might be useable in the task which follows.

Give students some class time to read the task. Explain that this is a very similar task to the one they have just read and discussed. Then put them in pairs, and get them to ask each other similar questions to the ones you asked about the task on the previous pages. This can be done spontaneously. Students should alternate between asking and answering.

Now students should be fully prepared to do this writing task.

Part 2: Article Page 196

If presenting the model answer in class time, draw attention to the comments, and add a few of your own. In particular you might mention:

- the fact that the Part 2 task gives the writer more scope to be creative and give opinions. (Whereas the compulsory Part 1 is mainly about task fulfilment.)
- the fact that the piece 'flows' very nicely – that is, the ideas follow logically from each other, and it is therefore very easy to read. This is because it is well organized and linked.
- the excellent range of language (*is equally ambivalent, cut us off from human contact, anti-social overweight couch potatoes* etc).
- the strong beginning and ending – very important!

Write the following useful language for articles on the board.

Rhetorical questions
Have you ever wondered/asked yourself why ... ?
Did you realize/Were you aware that ... ?
What would you do if ... ?
It's hardly surprising, is it?

Other ways of addressing the reader
As you can imagine ...
Let's look firstly at (the problem of ...)
Imagine you were trying to ...
I'm sure we've all been in the situation where ...

Attitude adverbials to express opinion
Worryingly, (the number of accidents in the home is increasing).
Not surprisingly, (many people are now choosing to use public transport).
Interestingly, (this 80-year-old actor is more popular with the younger generation).

Students might write the next task (Sporting Life) for homework.

Follow the same procedure for the remaining tasks in the unit if you are intending to go through them all in class time.

Alternatively, use the various sections as a reference guide for students to come back to as and when needed.

Or use the rest of the unit as an extended homework activity. Students choose one of the Part 2 tasks to write about.

Here are some additional comments:

Page 197 Essay. See also Unit 5 page 68 in the Coursebook and page 60 in Teacher's Book.

Page 198 Information sheet. See also Unit 10 page 136 in the Coursebook and page 107 in Teacher's Book.

Page 199 Contributions: brochure and guidebook entries. See also Unit 9 page 116 in the Coursebook and page 92 in Teacher's Book.

See also pages 116–117 for Useful language on brochures and guidebooks.

Page 200 Proposal – see also Unit 11 page 148 in the Coursebook and page 115 in the Teacher's Book.

Page 201 Report – see also Unit 3 page 34 in the Coursebook and page 34 in the Teacher's Book.

Page 202 Informal letter – see also Unit 13 page 170 in the Coursebook and page 132 in the Teacher's Book.

Page 203 Review – see also Unit 6 page 76 in the Coursebook and page 65 in the Teacher's Book.

Page 204 Character reference – see also Unit 4 page 56 in the Coursebook and page 51 in the Teacher's Book.

Page 205 Letter of Application – see also Unit 4 page 49 in the Coursebook and page 45 in the Teacher's Book.

Unit 1

Reading: Around the world in 94 days

Page 8

A Complete each sentence below with a noun from the box. Then, in your vocabulary book, make a note of the useful phrases in bold.

line	stride	roles	moment	sponge
inspiration	key	ambition		

1 Usually the winner of a sports competition receives all the praise and fame, while the runner-up is soon forgotten. However, when Ellen MacArthur came second in the Vendee Globe sailing race, **the** _____________ **were reversed**.
2 As a child, Ellen spent all her spare time reading sailing books, **absorbing information like a** _____________.
3 The thoroughness of Ellen's preparation was **the** _____________ **to her success**.
4 As her boat **crossed the finishing** _____________ Ellen was surrounded by thousands of spectators.
5 Ellen realized that she had **fulfilled the** _____________ that had dominated her life until then.
6 Now she could **savour that** _____________.
7 Ellen is as modest as ever; she has **taken** her new-found fame **very much in her** _____________.
8 Ellen is a heroine and **an** _____________ **to her generation**.

B Now reuse some of these phrases in a new context.

1 Colin had a phenomenal memory and could _____________________________.
2 Jacobs _____________________________ first, in a time of 1 minute 45 seconds.
3 Sue Estevan starred in the play 'Hamlet' while her sister Clare had a small part; but in 'Macbeth' _____________________________, and it was Clare who was the star.
4 The _____________________________ is hard work and a little bit of luck.

Unit 2

Listening 2: Multiple matching Page 26

A Underline the correct word, from the words in italics, to form useful phrases from the listening. Listen to the recording again to check your answers or read the listening script.

1 After six months of marital bliss, **it was all** ***done/over/finished*** between us.
2 When my children left home, I suddenly found I had **time on my** ***plate/clock/hands***.
3 When I finally got my big chance, **there was no** ***stopping/pausing/halting*** me.
4 **I** ***dragged/leapt/threw*** **myself into my work** with great enthusiasm.
5 **I worked my** ***track/way/path*** **up** to the position of supervisor.
6 The situation got really bad, and **it got to the** ***moment/point/place*** **where** I just couldn't sleep at night.
7 When I was offered a job working in Portugal, **I** ***jumped/rushed/dived*** **at the chance**.

B Complete each sentence below with a phrasal verb from the box in an appropriate form. These verbs were all used in the listening.

split up	end up	give up	put off
find out	come up to		

The band had been together for a good few years – we were **(1)** _________________ five years together, in fact. I guess we just gradually **(2)** _________________ that there are other things in life beyond music, and it became inevitable that we would **(3)** _________________. You see, we weren't pulling in the same direction anymore and we **(4)** _________________ trying to co-operate with each other. We had a lot of professional disagreements and we **(5)** _________________ fighting all the time. Nevertheless, we kept **(6)** _________________ the big decision – it wasn't an easy step to take.

Unit 3

Reading: Scents and sensitivity Page 38

A In the box you will see verbs from the text, which are often used in scientific journalism. Put the correct word, in an appropriate form, into the sentences.

link	regain	treat	acknowledge
draw	trigger	rectify	subscribe
alert	affect		

1 Doctors are ______ the three men for shock and hypothermia.
2 At the third attempt, the engineers managed to ______ the problem.
3 These days, however, few scientists ______ to such an extreme view.
4 The latest figures suggest that as many as five million people may be ______ by the flooding.
5 The researchers have ______ that some of their methods may have been faulty.
6 Scientists have ______ the outbreak of the disease with a similar case four years ago.
7 The behaviour of the mice ______ the researchers to another possible explanation for the disease.
8 Scientists now believe that this unusual weather event was ______ by cool air descending from the mountains.
9 With such a blow to the brain it may take the patient several minutes to ______ consciousness.
10 Dr Passmore says it is difficult to ______ any firm conclusions from the findings.

B Match the two halves of the sentences to show three expressions with 'take' used in a new context. The expressions are all in the reading text.

1 Fortunately I had **taken the precaution of**
2 Seeing those old photos again
3 If you **take into account** the money you borrowed from me last month,

a really **takes me back in time**.
b that makes £35 in all that you owe me.
c closing all the windows before I left the house.

C Use the nouns in the box to complete some further useful expressions with 'take'.

responsibilities	offence	pieces	point
credit	notice		

1 I hope you won't **take** ________________ **at** this, but I really don't think we can use any of your proposals.

2 I can assure you I **take my** ________________ **very seriously**, and I'm really sorry for this misunderstanding.

3 I banged on the door for ages but she **took no** ________________ **of** me whatsoever.

4 I **take your** ________________, but I still think it's unethical to behave in such a way.

5 I had to **take** the wardrobe **to** ________________ to get it through the door.

6 It was actually Colin who danced the best, but Mary **took all the** ________________ **for** their prize-winning performance.

Ready for Reading

The perils of pizza making Page 44

A Match the verbs in bold in sentences **1–6** with their meanings (**a–f**).

1 **Scoop up** a piece of dough from the tray.
2 **Press out** from the middle of the dough.
3 **Stretch** the dough into a circular shape.
4 **Twirl** the pizza to shake off the excess flour.
5 **Toss** the pizza in the air 'for show'.
6 **Slide off** the pizza from your paddle into the oven.

a pull/elongate
b throw vertically
c push out with your fingers
d tip up the object so that the pizza runs off
e place something underneath and lift up with a quick movement
f spin round and round

B What is the missing word in these useful expressions from the text?

1 I hadn't even got to the toppings, ____________ **alone** the tossing stage.
2 He **took one** ____________ **at** my sorry effort and sighed.
3 It **wasn't so** ____________ a circle **as** an early map of the world.
4 I thought I **was** ____________ **to something**.

Unit 4

Reading: The fast track to burnout Page 53

A Look at the words in bold, as they are used in the texts, and choose which option (**A, B** or **C**) best reflects the meaning of the words.

In text A

1 'I got **sucked in** too at first' means that
A Tanya wanted to be materialistic.
B Tanya was deceived by her colleagues.
C Tanya was embarrassed at her lack of possessions.

In text B

2 'Lily was **snapped up** by a retail chain' means
A they let her down badly.
B they considered her and rejected her.
C they asked her to work for them.

3 A '**performance appraisal**' is
A a formal meeting between an employee and their manager to discuss how well the employee is working.
B a computer programme which enables people to see what jobs they are best suited for.
C a report that every new employee has to submit as part of their training.

In text C

4 '**Perks**' means
A money paid to persuade somebody to do something for you.
B benefits for employees apart from salary.
C flexible work contracts for permanent staff.

5 '**High-flyers**' are
A employees who are identified as excellent and given special treatment.
B interviewees who are regarded as likely candidates for a job.
C managers who have little time for their staff

6 A '**sabbatical**' is
A a formal request to leave a company.
B a decision to award a pay rise to an employee.
C an agreed period of time off work to pursue some other interest.

Unit 5

Listening 1: Multiple choice — Page 61

A Complete the sentences from the listening, which contain useful phrases about love and marriage. Listen to the recording again to check your answers, or read the listening script.

The positive side

1 He got down on one ________ and asked me to marry him.
2 We have a good marriage based on ________ respect ...
3 We enjoy each other's ________ ...
4 I can see the two of us being ________ together.

The negative side

5 You've just got to ________ at it.
6 One in three marriages ________ in divorce.
7 Having my own business put a tremendous ________ on my first marriage.
8 Getting divorced is the easy ________ out.

B In bold are some other useful words and expressions to do with love and relationships. Put the correct word from the box into the two speakers' comments.

patch	separation	incompatible	hit
sight	commitment	chat	

When I first met Dave it was '**love at first** 1________________'. He didn't try to 2________________ **me up**, like all the other boys did, and we 3________________ **it off** immediately.

Sandra and I **went through a bad** 4________________ last year. She said I was afraid of 5________________, which wasn't true. So we had **a trial** 6________________, and I think we both realized that we **were** 7________________.

Unit 6

Reading: Multiple intelligences — Page 72

A Which word (**A**, **B** or **C**) completes the gap? The missing words are adjectives which form adjective-noun collocations from the text. Check your answers in the text if you are not sure.

1 There has been ______________ **debate** about how one defines intelligence.
A wild **B** severe **C** vigorous

2 To do mathematical equations ______________ **agility** is needed.
A mindful **B** mental **C** memorable

3 In my schooldays ______________ **achievement** was all-important.
A academic **B** studious **C** bookish

4 The likes of Einstein and Darwin show that ______________ **potential** is infinite.
A mortal **B** manly **C** human

5 This term describes people with a ______________ **understanding** of the natural world.
A deep **B** high **C** large

6 Einstein asked ______________ **questions** about the universe.
A primary **B** fundamental **C** organic

B In the box you will see formal verbs often used in scientific texts. Complete each gap with the appropriate form of a verb, then check your answers in the text. In some cases more than one verb may be used.

interpret	characterize	visualize
count	gauge	rate

1 'Spatial' intelligence is about being able to ________________ a world in one's head.
2 Artists and architects would ________________ highly in this category.
3 'Personal' intelligence is the ability to ________________ one's own mood, feelings and mental states.
4 These two categories could be ________________ as emotional intelligence.
5 Zoologists and botanists can ________________ themselves among this group.
6 'Existential' intelligence ________________ those who ask fundamental questions about the universe.

Reading: My constant fight to stay awake
Page 78

A Match the words in bold in the extracts from the text with the explanations/synonyms (**a–e**).

1 an incurable sleep **disorder**
2 a **deficiency** of hypocretin
3 overwhelming **fatigue**
4 sleep **paralysis**
5 **hallucinations** in his sleep

a tiredness
b shortage
c seeing imaginary things
d medical condition
e loss of feeling and movement

B Put the correct phrasal verb from the box, in an appropriate form, into the sentences or phrases from the text. The meaning of the phrasal verb is given in brackets.

put down to	turn up	level off
come round	turn down	

1 'I put a hand on his shoulder and he will ________________ … ' (regain consciousness)
2 Dan is remarkably fresh-faced. He ________________ this ________________ the new tablets … (attributes this)
3 Since he started taking Modafinil, his moods have ________________ … (stabilized)
4 A potential employer ________________ him ________________ because of his medical condition. (rejected)
5 Dan would probably ________________ late for work all the time. (arrive)

C Can you remember which adjectives were used in these extracts from the text? The first letter is given.

1 Dan's doctor was equally b______________. (means *puzzled*)
2 … these horrible noises in my head – babies crying and a h________-p______________ squeal.
3 'I used to be this h______________-g______________ -l______________ person who was always cracking jokes.

Unit 7

Reading: Multiple-choice extracts
Page 88

A Find formal language in text A which means the same as:

1 take part (1 word) ______________________
2 go to (1 word) ______________________
3 thing to do (3 words) ______________________
4 If (6 words) ______________________
5 rarely (3 words) ______________________

B Unscramble the words in italics to reveal useful spoken phrases from text B.

1 I've been meaning to phone the dentist for ages, but *round it I've got to never.*

____

2 I was sick a couple of times but the next day *normal back to was I.*

____

3 I'm a bit down at the moment – *things of top me getting on are* at work.

____

C Look again at the answer for A3 (*course of action*). Underline the correct words from the words in italics to reveal some more useful collocations which follow the pattern of noun + of + noun.

1 When Harry passed on confidential information to another company, he was sacked for **breach of *code/agreement/contract***.
2 It was a real **stroke of *fortune/luck/destiny*** that Dave happened to be passing us in his car.
3 I quit my job over **a matter of *principle/ honour/belief*** – I just didn't approve of the way management imposed new working hours on everybody.
4 By a strange ***change/turn/twist* of fate**, the man who rescues her at the end of the film turns out to be her long-lost brother.

Unit 8

Reading: Unplugged Page 104

A Find words or expressions in the text which mean:

(base text paragraph 3)

1 missing ______

2 obscure ______

(base text paragraph 7)

3 attractively unusual ______

4 offering products at a lower price than others ______

(base text paragraph 8)

5 able to be used even by people who understand nothing about computers ______

(paragraph D)

6 highly advanced ______

7 made to suffer ______

(paragraph E)

8 no longer used ______

B Match the linking phrases in bold, which can be found in the text, with phrases of similar meaning (**a**–**d**).

1 **As for** the actual equipment itself …

2 **It strikes me**, though, that the main reason …

3 **It has not escaped my attention that** …

4 **Seriously though**, there is, I suppose, an outside chance …

a Joking apart

b It seems to me

c As far as X is concerned

d I'm well aware that

Unit 9

Reading: Going it alone Page 112

A Match the idiomatic language in bold (in **1**–**4**) with the paraphrases (**a**–**d**).

1 I **handed in my notice** …

2 Everyone had to **muck in** …

3 You could easily **tag along with** another group …

4 I no longer want to **rough it** …

a share the work that needs to be done

b join together in doing something

c live without the usual home comforts

d told my boss I wanted to leave my job

B In section E of the text find words which mean:

1 spoiling yourself ______

2 beauty treatment of the face ______

3 beauty treatment of the nails ______

C These common colloquial ways of saying that you met and liked someone are taken from the text:

a We took to each other straightaway …

b The group really gelled …

c … we all got on like a house on fire.

d I hit it off with (her) …

1 Which one is the strongest – expressing the greatest liking? ______

2 Which one tends to be used of a larger number of people? ______

Ready for Listening
Part 4: Multiple matching Page 127

A Rewrite the second sentence, so that it is similar in meaning to the first, using the words in brackets. The bracketed words must be unscrambled to reveal useful phrases from the listening.

1 I couldn't speak the language very well.
I ______________________________
______________________________.
(two sentences barely together string could)

2 I felt stuck in a fixed and boring way of life.
I ______________________________
______________________________.
(in bit a was rut of a)

3 I owed a lot of money.
I ______________________________
______________________________.
(was debt up to eyes in my)

4 For the most part, we are very different.
We ______________________________
______________________________.
(in most worlds respects apart are)

B Underline the correct word, from the words in italics, to form further useful phrases from the listening.

1 I learned a lot about the culture by *combining/mixing/uniting* with the locals.
2 But there's a big *difficulty/defect/downside* to all this ...
3 Living in this country *suits/fits/matches* us to a tee.
4 I took the *dive/plunge/leap* and moved abroad.
5 I *set/went/put* up in business with a partner.
6 I decided to go it *solely/alone/by myself*, so I bought out my partner.

Unit 10
Reading: The joy of plumbing Page 130

A Find useful verb phrases in the text which mean:

1 wishes to remain anonymous (paragraph 3)
____
2 had a right to (paragraph 4)
____
3 say something you shouldn't have said (paragraph 5)
____
4 accepted as normal (paragraph 5)
____
5 so surprised they couldn't believe it (paragraph 6)
____
6 put things right (paragraph 6)
____
7 extinguishing a cigarette (paragraph 7)
____

B Find single words in the text which mean:

1 paragraph 1 'in poor condition' or 'badly looked after'
____
2 paragraph 2 'coming too late'
____
3 paragraph 7 '(has) mixed feelings'
____

C Complete the sentences using a word formed from the base word 'neighbour'.

1 It's a rather dangerous ______________ to live in.
2 Thanks a lot for the apples – very ______________ of you.
3 He married a girl from a ______________ village.

Unit 11

Reading: The trouble with modern audiences

Page 142

A Which word (**A**, **B**, **C** or **D**) best completes the gap? Look back at the text if you are not sure.

1 Mr and Mrs Fidget-Bottom were _______ their heads up and down in time with the music.

A tapping **B** shaking **C** bobbing **D** ducking

2 If you want to _______ through your programme, fine.

A tap **B** flick **C** click **D** whip

3 A performance was an event which we had no way of even attempting to _______.

A recreate **B** reflect **C** rectify **D** reclaim

4 The Fidget-Bottoms seemed oblivious to the _______ of social conduct.

A standards **B** norms **C** models **D** types

5 I felt that my _______ of temper was fully justified.

A outbreak **B** input **C** outburst **D** downpour

6 They were cocooned in their own world, with not the slightest _______ for anyone.

A worry **B** attention **C** involvement **D** concern

7 I doubt if it even _______ their mind that they were doing anything wrong.

A hit **B** crossed **C** struck **D** gripped

B The following verbs can all be found in the text, but which of them annoy the writer? Check your answers in the text.

coughing shouting wandering off conducting going out stroking kicking whistling chatting

Unit 12

Listening 2: Multiple matching

Page 158

Listen again to the first three speakers, or read the listening script. Then close your Coursebook. How were the following useful phrases used? The first one has been done for you.

Speaker 1

1 on every street corner
There was begging on every street corner.

2 I was in some way to blame
____

3 to persuade me otherwise
____

4 I put aside a certain sum of money
____

Speaker 2

5 all the suffering in the world
____

6 voluntary work overseas
____

7 I needn't have worried
____

8 could have done a lot more to help
____

Speaker 3

9 _______________________________
to raise money for
____

10 my first instinct was
____

11 _______________________________
it's not something I boast about

Unit 13

Reading: Multiple choice extracts Page 172

A As you read the second and third extracts, find words which mean:

1 made redundant (extract 2)

____

2 someone who takes the blame for something, even if it's not their fault. (extract 2)

____

3 search through something in detail (extract 3)

____

4 intended to deceive people in an illegal way (extract 3)

____

5 information to act on (extract 3)

____

6 directing its attention towards (extract 3)

____

7 deliberately disobey (extract 3)

____

8 make someone angry (extract 3)

____

B Look again at the first extract. Which five 'formal' verbs in the text have these informal synonyms?

1 got in touch with ____________
2 told ____________
3 get rid of ____________
4 stopped ____________
5 looks into ____________

Unit 14

Listening 2: Multiple choice Page 187

A Put the linkers in the box into the appropriate extracts from the text below.

presumably apart from anything but at the expense of

1 Buy Nothing Day is ____________ a day of militant action.
2 ... but this should not be ____________ the environment or developing countries.
3 ____________ then, Chris, you're against Christmas shopping, too?
4 What exactly will you be doing, ____________ not buying anything?

B

1 Which one means 'except for'? ______
2 Which one, in this context, means 'I imagine'? ______
3 Which one, in this context, means 'Absolutely not'? ______
4 Which one means that something/someone else suffers as a result of an action? ______

C Use these useful expressions from the listening in the new contexts below.

it's all very well a one-off you'll just have to wait and see saw the funny side of it word of mouth

1 Michelle was not amused when her boyfriend cancelled their date. But at least her brother ____________.
2 We get a lot of our business from personal recommendations and ____________.
3 ____________ for him to complain about rude people – he isn't exactly a model of politeness himself!
4 In my opinion Pele was ____________ – we'll never see a footballer of his talent ever again.
5 I'm afraid I'm sworn to secrecy. ____________ what happens.

Answers to photocopiable exercises

Unit 1
Reading: Around the world in 94 days

A **1** roles **2** sponge **3** key **4** line **5** ambition **6** moment **7** stride **8** inspiration

B **1** absorb information like a sponge
2 crossed the finishing line
3 the roles were reversed
4 key to success

Unit 2
Listening 2: Multiple matching

A **1** over **2** hands **3** stopping **4** threw **5** way **6** point **7** jumped

B **1** coming up to **2** found out **3** split up **4** gave up **5** ended up **6** putting off

Unit 3
Reading: Scents and sensitivity

A
1 treating
2 rectify
3 subscribe
4 affected
5 acknowledged
6 linked
7 alerted
8 triggered
9 regain
10 draw

B
1 c **2** a **3** b

C
1 offence
2 responsibilities
3 notice
4 point
5 pieces
6 credit

Ready for Reading
The perils of pizza making

A **1** e **2** c **3** a **4** f **5** b **6** d

B **1** let **2** look **3** much **4** on

Unit 4
Reading: The fast track to burnout

1 A **2** C **3** A **4** B **5** A **6** C

Unit 5
Listening 1: Multiple choice

A **1** knee **2** mutual **3** company **4** retired **5** work **6** ends **7** strain **8** way

B **1** sight **2** chat **3** hit **4** patch **5** commitment **6** separation **7** incompatible

Unit 6
Reading: Multiple intelligences

A **1** C **2** B **3** A **4** C **5** A **6** B

B **1** visualize
2 rate
3 gauge (*interpret* would also be correct)
4 interpreted (*counted* would also be correct)
5 count
6 characterizes

Reading: My constant fight to stay awake

A **1** d **2** b **3** a **4** e **5** c

B **1** come round **2** puts this down to **3** levelled off **4** turned him down **5** turn up

C **1** baffled **2** high-pitched **3** happy-go-lucky

Unit 7
Reading: Multiple choice extracts

A
1 participate
2 attend
3 course of action
4 In the highly unlikely event that
5 in exceptional circumstances

B
1 I've never got round to it
2 I was back to normal
3 things are getting on top of me

C
1 contract
2 luck
3 principle
4 twist

Unit 8
Reading: Unplugged

A **1** astray **2** esoteric **3** quaint **4** undercutting **5** idiot-proof **6** state-of-the-art **7** subjected to **8** obsolete

B **1** c **2** b **3** d **4** a

Unit 9
Reading: Going it alone

A **1** d **2** a **3** b **4** c

B **1** pampering **2** facial **3** manicure

C **1** c **2** b

Ready for Listening
Part 4: Multiple matching

A **1** could barely string two sentences together
2 was in a bit of a rut
3 was up to my eyes in debt
4 are worlds apart in most respects

B **1** mixing **2** downside **3** suits **4** plunge **5** set **6** alone

Unit 10
Reading: The joy of plumbing

A **1** declines to be named
2 were entitled to
3 speak out of turn
4 took for granted
5 shocked beyond belief
6 rectify the situation
7 stubbing out a cigarette

B **1** shabby **2** belated **3** ambivalent

C **1** neighbourhood
2 neighbourly
3 neighbouring

Unit 11
Reading: The trouble with modern audiences

A **1** C **2** B **3** A **4** B **5** C **6** D **7** B

B coughing, wandering off, conducting, stroking, whistling, chatting

Unit 12
Listening 2: Multiple matching

Possible answers (it is correct ideas rather than exact words used that are being tested here).

2 *I couldn't help feeling that, as a wealthy Westerner*, I was in some way to blame.
3 *I wanted to help the beggars, but my colleagues tried* to persuade me otherwise.
4 *Every day* I put aside a certain sum of money *to give to beggars*.
5 *I wanted to do something about* or *A friend of mine complained about* all the suffering in the world.
6 *I applied to do* voluntary work overseas.
7 I needn't have worried – *I didn't need to have any special skills*.
8 *The government there* could have done a lot more to help.
9 *I did a concert* to raise money for *an international charity*.
10 My first instinct was *to think how I would benefit*.
11 *I did the concert for free and helped to raise lots of money for charity but* it's not something I boast about.

Unit 13
Reading: Multiple choice extracts

A
1 laid off
2 a scapegoat
3 trawl
4 fraudulent
5 ammunition
6 homing in on
7 flout
8 make someone's blood boil

B

1 contacted
2 informed
3 dispose of
4 ceased
5 investigates

Unit 14

Listening 2: Multiple choice

A **1** anything but
2 at the expense of
3 Presumably
4 apart from

B **1** apart from
2 Presumably
3 anything but
4 at the expense of

C **1** saw the funny side of it
2 word of mouth
3 It's all very well
4 a one-off
5 You'll just have to wait and see

Progress test 1: Units 1–3

Reading CAE Paper 1

Part 3 Multiple choice

You are going to read a magazine article. For questions **1–7**, choose the answer (**A**, **B**, **C** or **D**) which you think fits best according to the text.

MEMORIES OF A GARDEN

I was brought up in a small village, which meant I was quite bored for most of my childhood. I did a lot of reading, but my main hobby was visiting a big old house on the edge of the village. Actually, it was the garden I visited. The woman who lived in the house was a bit of a recluse, but she told the gardeners to let us children come into the garden, so long as we left her in peace. She said a love of plants might rub off on us, and it was possible we'd learn something about growing things. It didn't work in my case – I was just interested in running on the lawns and climbing the trees that grew round the house. The gardeners were very busy, but they didn't seem to mind us noisy brats invading their territory.

We had theories about the owner of the house: she was an eccentric millionaire; she bred racehorses – there were always horses in the field next to the house; she was a famous artist (on the flimsy evidence that someone had seen sketch books lying around). But one day I was in the garden, up a tree as usual, and a group of people wandered past with one of the gardeners. They were American, and were saying they'd come to England to see some famous gardens, and this was their favourite. I couldn't believe my ears. The gardener said yes, the owner and her late husband had created the garden almost from nothing, and people visited from all over. Now I understood why there were sometimes strangers around, bent earnestly over the flower-beds.

The house itself was a no-go area. It was huge and dark. Village gossip maintained that most of it was closed up, and only two rooms were occupied. Looking inside from the top of a tall tree, I could see signs that the whole house was lived in, but the rooms looked like something from the 19th century, with heavy, ugly furniture. Though there was electricity and modern heating, the place looked uncared-for, almost dangerously so. There must have been holes in the roof from the number of buckets placed in strategic positions. The garden, on the other hand, was always immaculate, and must have swallowed most of the owner's income.

I grew up, moved away from the village, and became a journalist. One day I heard that the owner of the big old house had died, and soon after that I was sent by my magazine to interview the new owners. I went first to the village pub, to get the gossip. Rumours abounded. The house was going to be turned into an expensive retirement home, or a sort of health spa, or the neighbourhood's most exclusive restaurant. I went to meet the owners, who put me right. They were well-known figures in the catering industry, and envisaged the place as a holiday retreat for millionaires and film stars to stay in, a luxury hideaway. The garden was being preserved as a horticultural treasure, but where before it had been enjoyed by children and enthusiastic tourists, now it was to be appreciated exclusively by the super-rich.

Some months later I went back to discover what had happened to the house and garden. I had expected a transformation, but apart from fresh paintwork on the doors and windows, from the outside everything looked much the same. Inside, however, there were changes. No buckets for a start! The rooms were filled with antique furniture, and the decorations were elegant. There was an air of discreet luxury – and security cameras winked from every corner. I felt, with my meagre journalist's salary, perhaps I shouldn't be there at all. Was it just me, or was there a faintly unwelcoming air about the place?

But I was being unfair. The new owners were hospitality itself, and very anxious for my approval. They went out of their way to answer my checklist of questions, and not just, I felt, because they were desperate to acquire free publicity in the press. I got the genuine impression they would do anything to put a guest at ease and make him or her feel quite at home. As I left, and looked at the lights from the house flooding across the garden, I considered I should be happy that the place was still standing at all. Probably my memories of the old building with its eccentricities were romanticized. I was glad I'd been back, and I was sure the village was benefiting from the trade these newcomers brought, though no doubt there was plenty of grumbling in the pub about 'strangers' and 'change for change's sake'. Putting regret resolutely aside, I turned to shout, "Goodbye, and good luck!" to the owners waving from the doorway.

1 The writer liked visiting the garden of the old house because

A she enjoyed talking to the gardeners.

B she learnt about different kinds of plants.

C she and her friends were free to play there.

D she found it a peaceful place to spend time.

2 The writer found out that

A the garden was internationally famous.

B the owner of the house was a successful artist.

C the house had been inherited by the owner's husband.

D the grounds of the property were used for breeding horses.

3 What did the writer realize when she saw inside the house?

A The owner of the house lived in only two rooms.

B Nothing had changed in the house since the 19th century.

C More money had probably been spent on the garden than the house.

D No visitors were allowed to enter the house because it was dangerous.

4 After the owner's death, the house and garden were bought by people who

A planned to open a luxurious retirement home.

B intended to make the house into a first-class hotel.

C thought they would create the best restaurant in the area.

D wanted to make the garden into a popular tourist attraction.

5 What does the writer say about the alterations to the house?

A They were in good taste.

B They created a pleasant atmosphere.

C They were in contrast to the style of the garden.

D They transformed the external appearance of the house.

6 Which phrase is echoed by 'to put a guest at ease' (line 77)?

A were hospitality itself (line 71)

B anxious for my approval (line 72)

C went out of their way (line 73)

D desperate to acquire (line 75)

7 After her visit to the house and garden, the writer concluded that

A it can be a mistake to revisit places you once knew.

B traditions should be preserved as far as possible.

C it is important to be cautious about making changes.

D some childhood memories cannot be trusted.

Use of English CAE Paper 3

Part 1 Multiple-choice cloze

Read this article about an actor.

For questions **1–12**, read the text below and decide which answer (**A**, **B**, **C** or **D**) best fits each gap. There is an example at the beginning **(0)**.

MOVIE STAR

The restless, jiggling knee, the **(0)** __________ he says 'yeah yeah' impatiently, the **(1)** __________ tapping of cigarette over ashtray – all give the **(2)** __________ that Ewan McGregor has been, somehow, overwound. Perhaps this is how someone behaves when they are struggling to **(3)** __________ their ego in check – trying to **(4)** __________ to terms with being an international star.
Success seems to come naturally to McGregor. 'I've never been **(5)** __________ of work. I've been in a rush to get to the top, since I was a kid. I was always **(6)** __________ for success.'
He earns £5 million a film, and plays opposite Hollywood's most celebrated women actors. It's likely that, in the age-old Hollywood **(7)** __________ , film publicists encourage gossip about McGregor and his female co-stars, but the rumours are without **(8)** __________ . In fact, his wife and family always travel with him on location.
McGregor grew up in Scotland. When he and his older brother were at school, the young Ewan was **(9)** __________ hauled up before the headmaster for anti-social conduct. He thinks this was because he **(10)** __________ it hard to live up to his brother.
'There was some rivalry, I guess. My brother was academic and sporting – the important things at our school. I was keen on music and artistic studies, which didn't **(11)** __________ as serious activities. I realize now, all I cared about was being a performer, **(12)** __________ on a show.'

0	**A** <u>way</u>	**B** means	**C** method	**D** manner
1	**A** many	**B** varied	**C** numerous	**D** repetitive
2	**A** opinion	**B** viewpoint	**C** impression	**D** persuasion
3	**A** contain	**B** keep	**C** provide	**D** support
4	**A** go	**B** set	**C** reach	**D** come
5	**A** wanting	**B** minus	**C** short	**D** lacking
6	**A** envious	**B** selfish	**C** jealous	**D** greedy
7	**A** performance	**B** tradition	**C** nature	**D** procedure
8	**A** foundation	**B** discovery	**C** beginning	**D** establishment
9	**A** gradually	**B** radically	**C** steadily	**D** regularly
10	**A** found	**B** accepted	**C** saw	**D** realized
11	**A** depend	**B** rely	**C** count	**D** rest
12	**A** putting	**B** giving	**C** presenting	**D** producing

Part 2 Open cloze

For questions **1–15**, read the text below and think of the word which best fits each gap. Use only **one** word in each gap. There is an example at the beginning **(0)**.

JOHN LENNON'S CHILDHOOD HOME

Some of the best-loved songs of our time **(0)** ___*were*___ dreamt up in one small room. John Lennon's bedroom was his escape route, the place **(1)** __________ he would sit **(2)** __________ hours drawing, writing lyrics and dreaming. His mother Julia adored him, but felt she was not able to offer him the steady life he needed, and gave him up **(3)** __________ the age of five to **(4)** __________ raised by her sister Mimi. John's aunt was loyal and loving; however, these were **(5)** __________ 1950s, and she was also very strict. Her young charge must **(6)** __________ felt suffocated sometimes.

The modest house where John Lennon was brought **(7)** __________ by Mimi and her husband George was called *Mendips*, and it has recently become a museum. It was given to an organization called The National Trust by Lennon's widow Yoko Ono, **(8)** __________ stepped in because of rumours that the house **(9)** __________ going to be turned **(10)** __________ a honeymoon hotel. 'John was hugely famous,' says his cousin Mike Cadwallader. 'Otherwise, **(11)** __________ would be interested in a house like this.' It is not history rooted in the distant past, it is the story of life in an ordinary family 50 years ago. Every weekend **(12)** __________ would be a family gathering **(13)** __________ some sort. John's friends would come round to visit him. 'Sometimes there were **(14)** __________ many of us there wasn't room for everyone round the table and we **(15)** __________ to take it in turns to eat,' Cadwallader recalls.

Part 5 Key word transformations

For questions **1–8**, complete the second sentence so that it has a similar meaning to the first sentence, using the word given. **Do not change the word given.** You must use between **three** and **six** words, including the word given. Here is an example **(0)**.

0 I don't suppose you know if the last train has already left?
HAPPEN
Do *you happen to know whether* or not the last train has already left?

---

1 It's not likely that Maria will say no to such a well-paid job.
HARDLY
Maria ______________________________ down such a well-paid job.

2 You are more likely to get into university if you have private maths lessons.
CHANCES
By having private maths lessons, you will ______________________________ into university.

3 It seems that the fridge is no longer working.
IF
It looks ______________________________ down.

4 I last won a game of tennis against my brother years ago.
BEATEN
It's years ______________________________ at tennis.

5 David should have asked my permission before he used my laptop.
SOONER
I ______________________________ asked my permission before he used my laptop.

6 Mentioning my day off when the boss was in such a bad mood was a mistake.
QUIET
I wish ______________________________ my day off when the boss was in such a bad mood.

7 It's possible that the curtains started burning when a candle fell over.
HAVE
The curtains ______________________________ fire when a candle fell over.

8 It was only because of Mr Dyer's generous donation that we were able to rebuild the library.
BEEN
If ______________________________ Mr Dyer's generous donation, we could not have rebuilt the library.

Vocabulary

Decide which word fits the space in each sentence.

success motivation lifestyle behaviour method aroma

1 When I started my own business I had to adapt my __________ to a 60-hour working week.

2 This is the most efficient __________ of cooking rice I know – it always works.

3 It's not lack of intelligence, it's poor __________ that prevents some people from doing as well as they should.

4 Her concert was a resounding __________. She's been booked for next season.

5 There was a delicious __________ of roast chicken in the air when he came home.

6 She won't modify her __________ for anyone. She doesn't care what people think of her.

gather vary adjust smell end take up

7 We like to __________ the places we go to on holiday, to get new experiences.

8 The perfumes you buy in this shop __________ of the flowers I remember from my grandmother's garden.

9 You won't find out what you're capable of if you don't __________ challenges.

10 I'll have to get the optician to __________ my glasses, they keep slipping down my nose.

11 I had to __________ a lot of information for the project, and that was fascinating.

12 The children are getting over-excited – it's bound to __________ in tears.

lifelong welcome cost-effective misleading significantly conceivably

13 Information you find on the Internet can be __________ , so you have to treat it with caution.

14 This software might __________ be obsolete by next year, so we'd better be prepared to replace it.

15 Last weekend my mother fulfilled her __________ ambition to have a trip in a balloon.

16 When he visited his childhood home, he found that nothing had changed __________.

17 We have to look at more __________ methods of packaging our products.

18 I had a proper lunch at my parents' last Sunday, which was a __________ change from ready meals bought in the supermarket.

Listening CAE Paper 4

Part 2 Sentence completion

You will hear a man called Geoffrey Clifton talking on the radio about a major change in his life.
For questions **1–8**, complete the sentences.

A CHANGE IN LIFESTYLE

In 1998 Geoffrey was working as an [**1**] in London.

When he was young, Geoffrey's [**2**] was the only person to take an interest in his writing.

Geoffrey saw an advertisement for a writing course when he was in a [**3**].

The course was held in a building which had been used for making [**4**].

Geoffrey wanted to write [**5**] and children's books.

The students on the course spent the afternoons [**6**] and reading.

Back in England Geoffrey was helped by a [**7**] he first met at a party.

Geoffrey and his wife have left London to live in the south of [**8**].

Writing CAE Paper 2

Part 1

Write your answer in **180–220** words in an appropriate style.

You work for a company that owns a chain of hotels. The company has recently bought another hotel which it hopes will become more popular with young people. The company has sent you to inspect it. Read the description of the hotel from a current brochure and your notes below, and **write a report** for your manager, outlining your findings and making suitable recommendations for improvements.

Surrounded by peaceful, beautiful gardens and close to the local beach, the Coral Hotel is ideal for people looking for a quiet place to stay. Transformed from a 19th century mansion house, the hotel has a charming old-fashioned feel to it.
We pride ourselves on our excellent staff who make every effort to ensure you have a wonderful holiday. The hotel also boasts a wide range of facilities for you to enjoy at no extra cost.

true – but lots to do in the local area. (a quiet place to stay)

some rooms in poor condition. (a charming old-fashioned feel)

Not impressed with the service. (excellent staff)

old tennis court and dirty-looking sauna. (a wide range of facilities)

Write your **report**.

Progress test 2: Units 4–6

Reading CAE Paper 1

Part 4 Multiple matching

You are going to read an article about management training. For questions **1–15**, choose from the four courses (**A–D**). The courses may be chosen more than once.

Which course mentions the following?

Participants are involved in energetic physical activity.	1	
Participants are asked to outline their training goals in advance.	2	
Participants travel to several different locations as part of the training.	3	
Competitive behaviour is discouraged.	4	
Participants receive input from different kinds of experts.	5	
Participants are surprised to discover skills they did not know they possessed.	6	
Participants are taught how to relate physical signs to feelings.	7	
The trainer is sensitive to participants who are shy.	8	
A link is made between relaxation and original thinking.	9	
There is emphasis on the importance of patience.	10	
Participants learn to concentrate on the most important aspects of a situation.	11	
Participants are helped to deal with their weaknesses.	12	
Participants are trained to respond imaginatively to unexpected events.	13	
The learning process alternates between practical activities and problem-solving.	14	
There is an opportunity to work individually and as part of a group.	15	

Training for Business

If lawyers and banks use them, alternative training courses can't be all that daft, can they? EMMA DE VITA finds out about four courses on offer and invites you to decide for yourself.

A COURSE 1 SHEEPDOGS

Expert sheepdog handler Barbara Sykes offers business executives the chance to spend a day learning how to 'think like a canine'. She explains: 'You'd be surprised at the similarities between the workplace and a group of dogs acting as a pack – the hierarchies, the team bonding'. Sykes's aim is that by the end of the day, participants will – like her dogs – be able to read the body language of their colleagues. 'The idea is to develop self-learning and facilitate team-working. The dogs are the teachers', she says. 'But I have to warn you, it's quite strenuous. You and your colleagues spend a day on a farm working with sheep, trying to imitate the skills of the dogs. You learn how your body movements affect the animals. If in your mind you're unsure of what you're doing, the animals pick up on it. Similarly, if you go into the boardroom and feel unsure, your body sends that message out. Your mind and body must work together'. Each participant learns how to bring the sheep under control by himself, then the participants are formed into a team and given the task of moving the flock across the fields and into the farmyard.

B COURSE 2 COMEDY

'Comedy provides a powerful model for developing a range of qualities crucial for business and management: confidence, communication, teamwork and creativity', says trainer Gerry Thompson. He uses improvization, or invention to help his clients break down the barriers to their creativity. 'I've discovered improvization is a powerful thing if you know how to use it. It can show you how to deal with things that suddenly happen, that come out of the blue, and it shows people their possibilities.' Some people may feel uncomfortable at the idea of clowning around in front of their colleagues, but Thompson gives guidance on the appropriate use of humour in the office.

Participants start with a physical warm-up. 'I've devised exercises, nothing too demanding, which help people unwind – to encourage creativity.' Then participants are taken through simple exercises like those used in the theatre. These encourage people to express themselves, and work towards humour in an indirect way. People often astonish themselves by improvizing their own comedy sketch on stage. 'There isn't any pressure to be funny'; Thompson reassures participants who may feel inhibited. 'The exercises are gently progressive. I never put people in an embarrassing situation. They gradually find themselves doing things they didn't think possible, and learn that if they challenge themselves, they will overcome their deficiencies. It builds up confidence'.

C COURSE 3 WAR

The mission of this course is 'to deliver management development programmes, employing battlefield studies as the medium'. Business has long used the military as a source of inspiration, but what distinguishes this course, says director Ian Blackwell, 'is the enriching and moving experience participants receive from visiting the scenes of past battles.' Managers are invited to deal with the scenarios that the officers faced. They have to make life-or-death decisions. 'We provide a fast-paced management workshop, where issues are more black-and-white than the corporate world, but which help people to focus on essentials.'

'Participants can practise decision-making skills as though they were exposed to the risk-taking scenario of a battle,' explains Blackwell. 'But there's no physical engagement – the approach is intellectual.' The tour of battlefields, for example, involves a three-day visit of strategic battle sites combined with presentations from military historians, who recount the events of the battle. This is interspersed with discussions led by business consultants, who help participants apply military wisdom to their own situation. 'Let's not forget – running a business is like waging a war,' says Blackwell.

D COURSE 4 BREADMAKING

'Instead of training participants to climb mountains or find their way through forests,' says the course literature, 'this method of training strengthens business teams to meet the demands of corporate life by using bread-making and business-focused action learning.' Baker Andrew Whitley uses his bread-making courses to teach executives collaborative respect and the value of taking things calmly, not rushing. The focus is on the positive, and there's no room for rivalry in his course. Business results are achieved through camaraderie and enjoyment. Says Whitley: 'The process of baking is good fun, and tension-relieving.'

A questionnaire is sent out to the group of participants, who agree on a list of objectives. The two-day course starts in the bakery. 'We get straight into the first loaf of bread. It's both practical and symbolic, and it breaks the ice,' explains Whitley. After an hour of bread-making, the participants attend a session in the conference room with professional coaches, who discuss the group's objectives. Throughout the day, bread-making is interspersed with management sessions in which the main problems of work-related issues are identified and action points voted on. But the crunch comes at the end of the course when the bakers taste their wares, which apparently often reflect the baker's interpersonal skills. Would you want the creator of a burnt, misshapen loaf on your team?

Use of English CAE Paper 3

Part 3 Word formation

For questions **1–10**, read the text below. Use the word given in capitals at the end of some of the lines to form a word that fits in the gap **in the same line**. There is an example at the beginning **(0)**.

Life with my Father

My father's job as the only **(0)** *surgeon* in a rural hospital meant that there was	**SURGERY**
little **(1)** __________ in his working hours and that we rarely saw him at home. Our	**REGULAR**
(2) __________ was left to my mother; she washed and fed us, and dished out	**BRING**
comfort, particularly to me, who had a **(3)** __________ to cry at the slightest thing.	**TEND**
Even though my siblings and I outnumbered my mother by four to one, we didn't	
dare to **(4)** __________.	**BEHAVE**
If there was any sign of trouble breaking out, or a **(5)** __________ to follow orders,	**REFUSE**
my mother would threaten to inform my father, which was a very **(6)** __________	**PLEASE**
prospect! We all dreaded his stern face and look of disappointment. **(7)** __________,	**ADMIT**
there were times when he *did* show concern, particularly at our injuries and at	
school grades he thought were not **(8)** __________, but these were few. I believe that	**JUST**
my father actually had the capacity to be **(9)** __________ but he expressed his love	**AFFECTION**
through a lifelong **(10)** __________ to work hard and not complain about it, which	**WILLING**
was typical of his generation.	

Part 4: Gapped sentences

For questions **1–5**, think of **one** word only which can be used appropriately in all three sentences. Here is an example **(0)**.

0 William needs to make a greater ___effort___ if he wants to pass his driving test first time.
New credit card technology is being developed in a serious ___effort___ to stop fraud.
The new reserve is a joint ___effort___ between the council and the Natural Wildlife Society.

---

1 Once you've served your __________ in prison, you should be allowed to lead a normal life.
My daughter's only four so she hasn't learnt to tell the __________ yet.
She was six months pregnant at the __________ the photo was taken.

2 The gang kept a restaurant as a __________ for an illegal gambling house.
Politicians often maintain a united __________ even if they personally disagree with their party leader.
With her qualifications and personality, Sonia has a great career in __________ of her.

3 We didn't like the __________ of the hotel as it was rather dark and gloomy.
It doesn't __________ as if we'll get a break from the rain today.
I have no respect for people who __________ down on others with less money.

4 Emilio is __________ becoming the best player on our team.
My watch is a few minutes __________ so we should still be able to catch the train.
The children were __________ asleep by the time we finally got home.

5 The appeal judge ruled that the original sentence was too __________ and added a further two years.
You are invited to remain after the talk for __________ refreshments in the cafeteria.
Being a __________ sleeper means that you often feel tired in the morning.

Vocabulary

Decide which answer **A**, **B**, **C** or **D** best fits each space and underline it.

1 Both husband and wife worked long hours, which put a great ______ on their relationship.

A difficulty **B** trouble **C** strain **D** effort

2 I was rather ______ for time today, so I'm afraid I'll have to finish that report tomorrow.

A challenged **B** pressed **C** lacking **D** stressed

3 In our work-obsessed society, it's important to set ______ time for yourself.

A aside **B** up **C** off **D** back

4 The series became so popular that it was moved to the ______ time spot of 8pm.

A leading **B** prime **C** main **D** major

5 He didn't think he'd get to sleep, but eventually he ______ off.

A slept **B** shook **C** drifted **D** fell

6 We ______ like a house on fire from the moment we first met.

A broke up **B** fell out **C** took to **D** got on

7 She ______ in touch with her school friends for years and years.

A stood **B** put **C** kept **D** went

8 My brother was a gifted footballer, and all of us ______ up to him with respect.

A admired **B** looked **C** saw **D** watched

9 My mother ______ her feelings forcibly when we kicked the football through the kitchen window.

A expressed **B** said **C** told **D** talked

10 She's only nine, but she's already a ______ cook, and has produced some delicious meals.

A brainy **B** future **C** promising **D** dab

11 We're depending on you to come up with some ______ ideas. We need inspiration.

A bright **B** proficient **C** talented D gifted

12 I always sleep ______ when I'm at the seaside. It must be the healthy air.

A evenly **B** deep **C** soundly **D** hard

13 The children are still ______ awake. They're much too excited to settle down.

A wide **B** fast **C** light **D** openly

14 Please don't ask me to navigate, I'm ______ at reading maps.

A uninterested **B** incapable **C** disabled **D** hopeless

15 My sister's a very ______ swimmer; in fact, she's the school champion.

A rough **B** strong **C** hard **D** heavy

Listening CAE Paper 4

Part 4 Multiple matching

You will hear five short extracts in which people are talking about spending time with groups.

TASK ONE

For questions **1–5**, choose from the list **A–H** the purpose of each group.

A to organize sport

B to entertain

C to provide training

D to deal with emergencies

E to give advice

F to provide new employment

G to learn a skill

H to make a product

Speaker 1 [ ] 1

Speaker 2 [ ] 2

Speaker 3 [ ] 3

Speaker 4 [ ] 4

Speaker 5 [ ] 5

TASK TWO

For questions **6–10**, choose from the list **A–H** each speaker's feeling about being part of the group.

A Being in a group was difficult because I prefer solitude.

B The group gives me reassurance in a difficult situation.

C I am not sure that the group gives good value for money.

D It gave me renewed pleasure in my hobby.

E It is an enjoyable contrast to my daily life.

F I enjoy being the leader of a group.

G It was a pleasure to learn practical skills in a group.

H I was disappointed by the experience.

Speaker 1 [ ] 6

Speaker 2 [ ] 7

Speaker 3 [ ] 8

Speaker 4 [ ] 9

Speaker 5 [ ] 10

Writing CAE Paper 2

Part 2

Write an answer to **one** of the questions **2–4** in this part. Write your answer in **220–260** words in an appropriate style.

2 You have been asked by the owner of a sportswear and equipment shop to provide a reference for a friend of yours who has applied for a holiday job as a sales assistant.

The reference for your friend should include information about his or her
• character • previous experience • skills and interests • suitability for selling sports goods.

Write your **reference**.

3 You see the following announcement in an international magazine.

> **Young Entrepreneur of the Year Competition**
>
> *Are you between 18–25? Would you like to be your own boss and help other people at the same time? Are you looking for funding?*
>
> Write to us
> – outlining your idea for a new project, business or scheme
> – saying how it would benefit the local community
> – explaining why you would be a suitable person to run it.

Write your **competition entry**.

4 Your college magazine is taking part in an international survey on changes in family life over the last ten years. You have been asked to write a report for this survey, outlining what changes have taken place in family life in your country, and what factors have caused these changes. Suggest how the situation might change in the future.

Write your **report**.

Progress test 3: Units 7–9

Reading CAE Paper 1

Part 2 Gapped text

You are going to read an extract from a newspaper article. Six paragraphs have been removed from the extract. Choose from the paragraphs **A–G** the one which fits each gap **(1–6)**. There is one extra paragraph which you do not need to use.

Medicine and mortality: The dark world of medical history

Sir Henry Wellcome, the philanthropist and pharmacist, spent his life assembling an archive as gigantic as it is gruesome. Now it has gone on show. Jeremy Laurance reports.

It is one of life's constants: the heart beats approximately one billion times before it expires. What determines how long a creature lives is the speed at which its heart beats, whether it belongs to a whale, a humming bird or a human.

1	

Others without a personal interest will still find plenty to fascinate them. The collection contains three galleries displaying the curiosities amassed by the trust's founder, Sir Henry Wellcome, together with modern acquisitions and art works. Delicately carved Aztec sacrificial knives, Napoleon's silver-handled toothbrush, and Charles Darwin's walking stick are displayed alongside a Peruvian mummy.

2	

Known as a pharmacist, philanthropist and entrepreneur, Sir Henry founded the Burroughs Wellcome drug company that is now the multinational GlaxoSmithKline. As a child, he worked in his uncle's drugstore, and later, after graduating from the Philadelphia College of Pharmacy he worked as a travelling salesman in New York. He moved to London in 1880 to set up a pharmaceutical company with his friend, Silas Burroughs.

3	

Ken Arnold, curator of the Wellcome Collection, hopes that the exhibition achieves this but is keen to show that Wellcome was more than just a collector. He says: "Wellcome was a giant figure of the early twentieth century. He coined the word 'tabloid', for medicinal powders compressed into pill form, which was later applied to newspapers. He pioneered aerial photography and organized the biggest archaeological dig of the time."

4	

Steve Cross, the curator of Medicine Man said: "I don't think even Henry realized that within the dusty storerooms where he kept his collection lay one of the world's great museums. These objects tell us something fascinating about humanity's perennial fascination with our own bodies, but Henry would have wanted us to show 10 times more."

5	

Unlike the others, the last gallery houses changing exhibitions and is devoted to the heart. It includes intricate 16th-century drawings of the circulation by Leonardo Da Vinci, which remain astonishingly accurate four centuries later, displayed alongside MRI scans and a heart and lung machine.

6	

The explanation given for this is that our extra longevity is thanks to medicine. Perhaps that inflated claim is not surprising in a museum celebrating its achievements, but even Sir Henry might have added that better living conditions and improved diet have also made a difference.

A It is not these remarkable achievements however, that the public will learn about in the museum. Rather they will get to see the cream of almost two million collected artefacts on display in 'Medicine Man', one of two permanent galleries. Most of the items were amassed during the last 25 years of Wellcome's life, following the break-up of his marriage in 1910, when he became a recluse, focusing on his work, travel and collecting.

B It is here we learn that it is possible to calculate the length of any creature's life from its heart rate. Thus the tiny shrew, whose heart races at more than 1,000 beats a minute, lives little more than a year but has the rapid metabolism necessary to escape predators. The sperm whale's heart pumps at 10 beats a minute and keeps going for 70 years. Only humans defy nature by living not the 30-odd years that this formula suggests – as they did in medieval times – but far longer.

C Together, they provide the visitor with a rapid journey through the history of medicine, embracing everything from witchcraft to artificial iron legs. There are showcases featuring birthing implements and syringes, alongside a used guillotine blade. A dentist's signboard from China is strung with more than 100 teeth, testament to the skill of their extractor. What kind of a man would have brought these strange objects together?

D This was not Sir Henry's intention and not what he had in mind for his collection. The company continued to prosper and at his death, he left a bequest which has made the Wellcome Trust the wealthiest charity in the UK with an endowment of £14bn, providing medical research grants worth £520m this year.

E It was very successful, building groundbreaking research laboratories, and Sir Henry used a large part of the profits to finance his passion for collecting objects of medical interest, even dispatching teams of agents to find objects for him from around the world. At one stage, 1,000 objects a month were arriving at his offices, and many parcels were left unopened. His vision was for a "museum of man", which would cast light on the development of medicine and attitudes to the body and to health across time and in all cultures.

F To complement the collection and bring it up to date, a second gallery, 'Medicine Now', provides a contemporary take on present concerns with a focus on one rich-world epidemic, obesity, and one of the poor world, malaria. Interspersed through the space are red boxes in which artists display their response to experiences of illness and treatment.

G You can see an example of each of these on display at the stunning Wellcome Collection, the medical museum renovated at a cost of £30m. Designed to illuminate our own mortality and the efforts mankind has made to extend it, the exhibition, which has only just re-opened to the public, includes the heart of 22-year-old Jennifer Sutton who had a transplant two weeks ago. She plans a visit to see it.

Use of English CAE Paper 3

Part 1 Multiple-choice cloze

For questions **1–12**, read the text below and decide which answer **(A, B, C** or **D)** best fits each gap. There is an example at the beginning **(0)**.

POWERPOINT

Everybody agrees that **(0)** __________ the right company image is vital in today's competitive business environment. If you don't show customers and suppliers that your company is technologically up to **(1)** __________ , your business could **(2)** __________ . But learn how to get it right and you could be a **(3)** __________ ahead of the competition.

If your standard presentation at a meeting **(4)** __________ of handing out reams of paper to participants, why not maximize the **(5)** __________ of your message by **(6)** __________ of our state-of-the-art software? What you have to say would have a much **(7)** __________ effect if you could automatically change the colour schemes, alter the **(8)** __________ of the text, and include drawings and graphs throughout your document. If this element is **(9)** __________ from your presentations today, then PowerPoint is the **(10)** __________ to your prayers.

PowerPoint is one of the most popular presentation programmes on the market. It **(11)** __________ you to transfer your personal presentations, details and data onto a variety of mediums. From a set of ordinary facts and figures you can create a huge array of visuals that are **(12)** __________ to hold the attention of your audience.

0	**A** <u>projecting</u>	**B** impressing	**C** striking	**D** emphasizing
1	**A** period	**B** present	**C** date	**D** moment
2	**A** spoil	**B** worsen	**C** endure	**D** suffer
3	**A** pace	**B** step	**C** rate	**D** level
4	**A** consists	**B** comprises	**C** includes	**D** incorporates
5	**A** impact	**B** factor	**C** element	**D** outfit
6	**A** capacity	**B** ability	**C** means	**D** method
7	**A** higher	**B** greater	**C** farther	**D** longer
8	**A** sight	**B** view	**C** prospect	**D** appearance
9	**A** losing	**B** going	**C** missing	**D** failing
10	**A** answer	**B** reaction	**C** remedy	**D** solution
11	**A** approves	**B** allows	**C** accepts	**D** agrees
12	**A** concluded	**B** defined	**C** guaranteed	**D** decided

Part 4 Gapped sentences

For questions **1–5**, think of **one** word only which can be used appropriately in all three sentences.
Here is an example **(0)**.

0 There's a *fair* chance of snow over the weekend.

It was only *fair* that Matthew had to pay for the damage he caused.

I had *fair* hair when I was younger but it's got darker over the years.

---

1 The new bypass should help to __________ traffic congestion in the town centre.

My tennis coach told me to __________ my grip on the racquet between strokes.

The pain began to __________ off not long after I'd taken the medicine.

2 Steve made the __________ of his holiday even though it rained every day.

It will take half an hour at the __________ to reach the port.

For the __________ part, life in our town is fairly peaceful.

3 We don't know much about Anya as she tends to __________ to herself.

The explorers could no longer __________ going once their supplies had run out.

The young elephant tried hard to __________ up with the rest of the herd.

4 We know from __________ experience that the best pupils do not always perform well in this exam.

The witness said the thief ran __________ before he had a chance to stop him.

I stayed up way __________ my bedtime last night just to watch that horror film.

5 It was an accident so there's no point being __________ with him.

The animal known as a 'liger' is a __________ between a lion and a tiger.

It didn't __________ my mind that my business partner might be stealing from the company.

Part 5 Key Word transformations

For questions **1–8**, complete the second sentence so that it has a similar meaning to the first sentence, using the word given. **Do not change the word given**. You must use between **three** and **six** words, including the word given. Here is an example **(0)**.

0 The company intends to stop sponsoring any events in the future.
WITHDRAW
The company is *to withdraw its sponsorship from future* events.

---

1 I didn't do anything more than arrange a meeting between two single people.
DID
All ______________________________ up a meeting between two single people!

2 Even at a young age, I did not want to be criticized in front of other people and I still don't.
PUBLIC
Even at a young age, I objected ______________________________ and I still do.

3 Simon warned me to keep quiet if the boss got angry.
THAT
Simon warned ______________________________ his temper, I should keep quiet.

4 I'm sure the school will take more notice of safety issues after last week's accident.
BOUND
The school ______________________________ greater attention to safety issues after last week's accident.

5 After we returned home with the new video game, Jun said that I had to try it out first.
SHOULD
After we returned home with the new video game, Jun insisted ______________________________ a go first.

6 You will not be able to change Jill's mind about getting married next week.
AHEAD
You will not be able to dissuade Jill ______________________________ the wedding next week.

7 The food they served us was better than any I've ever eaten.
SECOND
The food we ______________________________ none.

8 I told Tim I would be happy to drive him to the station but he wanted to walk.
LIFT
I offered ______________________________ to the station but he wanted to walk.

Vocabulary

1 For each sentence, match one half of the sentence in BOX ONE (**1–9**) with the second half of the sentence in BOX TWO (**A–I**).

Example: 1–E

BOX ONE

1 He is unlikely to have such an extreme allergic reaction again
2 There's no limit to what my brother will do
3 Emma told us her father had terrified her
4 Leave him to his own devices;
5 He showed a great deal of interest in the project,
6 The lead singer rang up to say he'd got a blocked nose,
7 He tries not to lose his temper,
8 Sometimes I overhear some really strange conversations in the street,
9 It's a good thing to have a mind of your own

BOX TWO

A and wouldn't be able to perform that night.
B but I've known him get into terrible rages.
C and said he'd support it financially.
D with his sudden outbursts of temper.
E so long as he avoids any kind of contact with peanuts.
F and want to ask the people what they're talking about.
G to get his own way.
H so long as you can still get along in a team.
I he's happiest that way.

2 For each sentence, match one half of the sentence in BOX ONE **(1–9)** with the second half of the sentence in BOX TWO **(A–I)**.

Example: 1–D

BOX ONE

1 I was sent upstairs in disgrace,
2 Sally didn't have any medical complaints when she was young,
3 As a child she found it was better to be self-reliant
4 When Sonia Abigele won the marathon in record time,
5 Maggie is seething with anger over the terrible holiday she had,
6 She says she'll clean the car,
7 I'm absolutely furious about something,
8 After the garage repaired my car,
9 I get such swollen ankles in hot weather,

BOX TWO

A but I know she'll be too busy to get round to it today.
B and I had to ring you to let off steam.
C she put it down to her new training routine.
D and ate a solitary meal in my room.
E and intends to demand a full refund from the travel agency.
F but now she's always got something wrong with her.
G I have to wear sandals all the time.
H than to depend on other people for things.
I they put it through the car wash at no extra charge.

Writing CAE Paper 2

Part 2

Write an answer to **one** of the questions **2–4** in this part. Write your answer in **220–260** words in an appropriate style.

---

2 You write film reviews for your student newspaper. You have been to a film recently that was a box-office hit in your country. Write a review of the film, giving a brief synopsis of the story. Say whether you liked the film or not, and why, and include comments on the acting and the directing.

Write your **review**.

3 An English-language website has invited its readers to write an article entitled 'Technology – friend or enemy?' In your article you should comment on the effect of technology on people's daily lives, including the effect on two or more of the following: free time, health, work, relationships, education or sport.

Write your **article**.

4 A guidebook is being produced for young people visiting your country. You have been asked to write an entry about **either** coastal **or** lakeside resorts. You should recommend two or three resorts to visit, saying why they would appeal to young people.

Write your **contribution to the guidebook**.

Listening CAE Paper 4

Part 1 Multiple choice

You will hear three different extracts. For questions **1–6**, choose the answer (**A, B** or **C**) which fits best according to what you hear. There are two questions for each extract.

Extract One

You hear two people on a radio programme talking about a type of diet.

1 According to the man, following the diet means that you
A consume more raw food than cooked.
B eat only what Stone Age man ate.
C avoid large quantities of meat.

2 What did the man decide after trying the diet for a month?
A He would continue to follow the diet.
B It was not possible to give up certain foods forever.
C There had been no noticeable change to his waistline.

Extract Two

You hear part of an interview with an engineer called Angus Robson.

3 Angus built the trebuchet in order to
A break a long-standing record.
B gain publicity for his company.
C prove a point of scientific interest.

4 Angus says that children today are less interested in inventing because
A they are not encouraged to be creative.
B they are not taught physics well at school.
C they do not regard engineering as a rewarding career.

Extract Three

You hear part of an interview with Andrea Harris, a campaigner for green issues.

5 The purpose of the latest campaign is to
A reduce flights to particular tourist destinations.
B pressure airlines to use more fuel-efficient planes.
C fully inform people about air travel pollution.

6 What do Andrea and the interviewer agree about?
A There is little point in people deciding not to fly.
B There are greater sources of pollution than air travel.
C Tourists should not feel guilty about flying.

Progress test 4: Units 10–12

Reading CAE Paper 1

Part 1 Multiple choice

You are going to read three extracts which are all concerned in some way with the theme of learning from Nature. For questions **1–6,** choose the answer **(A B, C** or **D)** which you think fits best according to the text.

Make our website work for your project

With many thousands of regular local and overseas visitors a month, the New Zealand Trust for Conservation Volunteers website will connect you with many volunteers who will enjoy the experience of helping your project if they can get the information in a way that interests them. You are not limited in the information you can place on the website – and there is no charge. Where else do you get such an advertising opportunity? One of the better examples of project descriptions now on the site is that for the Shorebird Sanctuary Society. Look it up. If you have any problem, just email us, send us as much information as you wish, and we'll dress it up for publication so it looks really impressive.

The form we ask you to fill in is basic – bare facts. When you describe the attractive features of your project and the local environment, you will inspire volunteers to come to you, and take the trouble to ask for more details. Suitable photographs make a big difference! The scope and social benefits of participation are much increased if you also have a few interesting helpers who have come from other regions of New Zealand or from overseas. Make sure your information is revised at least every four weeks so that all details are currently accurate. This is essential as some volunteers plan trips six months ahead, while some make decisions for the next weekend.

1 One advantage of using the website is that
- **A** the organizers will improve your project presentation.
- **B** there is only a small fee for registration.
- **C** the volunteers it attracts tend to be skilled.
- **D** it has a section giving advice on setting up a project.

2 Project descriptions which are features on the website should
- **A** contain pictures of the project.
- **B** be as detailed as possible.
- **C** be updated on a monthly basis.
- **D** offer work to non-New Zealanders.

Extract from a travel supplement

We were halfway through dinner when the neighbour rang to tell us the cows had got out on to the road. Doug the farmer and I leapt into action; he went on the farm bike to head the cows off, while I held them at the other end. An engine's roar broke the silence with a crescendo of gears. Taking a chance, I stepped out in front of the oncoming vehicle, waving my arms for the driver to stop. The car screeched to a halt, its lights dazzling my eyes, and two dark figures jumped out and strode towards me, shouting incomprehensibly. I was frozen to the spot, the only movement being that of my thoughts which, in a split second, had invented escaped prisoners on a murderous rampage, and headlines to match. In another split second the two silhouetted figures revealed themselves as my fellow "wwoofers" from the Czech Republic, who had sped up in their car to help.

Wwoofers are volunteers on the WWOOF scheme (officially, World Wide Opportunities on Organic Farms, but still commonly known by its former name, Willing Workers on Organic Farms). For young – or not so young – environmentally-aware visitors on a budget, "wwoofing" is a great way to see the country. WWOOF is an international movement that connects volunteers with host farmers, in an exchange that benefits both. The wwoofers get a place to stay and learn about farming and growing; the hosts get a hand with the myriad jobs around their farms.

3 When the writer first saw the people getting out of the car, her main feeling was one of
- **A** relief.
- **B** fear.
- **C** failure.
- **D** embarrassment.

4 The writer suggests that volunteers on the WWOOF scheme
- **A** might feel misled about the purpose of the scheme.
- **B** often perform a greater range of tasks than they expect.
- **C** probably gain more from the scheme than the farmers.
- **D** are unlikely to have a lot of money to spend travelling.

Extract from a newspaper

The dozen jumping spiders in a laboratory at Canterbury University have just become high earners – to the tune of $730,000 in fact. That's how much money researcher Duane Harland has secured for research into the fly-sized creatures. But he is interested only in one part of the spider: its eyes, and how it assembles its view of the world. Obscure, you might think. What's the point? Valid question, says Dr Harland, 31. 'Why study spiders? Where is that going to get you? How is that going to get you a better job, or increase your wages by $2 an hour?' Dr Harland, an animal behaviour researcher, explains
13 it thus: "Most spiders have eight eyes but can't see well, relying on environmental cues like vibrations to make sense of their world. But two of the jumping spider's eight eyes can discern colour and shape. Also, despite its tiny brain, this variety is clever – solving problems and thinking ahead."

Dr Harland believes people can't always see that such apparently obscure research can bring great benefits; if New Zealand has an anti-intellectual streak, he says, it is because people can have difficulty ascribing worth to something that doesn't lead directly to financial gain. So let's speculate where spider vision research could go. It could eventually lead to the development of robots that use vision-directed decision-making. Those robots could then become part of, say, an unmanned, model-
29 sized helicopter, giving an invaluable advantage to rescuers when searching for people lost in the wilderness – its artificial vision capable of spotting human forms while avoiding obstacles.

5 *It* (line 13) refers to
- **A** the amount of money required for the research.
- **B** the particular kind of vision a spider has.
- **C** the reason for some people's scepticism.
- **D** the purpose of the spider research.

6 Which phrase is echoed by the writer's words 'an invaluable advantage'? (line 29)
- **A** apparently obscure research
- **B** bring great benefits
- **C** difficulty ascribing worth to something
- **D** lead directly to financial gain

Use of English CAE Paper 3

Part 2 Open cloze

For questions **1–15**, read the text below and think of the word which best fits each gap. Use only **one** word in each gap. There is an example at the beginning **(0)**.

BEACH HOUSE

With five children aged from 16 to 5, Kate Barton doesn't have too **(0)** *much* time on her hands – and **(1)** __________ she has, she doesn't like to waste. When she bought a beach house two years ago, **(2)** __________ entire transaction took her less than seven days, and the transformation **(3)** __________ what had been a dingy shack, into a bright and cheerful seaside retreat was completed in **(4)** __________ matter of weeks. 'I wanted a family escape for the school holidays **(5)** __________ we could reach easily from our flat in the town', she says, 'a place **(6)** __________ all the children to enjoy an outdoor life.'

A far cry from the traditional beach chalet, this intriguing house consists **(7)** __________ two old railway carriages, which house five small bedrooms. In the 1930s, a number of carriages had been brought down to the beach and given a new lease of life **(8)** __________ holiday homes. When Kate and her husband bought the house, it was decorated from top to toe **(9)** __________ a depressing shade of chocolate; so first of **(10)** __________ they painted the walls off-white to create a light, bright background.

'I had a picture in my mind of **(11)** __________ I wanted the house to look,' said Kate. 'But my main priority **(12)** __________ that we would be able to live in it **(13)** __________ worry, so I only chose materials that would be able to stand up to the rough seaside weather. And it **(14)** __________ to be somewhere we could feel on holiday.' **(15)** __________ the unconventional nature of this seaside home, Kate has indeed created a comfortable, homely escape for her large family.

Part 3 Word Formation

For questions **1–10**, read the text below. Use the word given in capitals at the end of some of the lines to form a word that fits in the gap **in the same line**. There is an example at the beginning **(0)**.

Where's the culture?

These days I do most of my travelling via the televison: for a start it's	
(0) *inexpensive*, it's far less harmful to the environment, and it also	**EXPENSE**
(1) __________ us to see places that would not appeal to our two under-fives.	**ABLE**
The **(2)** __________, unfortunately, is the kind of travelling companion we end	**SIDE**
up with. In Channel 2's new series 'Adventures', each programme is hosted by a	
different celebrity, **(3)** __________ because they are supposed to be 'interesting'.	**PRESUME**
I can honestly say that I felt nothing but **(4)** __________ for Jane Kinnear	**ADMIRE**
who provided viewers with some fascinating and **(5)** __________	**SUBSTANCE**
background information on Turkey and **(6)** __________ ate the almost-raw	**READY**
meat dishes her local hosts served up, despite being a vegetarian.	
Henry Moore, however, was quite willing to offend his guide by describing the	
local folk music as a really **(7)** __________ din. We then had to witness his	**BEAR**
(8) __________ of anger when the hotel electricity supply failed. What did he	**BURST**
expect the guide to do about it? A good travel programme host can	
(9) __________ the bonds between people of different cultures; a bad one just	**STRONG**
(10) __________ people.	**ALIEN**

Vocabulary

Decide which word fits the space in each sentence. You will not need to use all the words in each group.

upbringing progress nightmare tide setback opportunities charges suggestions arrests

1 The police chief declared war on the rising __________ of crime in the city.

2 She had a wealthy __________, which was no preparation for her hard life on the farm.

3 I advise you to deny all __________ until you have seen a lawyer.

4 Their plans suffered a __________ when they temporarily ran out of funds.

5 We're having an away-weekend for office staff in June, and I'd welcome __________ for good places to go.

6 Let's get a bus into town, rather than drive it's a __________ to park at this time of day.

grant make arrive write stretch involve catch acquire slam

7 My parents refused to __________ my one wish to go to drama school.

8 The fishing villages __________ along either side of the harbour.

9 When you __________ the door like that, the whole house shakes.

10 If you can't __________ neatly, copy your essay out on the computer.

11 I'm hoping to __________ sight of Emma at college today, so I can ask her to the party.

12 I'm sorry I didn't __________ it to your party but I felt too ill to go out.

deafening ready widely solidly constant strangely in-depth swiftly late

13 The house was nothing unusual, __________ built in stone, and painted white.

14 We jumped out of our skins at the sudden __________ noise of a gun going off nearby.

15 The documentary offers us a fascinating __________ look at the fast food industry.

16 The film got terrible reviews, but __________ enough, everyone I spoke to absolutely loved it.

17 When he was in hospital, he had a __________ stream of visitors.

18 She's not __________ read, but she has an extraordinary knowledge of music.

Listening CAE Paper 4

Part 2 Sentence completion

You will hear an author called Sandra Gray giving a talk to people who wish to become writers.

For questions **1–8**, complete the sentences.

WRITING AND PUBLISHING

Sandra Gray was commissioned by a magazine to write a [**1**].

Sandra attended a writing class that was run by an author of [**2**].

Sandra saw an advertisement for a competition with a little [**3**] as the prize.

It takes Sandra a lot of effort to do [**4**] for her novels.

Sandra's second novel was completed in less than [**5**] months.

The Power of Light is a novel set in [**6**].

Sandra says publishers like to receive letters with an unusual [**7**] from writers.

According to Sandra, writers should not hesitate to ask [**8**] for advice.

Writing CAE Paper 2

Part 1

Write your answer in **180–220** words in an appropriate style.

You recently worked as a group leader for a company called *Back to Nature*, supervising young teenagers on a conservation-awareness programme. Read the extract from the company's leaflet and the notes you have made on it below, and write to the director, giving feedback on the programme and proposing ways it could be improved.

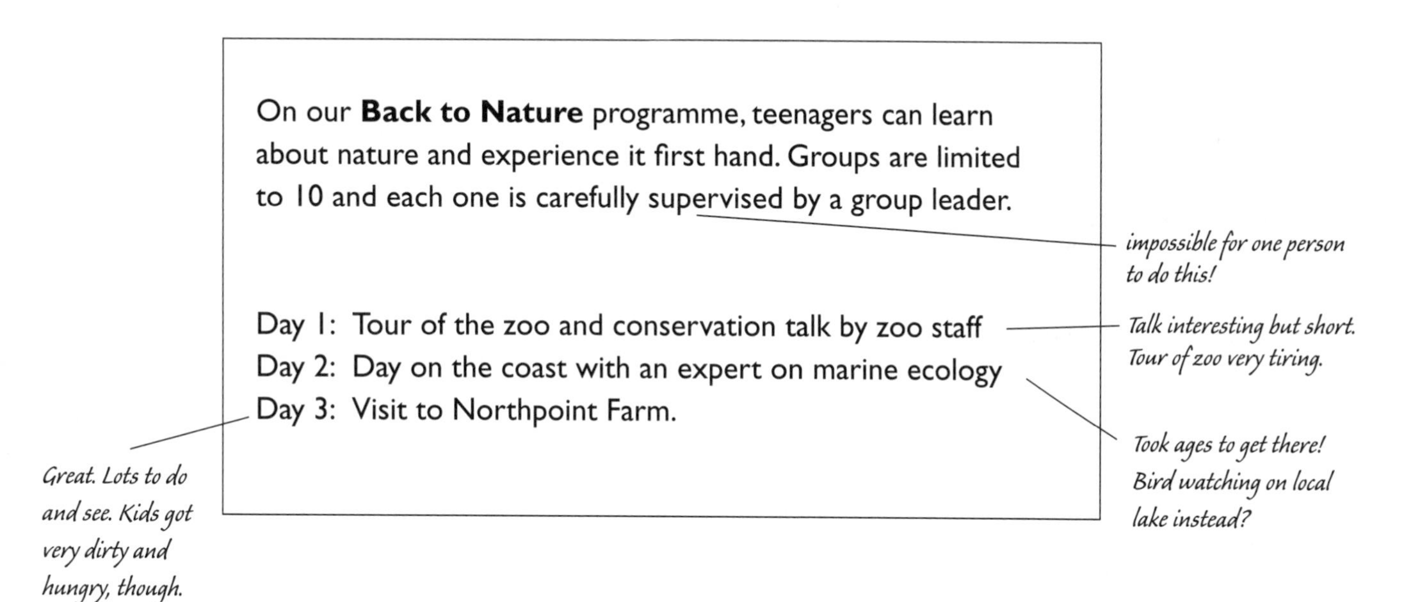

On our **Back to Nature** programme, teenagers can learn about nature and experience it first hand. Groups are limited to 10 and each one is carefully supervised by a group leader.

Day 1: Tour of the zoo and conservation talk by zoo staff
Day 2: Day on the coast with an expert on marine ecology
Day 3: Visit to Northpoint Farm.

impossible for one person to do this!
Talk interesting but short. Tour of zoo very tiring.
Took ages to get there! Bird watching on local lake instead?
Great. Lots to do and see. Kids got very dirty and hungry, though.

Write your **proposal**.

Progress test 5: Units 13, 14

Reading CAE Paper 1

Part 3 Multiple choice

You are going to read a newspaper article. For questions **1–7**, choose the answer (**A, B, C** or **D**) which you think fits best according to the text.

Fortune Hunter

A successful entrepreneur for many years, Barry Colman now helps others develop their business ideas

For Barry Colman, appearing on *Dragons' Den* – the reality TV show where would-be entrepreneurs present their inventions to experienced investors – was a reminder that the entrepreneurial spirit is alive and well in New Zealand. "I just don't know where all these ideas come from," Colman says, reflecting on his time as one of the five investors charged with evaluating the business proposals of entrepreneurs seeking finance and mentoring. "There was a stunning array of personalities," he says. He agreed to invest $725,000 of his own money in five businesses. While some of his fellow investors pulled out of similar agreements after conducting further research, Colman remains committed to four of his new ventures. "Everything takes a while and you've got to get the marketing right but I'm looking forward to great things from their proposals."

Colman's approach appeared to be to talk less than the other investors, often piping up near the end of a presentation with a surprise offer to invest. One of the series' more poignant moments was when he agreed to finance a clothesline system for people with disabilities, designed by accident victim Bernie Wadell. Wadell broke down when Colman agreed to invest $100,000 in his business. "I thought, 'There's a case of a guy who's got a product that is actually going to help a lot of people, and in doing that will return some good profits for all of us as well," says Colman. "I didn't expect him to burst into tears – it was almost as if his life's work was at stake."

Colman began his working life as a reporter in 1965 but eventually took the plunge into self-employment in 1977, launching a community newspaper. "It was really difficult for me because I enjoyed journalism, but it was quite clear you were never going to accumulate any wealth that way," he says. "I deliberately tried to find a business in which I would be significantly better off. The newspaper publishing business looked good at that point but I admit I was rather ignorant about newspapers and advertising. Previously I'd only ever been on the editorial side and I found out after the first four days that I had to turn to being the chief salesman as opposed to the editor. That was the first shock," he recalls. "The sales force we hired wasn't up to the job, and so I went to the library, read a book on selling, and away I went. We launched on time and on budget, but it was a steep learning curve!"

That first community paper grew into a collection of 30 titles with a combined circulation of a million issues a week. Colman says the key to his success relates to setting firm financial targets before embarking on a new venture. "Any entrepreneur has got to work out what their financial goal is in very specific numbers, not just round figures like 'I want to make a million dollars.' If I hear that at the end of someone's presentation, I know it's not going to work because it's obviously such a rounded number. They've got to work out exactly what it is they want financially and when they want it by," he says. "There are so many things to consider – production costs, staff and wages, marketing expenses – all of which need to be worked out before making your presentation."

"Creating wealth is really a mental process more than anything else. The three per cent of people who really make it in this world are not distracted from their goals," Colman insists. "Entrepreneurs starting out will come across numerous obstacles and they can count on everything going wrong because it nearly always does. But in the long term it doesn't matter." He says there is a myth that entrepreneurs need to be driven by a positive mental attitude. "You've got to have a good negative attitude in order to overcome everything that goes against you. If you have a negative expectancy, it's a very good part of your self-defence system because it simply means nothing is going to hold you back."

Colman says another key lesson for entrepreneurs is that the path to success is never straightforward. "If someone is adamant that the strategy they're following is the only way of achieving their goal, then they often don't succeed. But if you've got your mind on a particular goal, and you're prepared to be open and take alternative routes in order to get where you want to go, your chances are favourable." He says the best entrepreneurial ideas are, almost without exception, those that break new ground. "It's that old rule that you get paid a fee for service but you make a profit from innovation. You've got to provide something unique unless you want to end up with the same profit margin that conventional services get."

Not all Colman's ventures have been successful, however. His retail chain *Pack & Pedal* closed down in 2005. He says one of the secrets to surviving in business is knowing when to abandon a project, a move which may be emotionally hard to make. "We've had quite a number of projects that were almost at the point of launching but we turned back," he says. "Once you've made that decision, you free up all this energy that you and your people have to then go on to another project because there is never any shortage of those."

1 What did Barry Colman find particularly surprising during his participation on *Dragon's Den*?

A The attitude of the other investors.
B The ability to think of new ideas and inventions.
C The amount of time inventors spent on their work.
D The lack of business experience amongst the inventors.

2 Bernie Wadell is used as an example to demonstrate

A what kind of product is worth investing in.
B that Colman will finance projects most investors would reject.
C how people tend to react to Colman's offer to invest.
D the amount of money usually needed to finance a new project.

3 Colman's main reason for giving up journalism was that he was seeking greater

A authority.
B variety.
C financial reward.
D challenges.

4 In Colman's opinion, potential entrepreneurs say that they want $1million when

A they are overly-confident about their idea.
B they want to prove to Colman that they are ambitious.
C they are unrealistic about their own business skills.
D they have not put enough thought into their business plan.

5 What does Colman recommend about the attitude of entrepreneurs in paragraph 5?

A They must be willing to give up on a first project if necessary.
B They should be able to predict what can go wrong.
C They have to accept responsibility for mistakes they have made.
D They cannot allow anything to prevent them achieving their aims.

6 What advice does Colman give entrepreneurs in paragraph 6?

A Their idea must be one that no one else has thought of.
B They must come up with a plan and stick to it.
C Their product should make an immediate profit.
D They have to accept the input of others they work with.

7 In the final paragraph, Barry Colman concludes that

A employing the wrong people can take up all your energy.
B becoming emotionally involved in business is a bad idea.
C recognizing when a project is likely to fail is essential.
D making a loss in business is sometimes unavoidable.

Use of English CAE Paper 3

Part 3 Word formation

For questions **1–10**, read the text below. Use the word given in capitals at the end of some of the lines to form a word that fits in the gap **in the same line**. There is an example at the beginning **(0)**.

A Meal Out

I have never had a problem with **(0)** *loss* of appetite.	**LOSE**
I can eat anything, even the fatty, **(1)** __________ food they served	**TASTE**
up in my college canteen. Now I try to eat **(2)** __________, but	**HEALTH**
basically, I'll wolf down whatever is put on my plate. There has	
only ever been one **(3)** __________ and this was when I went to a meal	**EXCEPT**
in a restaurant run by a famous chef. I was one of about forty	
(4) __________ at this gala occasion. The first dish looked delicious,	**DINE**
but its taste was quite different from its **(5)** __________ – it was	**APPEAR**
disgusting. I managed two **(6)** __________, then gave up. The main	**MOUTH**
course was equally **(7)** __________, with succulent-looking lamb chops	**DECEIVE**
that turned out to be inedible. The dessert looked **(8)** __________ and	**PROMISE**
smelt good, but by now I **(9)** __________ everything that was put in front	**TRUST**
of me. I left feeling that 'fine-dining' was completely **(10)** __________,	**RATE**
and headed for the nearest pizza place.	

Part 4 Gapped Sentences

For questions **1–5** think of **one** word only which can be used appropriately in all three sentences. Here is an example **(0)**.

0 People in our office tend to *go* out for a drink most Fridays.
Do you think this blouse will *go* with my new skirt?
Maria can *go* on talking about her health problems for hours!

1 My car's being repaired so could you possibly __________ me up tomorrow?
I did not have much of an appetite and could only __________ at my dinner.
He doesn't usually __________ the team until an hour or so before the game.

2 Pacific and Australasian history __________ outside my area of expertise, so ask Professor Moore instead.
It's easy to __________ for a trick when the other person seems genuinely kind.
We watched the rocks __________ before they crashed into the river.

3 We'll __________ what happens with the weather before making plans.
Jenny didn't __________ through Martin's false promises until it was too late.
I'm sorry but I don't think we should __________ each other anymore.

4 I admit that I found the film __________ to understand in places.
The government is encouraging people to save __________ for the future.
The desert has a dry, __________ surface which can sustain little life.

5 We need to __________ out a way to reduce costs without firing anyone.
I usually __________ up a big appetite after patrolling the streets all day.
This video game doesn't __________ the way it's supposed to.

Vocabulary

Decide which word fits the space in each sentence.

---

1 Would you like a soft __________ with your meal, or something stronger?
A food **B** menu **C** drink **D** dish

2 My mother is in her eighties, and she's not a big __________ these days.
A eater **B** stomach **C** hunger **D** appetite

3 She's a smooth talker; she can __________ most people with her charm.
A take for **B** take in **C** see through **D** fall for

4 I don't think he's dishonest - he's never told me a __________ as far as I know.
A deception **B** swindle **C** trick **D** lie

5 After finishing the marathon, Dave just wanted to __________ his thirst with a cold drink.
A soak **B** fulfill **C** extinguish **D** quench

6 There isn't a scrap of __________ to support his accusations.
A evidence **B** progress **C** criteria **D** advice

7 I'm going to the Saturday market, to see if I can __________ up a few bargains.
A cut **B** make **C** pick **D** offer

8 The village they live in is __________ enough, but I'd find it a bit boring after a while.
A satisfied **B** contented **C** winning **D** pleasant

9 Why don't you go for a swim and __________ up an appetite for lunch?
A pick **B** work **C** lose **D** heat

10 She was absolutely __________ when the children came home covered in mud.
A dirty **B** furious **C** tired **D** frightened

11 He was ordered to pay the fine in __________ within 60 days.
A full **B** complete **C** total **D** all

12 It was only a two-star hotel, but it seemed the __________ of luxury to James.
A peak **B** summit **C** height **D** top

13 This beach is nowhere __________ as good as the one we went to yesterday.
A close **B** much **C** half **D** near

14 He was obviously not __________ aware of the dangers of going up into the mountains alone.
A utterly **B** highly **C** fully **D** fairly

15 Her earnings were low that month and she was not able to spend quite as __________ as she would have liked.
A loosely **B** freely **C** openly **D** greatly

Writing CAE Paper 2

Part 2

Write an answer to **one** of the questions **2–5** in this part. Write your answers in **220–260** words in an apropriate style.

---

2 There is going to be an exhibition in London called 'Food Around the World'. Your country is going to contribute to the exhibition and you have been asked to write a proposal for the display. You should include information about different aspects of food in your country:

- Typical everyday dishes
- Food and drink for celebrations
- Shopping for food.

In your proposal, include ideas on how to present this information in the display.

Write your **proposal**.

3 Your college is producing an orientation pack for new students, and you have been asked to write an information sheet on sport and fitness facilities in and near the college.

You should mention the following points:

- the facilities available
- their location in relation to the college
- information about membership eg cost, conditions etc.

Write your **information sheet**.

4 Your best friend is at college, and he has written to you saying that he is getting into money difficulties, and he is not sure if he will have enough money to last for the rest of the course. Write back to him suggesting ways he can solve his problem, and advising him on how to manage his money.

Write your **letter**.

5 Answer **one** of the following two questions.

(a) Your teacher has asked you to write an essay about the importance of the beginning of a story. Briefly describe what happens at the beginning of the set book you have read and discuss how important it is to the development of the rest of the story.

Write your **essay**.

(b) A literary magazine has recently featured a series on characters in popular fiction and has invited readers to send in an article about a minor character that they know well. You decide to write an article, describing a minor character in the set book you have read and explaining the part he or she plays in the development of the story.

Write your **article**.

Listening CAE Paper 4

Part 3 Multiple choice

You will hear part of an interview in which television producer, Carrie Beale, is talking about a crime series called 'Nice Work'.

For questions **1–6**, choose the correct answer (**A**, **B**, **C** or **D**) which fits best according to what you hear.

---

1 Why did Carrie Beale decide to make a crime series about fraud?

A She was bored with making programmes about violence.
B She had always wanted to base a series on old crime films.
C She thought it was a formula that would help her regain popularity.
D She wanted to do something different from other crime programmes.

2 What does Carrie say about the gang?

A They will not get caught because they are very creative.
B They are innocent because they only cheat greedy people.
C They are involved in activities that cannot be excused.
D They will pay for their crimes before the end of the series.

3 The deceptions require careful planning because

A there is a great deal of travelling involved.
B the gang has to employ other criminals as assistants.
C the whole operation has to be carried out very quickly.
D it is necessary to create an appropriate setting for the crime.

4 What does Carrie mean by 'the psychology of greed'?

A Greed can lead people to criminal acts.
B People can be blinded to reality by their greed.
C Greedy people believe that money can solve all problems.
D Greed is the weakness that is most easy for criminals to exploit.

5 Carrie agrees that the gang is cruel because

A they deprive their victims of their self-respect.
B they laugh at their victims for being so stupid.
C they use their victims to fund an extravagant lifestyle.
D they want to have excitement at their victims' expense.

6 What does Carrie say about television audiences?

A They like programmes that give them a challenge.
B They tend to be critical of new programmes initially.
C They expect a greater variety of programmes than in the past.
D They are knowledgeable about techniques for producing programmes.

Final Test

PAPER 1 READING

Part 1

You are going to read three extracts from different sources. For questions **1–6**, choose the answer (**A, B, C** or **D**) which you think fits best according to the text.

Colleges Documentary Competition

This is the tenth anniversary of the Colleges Documentary Competition and the theme this year is 'Days Gone By'.

Entry Requirements and Rules

As with a 'real' documentary, students are expected to work as part of a team. A minimum of five people per group is acceptable, and there is no limit to the number of teams per college wishing to participate. Students who have submitted work to the competition in previous years are welcome to take part again, whether they were successful or not. Once a team has brainstormed the content and focus of their documentary, they are expected to prepare a proposal to accompany the film, both of which should be complete on submission. The winning team will get to see their documentary turned into a 40-minute programme to be screened on Channel Three.

College documentaries are to be set in the local area and may cover the history of the town any time from its origins to the end of the twentieth century, or even just a single year. Whether a team chooses to involve the local people – perhaps by recording conversations or by borrowing diaries and photo albums – or bases their film purely on academic research, what the organizers are really looking for is an insight into life as it truly was for people. Successful teams in the past have investigated single themes such as work or childhood experiences, rather than overcrowd their documentary with many influences. Finally, the emphasis in a documentary should be on the story, and this takes priority over special effects and clever editing with the camera.

1 In order to enter the competition, students must
- **A** finish the whole documentary.
- **B** wait for their proposal to be approved.
- **C** be first-time film makers.
- **D** be the winners over other groups in their college.

2 When making their documentary students are advised to
- **A** interview people from a variety of backgrounds.
- **B** focus their attention on a limited period of time.
- **C** be as creative as possible with their camera work.
- **D** concentrate on a specific aspect of local life.

Extract from a newspaper article

Recent research suggests that our memories are hardly as perfect as one might think. Studies show that memory after a day is a near accurate record of events, but that after a week all that remains are general details. Recollections of when and where an event occurred, or who said what, tend to be especially transient, says memory expert Daniel L Schacter in his book *The Seven Sins of Memory*. "With the passing of time, the particulars fade and opportunities multiply for interference – generated by later, similar experiences – to blur our recollections. We thus rely more on our memories for the gist of what happened, or what usually happens, and attempt to reconstruct the details by inference and sheer guesswork."

Because transience and some other memory problems increase with age, people in late middle age are starting to worry that those moments of absent-mindedness are the first signs of Alzheimer's disease, a condition affecting the memory that is rarely diagnosed before age 75. It doesn't help that there are plenty of entrepreneurs keen to exploit
23 that anxiety with herbal remedies and dietary supplements to boost mental performance.

3 What do we learn about memory in the first paragraph?
- **A** People deliberately choose to forget certain events.
- **B** People have clearer memories of conversations than events.
- **C** People invent details in order to complete a distant memory.
- **D** People may recall the same event differently from one another.

4 The writer mentions two treatments in line (23) in order to emphasize
- **A** the fear that many people have of memory loss.
- **B** the fact that not all instances of memory loss are serious.
- **C** the realization that Alzheimer's disease doesn't just affect the elderly.
- **D** the effectiveness of alternative medicine in treating memory problems.

Extract from a non-fiction book

People develop emotional bonds with sweets that date back to their earliest memories of childhood, locality and the family home. Sweets are the memorials of our innocence. They remind us of the time when the world could be measured out in sweet little objects of desire. Particular brands can conjure up memories of specific moments of childhood in a way that nothing else can. It is a truism that smell is the sense most intimately connected with memory, but perhaps sweets are the objects connected most closely with our childhoods. The extraordinary brand loyalty of confectionery customers over decades and, in many cases, lifetimes, is commercial testimony to this resonant quality.

With sweets, the distinction between adulthood and childhood is blurred. We joyfully regress when offered a sweet – just for a moment your boss can look like a five-year-old. Sweets are one of the best conduits of communication between grown-ups and children – we all like them, and we all know what is good about them. Sharing sweets, a grandfather and a grandson can be united in olfactory heaven on earth, a quality exploited by advertisers. There is also a sense that some sweets have been around so long they are immortal, and that quality can be conferred on us; the world is alright if your favourite sweet tastes the same now, at the age of ninety, as it did when you were five.

5 In the first paragraph, the writer suggests that people
- **A** remember the taste more than the smell of sweets.
- **B** tend to exaggerate the pleasure they got from sweets as children.
- **C** continue to appreciate sweets they first encountered as children.
- **D** think that old-fashioned sweets are superior to modern ones.

6 What are we told about the effect of sweets in the second paragraph?
- **A** They may improve relationships at work.
- **B** They allow people to share a similar experience.
- **C** They can make people feel more aware of their age.
- **D** They can cause people to misjudge one another.

Part 2

You are going to read an extract from a magazine article. Six paragraphs have been removed from the extract. Choose from paragraphs **A–G** the one which fits each gap (**7–12**). There is one extra paragraph which you do not need to use.

HONEY

The bee-keepers of a village in the African country of Zambia are getting a fair deal for their produce, thanks to the help of a world-wide organization. Ben de Pear reports.

It is very early in the morning as Chingangu Chimwanga emerges from his house with his two wives, Catherine and Josephine. Over Chingangu's shoulder is an axe and a mesh hood. Catherine is carrying a large coil of rope, while Josephine carries a large, lidded plastic bucket. It's 4.45am and the Chimwanga family, champion bee-keepers of Samasati village in North-West Zambia, are ready to do what they do best. They're going to harvest honey.

7 ______

This is because their honey is now sold in Europe under the umbrella of a worldwide movement that guarantees prices for farm products, so that suppliers like the Chimwangas are not at the mercy of global price fluctuations. Small farmers have always been vulnerable to such market forces. Commodity values can swing so wildly that sometimes producers receive less for their crops than it costs to produce them. Being part of a fair-trade scheme means that the farmers aren't exploited, because they receive a fair price which gives them the freedom to plan ahead for the next year.

8 ______

In spite of this, life is not easy. Sixty miles from a source of electricity, the 300 inhabitants make their living from forest and rivers, and the only income available to villagers is from selling their honey. Chingangu Chimwanga is the wealthiest farmer in the community. He owns a small house and can afford to send his children to school. His prosperity comes from the 255 beehives he owns, and the one we are heading towards is a half-hour walk from the village.

9 ______

The effect of this is two-fold. As well as slowing the bees down, the smoke from the burning leaves forces them to take action to protect their crop. When the bees smell smoke their instinct tells them the hive is on fire and they take on board as much honey as they can – and this disables them from attacking predators. In order to sting, the bee needs to bend its body into the correct position, and with such a swollen abdomen this is difficult.

10 ______

We tuck into it with glee. It is the most delicious honey I have ever tasted, less sweet but more fragrant – as a result of the hundreds of wildflowers the bees feast on in the forest – than the honey I buy in the supermarket back home.

11 ______

He is a popular visitor to the village, and is passionate about Zambian honey. 'Its quality is greatly appreciated by our customers,' he says. 'We buy from thousands of bee-keepers, and the revenue is vitally important to this region. The farmers take care of the environment because they know that if the forest is damaged, their source of income will be gone. I believe honey is Zambia's future.'

12 ______

I was sad to leave Samasati that evening. Back in the city I thought of the pristine environment I had so recently left, and of the beautiful golden honey, as sweet and pure now as it was centuries ago.

A Catherine explains this to me while we wait below. We can see the bees circling round Chingangu's head, and their low, unrelenting hum. Undeterred, Chingangu pulls up the bucket and fills it with the precious honeycomb, first dropping a large chunk down to us.

B After this the lids are removed and a sample is taken from each bucket, to check its purity. Then the buckets are weighed, and the owners paid. Today is Sunday, and after receiving their money the men go off to spend the rest of the day with their families.

C Armed with their few tools, they head to the forest interior, where their hives are placed 10 metres or more up in the branches of the trees. It seems a hazardous way to make a livelihood, but for as long as anyone can remember, people here have kept bees. And now, at last, things seem to be taking a turn for the better.

D And the knock-on effect is that once the farmers are released from the day-to-day worry of subsistence, and can think in terms of future development, there is a real incentive to farm in sustainable ways. And Samasati is a beautiful place, an environmental idyll where nature is a bountiful provider and pollution is non-existent.

E Bob Malichi likes it too. He is the CEO for the North-West Bee Products (NWBP), and the vital middle man for the bee-keepers. His organization buys the honey from the farmers, takes it to a factory where it is put in barrels, and transports it to Europe.

F I wonder whether the villagers agree with this, so I ask them if they think that honey is the key to the country's prosperity. 'Yes,' they say. 'Honey is always there. If we look after the bees, they'll produce for us. Our honey is unique because it's organically produced and comes straight from the forest.'

G As soon as we arrive, Catherine and Josephine start stripping trees of their low, leaf-covered branches. These are placed in a pile and tied into a bundle with some dried grass in the middle. It is set alight, and Chingangu climbs up the tree trunk. Hanging from his waist on the end of a long piece of twine is the smouldering bundle, which Chingangu pulls up and places near the hive's entrance.

Part 3

You are going to read a magazine article. For questions **13–19**, choose the answer (**A, B, C** or **D**) which you think fits best according to the text.

Mind Reading

Whether we know it or not, we all practise the skill of guessing people's thoughts and feelings.

If a baby starts to cry several hours after drinking his last bottle, his mother knows he's hungry. But suppose a woman's eyes brim with tears while she watches a DVD. Her husband wonders what she is so upset about. She might tell him directly: "This movie is all about a doomed romance." That may be true but she could be thinking about how the story reminds her of her own marital troubles. Maybe she's feeling hurt because she thinks her husband should realize what's bothering her. Or maybe she isn't even aware that her real-world concerns are intensifying her reaction to the fictional couple. Quickly he searches his mental files – on his wife's relationship history, on her reaction to their last row, on the way she reacts to similar movies. He watches the expressions flickering across her face and it finally it hits him: she knows about his girlfriend!

Every day, whether we're pushing for a raise or judging whether a friend really likes our redecorating spree, we're reading each other's minds. Drawing on our observations, our memories, our powers of reason, and our wellsprings of emotion, we constantly make educated guesses about what another person is feeling. Throughout the most heated argument or the most lighthearted chat, we're intently collecting clues to what's on the other person's mind. "It's a perceptual ability I call mindsight," says Daniel Siegel, psychiatrist at UCLA. Mind reading of this sort – not to be confused with the infallible superhero kind of telepathy – is a critical human skill. It enables us to negotiate, compete, co-operate, and achieve emotional closeness with others. Mind-reading ability is perhaps the most urgent element of social intelligence.

It's astonishing that we can peer into each other's minds at all, but in truth we generally don't do it all that well. Strangers (who are videotaped and later report their thoughts and feelings, as well as their assessments of their counterpart's thoughts and feelings) read each other with an average accuracy rate of 20 per cent. Close friends and married couples nudge that up to 35 per cent. And "hardly anyone ever scores higher than 60 per cent," reports psychologist William Ickes, the father of empathic accuracy, who is based at the University of Texas at Arlington. Ickes is eager to shoot down one of the oldest myths about mind reading – that women have some intuitive advantage. He explains why the gender stereotype persists. "It may be not an ability gap, but an incentive gap." Support for such an interpretation comes from a study in which researchers offered cash bonuses to participants for accurately reading others' minds. The payments "wiped out any difference between men's and women's performances," suggesting that men can read minds when they want to.

Our ability to mind read has ancient roots, says Ross Buck, a professor of communication sciences at the University of Connecticut. Over thousands of years of evolution, human systems of communication grew more sophisticated, as living and working arrangements became more complex. Mind reading became a tool with which to "create and maintain the social order," as Buck puts it. It helped to know when to affirm a commitment to a mate or defuse a dispute with a neighbour. Of course, in order to advance our own interests, we still needed to conceal feelings at times, and even to lie. "We didn't always want to show exactly what we were thinking, because others could use that to gain the upper hand," says Buck. Our merely adequate mindsight, then, can be thought of "as the product of a compromise between the need to show and the need to hide our true selves."

This delicate balance between perceiving and concealing has served humans well, but Siegel worries that mind-reading ability is now on the decline in our culture. Today's obsessed-with-success parents spend so much time stimulating their children with structured activities, noisy toys, and 'Baby Einstein' DVDs, they are not sitting still and being "present" with their kids. As a result, they deny children the opportunity to learn how to get in tune with another person, physically and emotionally – that is, to develop mindsight. A reasonable degree of mindsight is required, he says, for a civil society in which adults are kind to one another.

Reading body language is a core component of mind reading. Researchers have shown that when watching a body's movements reduced to points of light on a screen, observers can still read sadness, anger, joy, fear and romantic love. After so many years of mind-reading evolution, we're primed to read emotion into movement, even when there's very little to go on. Facial expressions are also cues. Despite the 3,000 different expressions we may deploy each day, it's the fleeting micro-expressions that betray many feelings. Unfortunately, the vast majority of us are terrible at detecting them. Still, we tend to focus on others' eyes, and that helps us. The many surrounding muscles make them a richer source of clues than other parts of the face: downcast in sadness, staring hard with jealousy, or glancing around with impatience. We know even more about someone's mind from the way the components of conversation fit together – someone's words, gestures, and pitch of voice may seem either compatible or incongruous. But despite all we glean from body language and voice tone, Ickes finds, it's the content of speech that contributes most to our success at mind reading. Words matter.

Part 3

13 What point is exemplified by the description of the husband and wife's behaviour while watching the DVD?

A Women are more emotional than men.

B Adults have more complex needs than children.

C People can easily misinterpret each other's feelings.

D Relationships require honesty to be successful.

14 What do we learn about the way that mindsight works in the second paragraph?

A People are often unaware that they are reading another person's mind.

B People use both an intellectual process and an emotional one to read minds.

C People make greater efforts to mind read in formal situations than in informal ones.

D People often believe that their ability to read minds is a supernatural one.

15 What does William Ickes suggest about people's ability to read minds?

A It decreases under the stress of test conditions.

B It works well in long-established relationships.

C It is something which is predetermined by gender.

D It is affected by an individual's motivation.

16 Which of the following best summarizes Ross Buck's theory about mind reading?

A The ability to mind read probably developed before speech.

B Communities could function effectively because of mind reading.

C Mind reading is a form of dishonesty which is unique to humans.

D Good mind readers tend to reveal little about themselves.

17 According to Daniel Siegel, people are losing their ability to read minds because modern parents

A fail to interact effectively with their children.

B do not spend enough time with their children.

C expect greater academic achievement from their children.

D are often too stressed to be positive role models.

18 What are we told about the influence of visual information on our ability to read minds?

A People are instinctively able to interpret the meaning of gestures.

B Some people have difficulty interpreting the full range of human expression.

C Eye movement is the most significant source of information for mind reading.

D It is harder for a person to fake their body language than the tone of their voice.

19 In these paragraphs, the writer is

A demonstrating ways to improve our mind-reading ability.

B suggesting when mind reading is most valuable.

C explaining how the ability to read someone's mind works.

D expressing doubt about people's claims to be good mind readers.

Part 4

You are going to read an article about the work of four modern authors. For questions **20–34**, choose from the authors (**A–D**). The authors may be chosen more than once.

Which author

describes novel-writing as the weaving of a complicated design?	20	
organizes a regular routine for creative writing?	21	
mentions the importance of creating characters that people can relate to?	22	
has different professional activities related to one type of literature?	23	
writes historical novels with an urban setting?	24	
had the courage that was needed to give up a regular job?	25	
writes novels for two distinct categories of reader?	26	
believes in writers having an unbiased assessment of their work?	27	
finds time to write in spite of domestic distractions?	28	
earns money entirely from writing fiction?	29	
believes that many subjects of novels are suitable for everyone?	30	
disapproves of continuing a story into a second book?	31	
has recently published a book on an aspect of literature?	32	
found new opportunities for a writing career after relocating?	33	
got inspiration for writing from watching colleagues at work?	34	

Part 4

We invited four authors to tell us about their work, and the other jobs they do.

A Jeannie Johnson

Jeannie Johnson writes novels about places – their past, and the people who live in them. 'It's important to have a feel for the place if you're going to write a regional saga', she says. 'Your readers need to be able to taste the city you're writing about.' The city that Jeannie writes about is Bristol, and her first novel, *The Rest of our Lives*, was published in 2002. The book was about men coming home from the war, written from the viewpoint of the women waiting for them. Now Jeannie has written a sequel called *A Penny for Tomorrow*. 'A sequel obviously relates back to the previous book, but it also needs to stand alone. I've read some sequels which have been pretty terrible because at least three chapters of the sequel seemed to belong more properly with the previous book.' She likes plenty of things happening in her books, and plenty of characters with complicated relationships. 'To me, writing is like knitting, using a whole mix of varied colours, but needing to end up with a pattern.' Apart from writing, Jeannie has a career as an actress, with walk-on parts in television dramas. 'It gets me out of the house and mixing with other people, which writing can't do. And I learn from the actors, how they identify with their characters – it's what a writer needs to do.'

B Michael Schmidt

Michael Schmidt sees creative writing as one of four jobs he does. He is also director of a publishing house, a university teacher, and an editor of a literary magazine. The common factor across these roles is that they are all concerned with poetry. 'Most writers have another job,' Michael says. 'And that can make it difficult to fit in time for their writing. I handle this problem by starting my writing day at 4.30 or five o'clock in the morning, and writing through to eight. Then in the evening, I'll get home around 6pm, and after watching television, will probably put in a couple of hours in the evening.' It is a demanding but productive schedule and has seen Michael successfully put together several collections and anthologies. His latest published book is volume two of *The Story of Poetry*. This book is divided into two parts: part one is what he calls 'a mixture of biography and literary criticism – a mix that makes it interesting for the general reader,' whilst part two is an anthology of the poets discussed in the first part. Interestingly, he does not publish his work at his own publishing house, because he feels it would not be handled with the objectivity that is essential for writers.

C Susan Poole

Thirty years ago, American writer Susan Poole left behind the bright lights of New York City to start a new writing life in Ireland. 'My move to Ireland has proved to be one of the happiest developments in my life,' she said. 'On my first trip here I stepped off the plane into chilly, lashing rain and knew I was home. Living here has made possible a lifestyle I'd always yearned for, and words come so quickly I can hardly get them down on paper.' In a lucky break, Susan was given a commission by a travel publishers which led to a stint of travelling and multiple guide books, as well as contributions to magazines and newspapers. 'Somehow I found the nerve to chuck the security of a steady job and strike out on the rocky freelance road, and I've never looked back,' she said. She wrote her first novel *The Town* whilst travelling for the guide books. 'It was such a relief to unwind in the evening and work on my own stuff,' she said. At nearly eighty Susan has plenty of other commitments: 'Life conspires against you when you're trying to write. I'm a busy wife, mother, grandmother and great-grandmother. But I manage somehow'.

D Adèle Geras

Adèle Geras gave up teaching in order to raise her family, and took up writing for children when she won a competition for a children's story in a magazine. Now she is fully employed as an author, writing both for children and adults. Her latest novel for young readers is *Troy*, about young people in Troy during the Trojan War, and her new adult novel is *Facing the Light*. Asked how she manages to write the two types of book, Adèle argues that there is surprisingly little difference between them. 'Once a young reader is aged over ten or eleven, the fiction they read is similar in many ways to the fiction that adults read.' However, she does identify two differences – the length of the book and age of the characters. 'Children's novels obviously have to be shorter, but I believe that children are now reading longer and longer books. My new novel, for example, is 87,000 words – not adult-novel length – but substantial enough. Then, you need to give your readers a main character who is much the same age as them, someone they will identify with.' Apart from these differences, Adèle maintains that the big themes like love, loss, anger, jealousy, sorrow make equally good material for children's or adults' books.

PAPER 2 WRITING

Part 1

1 Write your answer in **180–220** words in an appropriate style.

Your college has received funding from the Council to build a new arts and leisure centre for your students.

Read the memo from your Principal and your survey notes below, and write a letter to the Education Officer of the Council, expressing appreciation for the funding, and putting forward the students' suggestions.

MEMO

To: Student Representative

From: Principal

Re: New Arts and Leisure Centre

The Council wishes these facilities to be included in the plans:

- a hall with a stage and seating for theatre productions
- a library
- an exhibition space for art

Please ask the students for suggestions for the Centre, then write to the Council's Education Officer with the survey results. You should invite him to meet the student committee for discussions.

Students' Survey: suggestions for Centre

Hall – need standing room for concerts
Library – we've already got the main library. Quiet reading room instead?
Exhibition space – why not use the hall?

Plus:
Internet café – a must

Now write your **letter**. You do not need to include postal addresses.

Part 2

Write an answer to one of the questions **2–5** in this part. Write your answers in **220–260** words in an appropriate style.

---

2 An environmental magazine, *World Environment*, has asked its readers to submit articles about the problems caused by the energy needs of modern society. In your article you should:

- mention some of the problems which your country faces
- say what people are doing to solve these problems
- suggest what will happen in the future regarding the use of energy in your country.

Write your **article**.

3 There will be a festival of sport in your town next year, and your college hopes to be chosen as one of the venues for the festival. You have been asked to write a proposal which will be sent to the festival organizers, saying why your college would be suitable. You should include information on sports facilities, accommodation and catering facilities, and transport.

Write your **proposal**.

4 You see the following announcement in an international magazine.

> **Channel 6 / New travel series**
>
> 'Presenters Wanted' Competition
>
> Channel 6 is looking for local presenters to help us host a travel programme in their country. To enter the competition, all you need to do is:
>
> • *explain why you would make a good presenter*
>
> • *say what things you would include on the travel programme*
>
> • *say why these things would make the travel programme worth watching.*
>
> The six best entries will be called for an audition in January.

Write your **competition entry**.

5 Answer **one** of the following two questions.

(a) Your teacher has asked you to write an essay giving your opinions on the following statement:

Readers tend to prefer novels in which they can identify with the main character.

Write an essay explaining your views with reference to the set book you have read.

Write your **essay**.

(b) A literary magazine is running a series on the role of key relationships in a novel and has asked readers to send in articles on the topic. You decide to send in an article describing the relationship that the main character has with another character in the set book you have read, and saying what this relationship reveals about the main character's personality.

Write your **article**.

PAPER 3 USE OF ENGLISH

Part 1

For questions **1–12** read the text below and decide which answer (**A, B, C** or **D**) best fits each gap. There is an example at the beginning **(0)**.

Viking warship sails to Ireland

The Vikings are coming but this time it's in **(0)** __________ of scientific knowledge rather than conquest. For the first time in almost 1,000 years, a Viking warship **(1)** __________ sail yesterday from Denmark on a non-stop **(2)** __________ across the North Sea to Ireland. The new Sea Stallion of Glendalough is an accurate **(3)** __________ of an original 30-metre-long warship that was sunk in the 11th century, and which was first **(4)** __________ by Danish archaeologists 50 years ago. Although the **(5)** __________ boat has a GPS navigation system and radar, it was built with Viking-era tools using oak and iron rivets. This is because the 1,200-mile voyage is being **(6)** __________ as a unique large-scale archaeological experiment. "We want to discover how Viking maritime technology worked in **(7)** __________," said Preben Sorensen of the Viking Ship Museum in Roskilde which is spearheading the project. "For example, how well the structure of the vessel **(8)** __________ to the movement of the sea." So there will be no **(9)** __________ from crashing waves for the crew until the boat **(10)** __________ the Irish capital, Dublin, which the Vikings helped to **(11)** __________ almost 12 centuries ago. The original vessel was built there exactly 965 years ago, after one of the city's Viking kings, Ivar Haraldsson, **(12)** __________ to power in a military coup.

0	**A** inquiry	**B** search	**C** investigation	**D** study
1	**A** set	**B** raised	**C** made	**D** started
2	**A** navigation	**B** journey	**C** passage	**D** channel
3	**A** reconstruction	**B** rebuilding	**C** renovation	**D** restoration
4	**A** erected	**B** uplifted	**C** expelled	**D** excavated
5	**A** fake	**B** model	**C** replica	**D** imitation
6	**A** undergone	**B** undertaken	**C** underdone	**D** underrated
7	**A** use	**B** life	**C** practice	**D** method
8	**A** transforms	**B** settles	**C** modifies	**D** adapts
9	**A** shield	**B** shelter	**C** prevention	**D** barrier
10	**A** reaches	**B** arrives	**C** sails	**D** achieves
11	**A** originate	**B** found	**C** situate	**D** launch
12	**A** took	**B** got	**C** came	**D** went

Part 2

For questions **13–27**, read the text below and think of the word which best fits each gap. Use only **one** word in each gap. There is an example at the beginning **(0)**.

Robots to the rescue?

Japanese researchers are racing **(0)** _*against*_ time to design and build robots smart **(13)** __________ to serve the needs of its senior citizens in a country in **(14)** __________ 40% of people will be over 65 by 2055. The researchers say new types of robots will one day play a major role because **(15)** __________ simply won't be a sufficient number of young people available to do the kind of jobs that **(16)** __________ elderly can no longer do for themselves. Isao Shimoyama, dean of the University of Tokyo's Graduate School of Information Science and Technology, **(17)** __________ among a group of researchers who are working to develop robotic and information technology that will lead **(18)** __________ a new generation of robots. He hopes that prototypes of new robots capable **(19)** __________ performing a range of mundane tasks **(20)** __________ picking up clothes and putting them in the washing machine will be unveiled sometime **(21)** __________ the near future. Such machines do not need to be humanoid, **(22)** __________ robots that resemble people have some advantages, said Shimoyama. For instance, they are likely to have an easier time climbing up stairs inside homes **(23)** __________ a robot that moves on wheels. However, Shimoyama expects **(24)** __________ will be a few more years **(25)** __________ the first machines are ready to make **(26)** __________ way into people's homes. "They may look smart, but **(27)** __________ to humans, they are still quite stupid," Shimoyama said. "I don't think robots will ever be as smart."

Part 3

For questions **28–37**, read the text below. Use the word given in capitals at the end of some of the lines to form a word that fits in the gap in the same line. There is an example at the beginning **(0)**.

JOB ADVERTISEMENT

Simpson Electronics Ltd

This dynamic company is seeking a Sales Director to sell its new	
range of engineering **(0)** _*products*_ in South America. The	**PRODUCE**
successful **(28)** __________ will be fluent in Spanish and competent in	**APPLY**
Portuguese, and will **(29)** __________ have recent experience of this	**PREFER**
(30) __________ competitive market. We are looking for candidates	**INCREASE**
who are highly **(31)** __________ and who are able to demonstrate	**MOTIVE**
(32) __________ qualities. The Sales Director will mainly be	**LEADER**
responsible for putting strategies in place for the **(33)** __________	**DEVELOP**
of new business, for setting **(34)** __________ sales targets, and for the	**ACHIEVE**
(35) __________ of good relationships with key clients.	**MAINTAIN**
To apply for this position, please send a covering letter	
(36) __________ by your CV, and details of at least two referees.	**COMPANY**
For **(37)** __________ details, please contact Carolyn Patten	**ADD**
on 07 523 4102.	

Part 4

For questions **38–42** think of **one** word only which can be used appropriately in all three sentences. Here is an example **(0)**.

0 The painting would look more *level* if you lifted it up a bit at the left.

The two horses are now *level* and the race is almost over!

Petrol prices have remained *level* for the last three months.

---

38 Desperate to find his missing dog, Geoff decided to __________ an advertisement in the local newspaper.

A restaurant meal should be served ten minutes after you __________ your order.

I felt my father __________ his hand on my shoulder as we waited for the news.

39 The stone columns were designed to __________ a heavy ceiling.

There is not enough evidence to __________ the claim that the drug lowers blood pressure.

Our survey shows that most people __________ the idea of flexible working hours.

40 The country grew __________ after the discovery of oil off its coastline.

The sky over the Pacific is a __________ blue, unlike the pale colour of European skies.

The country has a __________ cultural history which the people are proud of.

41 The deadlines are usually __________ in our kind of work.

I held on __________ to Jim's hand while we waited for help.

I tried the jeans on but they were too __________ around the waist.

42 I gave Marta a final __________ goodbye before she disappeared through the departure gate.

He was knocked down by a strong __________ and had to be rescued.

A __________ of crime and violence has struck the town in recent weeks.

Part 5

For questions **43–50**, complete the second sentence so that it has a similar meaning to the first sentence, using the word given. **Do not change the word given**. You must use between **three** and **six** words, including the word given. Here is an example **(0)**.

0 The firefighters could not control the flames because of the very strong wind.

SUCH

There *was such a strong wind* ____________ that the firefighters could not control the flames.

---

43 Few films have won the number of awards that this one did today.

FILM

Seldom ______________________________ many awards as this one did today.

44 They think that the drawing was done sometime in the 16th century.

HAVE

The drawing is ______________________________ sometime in the 16th century.

45 It was some time before I felt comfortable being the driver of a manual car again.

USED

It took me a ______________________________ a manual car again.

46 I'm sure you were shocked to hear that your boat had been stolen.

COME

It ______________________________ shock to hear your boat had been stolen.

47 We were unable to extinguish the fire sooner because we couldn't find the hose.

PUT

We ______________________________ sooner if we'd been able to find the hose.

48 It would be pointless to ask Tom for help with your essay.

USE

It ______________________________ Tom for help with your essay.

49 I wasn't planning to stay for long in Australia, but I'm still here.

INTENTION

I ______________________________ for long in Australia, but I'm still here.

50 Please could you not smoke inside the house?

PREFER

I ______________________________ didn't smoke inside the house.

PAPER 4 LISTENING

Part 1

You will hear three different extracts. For questions **1–6**, choose the answer (**A, B** or **C**) which fits best according to what you hear. There are two questions for each extract.

Extract One

You hear part of an interview with Anita Rutherford, a successful writer.

1 According to Anita, the most difficult aspect of writing a short story is
- **A** working out its structure.
- **B** creating its characters.
- **C** keeping the balance between conversation and description.

2 The writer wrote about immigration because
- **A** it had recently become a serious issue in her country.
- **B** her own experience as a migrant had been negative.
- **C** she had been inspired by the story of someone she met.

Extract Two

You hear two people talking about the involvement of young people in crime.

3 The man blames his criminal behaviour on the fact that
- **A** he had never been disciplined.
- **B** his older brother had been involved in crime.
- **C** he was not afraid of being caught.

4 The man decided to live in an honest way because
- **A** he was offered a reasonable job.
- **B** he did not want to disappoint his family.
- **C** he couldn't face returning to jail.

Extract Three

You hear part of an interview with Jeanette Macfie, a designer and owner of a fashion company.

5 Jeanette decided to make her company more environmentally-friendly after
- **A** seeing 'green' products on sale on holiday.
- **B** becoming frustrated with poorly made goods.
- **C** realizing that the changes could be quite profitable.

6 After making her decision, the first thing that Jeanette did was to
- **A** get all her fabrics from Australia.
- **B** use only recycled products in the office.
- **C** switch to buying material that was environmentally-friendly.

Part 2

You will hear someone who works in an ecological theme park called The Eden Project, giving a talk to a group of visitors.

For questions **7–14** complete the notes.

EDEN PROJECT

The Eden Project is situated in a pit where material for manufacturing [**7**] was once extracted.

The speaker describes the constructions in the Eden Project as the biggest [**8**] in the world.

The roofs of the domes consist of [**9**], which are made from a transparent material.

In the larger dome you walk past [**10**], falling among big rocks.

In the smaller dome there are plants that grow in regions of the Mediterranean, [**11**] and California.

There is a walkway with a café and a [**12**] between the two domes.

It is possible to walk, or go by [**13**] from the visitor centre to the main entrance.

Visitors can see works of art made from such unusual materials as [**14**] and rubbish.

Part 3

You will hear a sports historian, Tim Campbell, being interviewed about an athlete called Roger Bannister, who broke a record by running a mile (1.6 kilometres) in four minutes.

For questions **15–20**, choose the answer (**A**, **B**, **C** or **D**) which fits best according to what you hear.

---

15 In 1954 Bannister thought he could run the four-minute mile because

A it was a favourable time for athletic achievement.
B he was mature enough to take on a major challenge.
C he would not have another opportunity for several years.
D there were no other athletes capable of making the attempt.

16 What does Tim Campbell say about Bannister's preparations for attempting the record?

A He insisted on doing most of his training alone.
B He employed a coach to give him intensive training.
C He changed his training schedule from month to month.
D He used a new training technique to improve his performance.

17 What happened when Bannister and his fellow runner went on holiday?

A They injured themselves by taking part in a dangerous sport.
B They left early because they thought they were wasting time.
C They benefited from having plenty of rest and good food.
D They took part in an activity that had unexpectedly good results.

18 After he decided on the date to try for the record, Bannister

A began to make detailed plans for the race.
B started to train at the venue of the race.
C experienced problems with nervousness.
D lost confidence in his ability to achieve his goal.

19 What problems did Bannister face because of the weather?

A The extreme conditions could cause the race to be cancelled.
B The strength of the wind could affect his performance.
C The surface of the track was in bad condition because of rain.
D The other runners were unwilling to race in such bad conditions.

20 What does Tim Campbell say about the race?

A Bannister was not prepared to consider the possibility of failure.
B The record was achieved in spite of a mistake in the race plan.
C Bannister had decided to try for the record a long time previously.
D There was not a large crowd of spectators because of the weather.

Part 4

You will hear five short extracts in which people are talking about speaking in public.

TASK ONE

For questions **21–25**, choose from the list **A–H** the situation each speaker is describing.

A I was asked to speak about an experience I had had.

B I had to speak to a critical audience.

C I had never spoken on such a formal occasion before.

D I had to make a speech about somebody I did not like.

E I was asked to do a series of talks on television.

F I gave a talk at short notice.

G I had to give a speech when I had a health problem.

H I gave a talk to people in the same profession as me.

Speaker 1 [ ] **21**

Speaker 2 [ ] **22**

Speaker 3 [ ] **23**

Speaker 4 [ ] **24**

Speaker 5 [ ] **25**

TASK TWO

For questions **26–30**, choose from the list **A–H** each speaker's feeling about the occasion when he or she spoke in public.

A It was sometimes a challenge to convince the audience.

B I felt doubtful that my audience would be interested.

C I was nervous because I thought I would make a mistake.

D I felt confident because I was well prepared.

E I was embarrassed by my performance.

F I felt bored because I didn't have anything new to say.

G I was angry that I had been put in this position.

H I felt calm because I was given a lot of support.

Speaker 1 [ ] **26**

Speaker 2 [ ] **27**

Speaker 3 [ ] **28**

Speaker 4 [ ] **29**

Speaker 5 [ ] **30**

PAPER 5 SPEAKING (approximately 15 minutes)

PART 1

This section lasts about three minutes. The Examiner asks the candidates questions about themselves, in turn. Possible questions include:

Where are you from?
What do you do?
What is it like living in your town?
How long have you been studying English?

Then the examiner asks one or more questions from any of the following categories. Possible categories include:

Leisure Time
What do you enjoy doing in your free time?
What activities or sports would you like to try?
How important is television in your life?
What kind of thing do you like reading?

Learning
What do you enjoy most about learning English?
If you could learn something new, what would it be?
What is the most positive learning experience you have had?
What advice would you give to someone who wanted to learn your language?

Relationships
What is your earliest memory of a childhood friend?
How do you stay in touch with family and friends?
How important is it to you to have a busy social life?
What makes you choose another person as a friend?

Future Plans
What are your plans for the next twelve months?
In what way might you use English in the future?
If you had the opportunity, what changes would you make to your life in the next couple of years?
Where do you think you'll be living in ten years' time?

Culture
What would you recommend people visit or do in your country?
To what extent have TV and the Internet influenced your culture?
In what ways is your country unique?
If you could live abroad for a year, where would you go?

PART 2

1

The first set of pictures show people in aircraft of different kinds.

Candidate A Compare **two** of these pictures and say how important flying is in the modern world, and how the people in the pictures might be feeling.

(You have approximately one minute to do this.)

Candidate B Can you say which photograph best illustrates the importance of flying today?

(You have approximately 30 seconds to do this.)

2

The second set of pictures show people saying goodbye to each other.

Candidate B Compare **two** of these pictures and say how the people might have spent their time together and how they might be feeling.

(You have approximately one minute to do this.)

Candidate A In which picture do you think people have the closest relationship?

(You have approximately 30 seconds to do this.)

Part 2

- How important is flying in the modern world?
- How might the people be feeling?

1

Part 2

- How might the people have spent their time together?
- How might they be feeling?

2

PART 3

Here are some suggested activities for a programme of adult education in your area.

First talk to each other about how useful these activities might be as part of an adult education programme. Then decide which two activities you would recommend for inclusion in the programme.

You have about three minutes for this.

- How useful might these activities be as part of an adult education programme?
- Which two activities would you recommend for inclusion in the programme?

PART 4

The examiner asks the candidates to discuss some questions which relate to the theme in Part 3.

This section lasts about four minutes.

Are there any other subjects you would recommend for inclusion in an adult education programme? (Why?)

Is it important for people to continue their education throughout their life? (Why?)

Is adult education an important investment for local communities? (Why?)

What can be done to attract adults to participate in an education programme?

Do you think that people change the way they learn as they get older? (Why?)

Progress test 1

Reading CAE Paper 1

Part 3: Multiple choice

1 C 2 A 3 C 4 B 5 A 6 A 7 D

Use of English CAE Paper 3

Part 1: Multiple-choice cloze

1 D 2 C 3 B 4 D 5 C 6 D
7 B 8 A 9 D 10 A 11 C 12 A

Part 2: Open cloze

1 where
2 for
3 at
4 be
5 the
6 have
7 up
8 who
9 was
10 into
11 nobody/no one
12 there
13 of
14 so
15 had/used

Part 5: Key word transformations

1 is hardly likely/going to turn
2 improve/increase your chances of getting *or* have more chances of getting
3 as if the fridge has broken
4 since I have beaten my brother
5 would sooner David had
6 I had kept/remained/stayed quiet about
7 might/may/could have caught/been set (on)
8 it hadn't/had not been for

Vocabulary

1 lifestyle
2 method
3 motivation
4 success
5 aroma
6 behaviour
7 vary
8 smell
9 take up
10 adjust
11 gather
12 end
13 misleading
14 conceivably
15 lifelong
16 significantly
17 cost-effective
18 welcome

Listening CAE Paper 4

Part 2: Sentence completion

1 accountant
2 best friend
3 coffee-shop/café/cafeteria
4 wine
5 short stories
6 swimming
7 publisher
8 Spain

Listening script Part 2 Sentence completion

It was in early summer of 1998 that a massive upheaval began in my life. Over a few months there was to be a change in my house, country and career. At the time I lived in London and worked as an accountant in the City. My wife was an architect, and our son was studying architecture at university. A respectable, comfortably-off family.

As a child, I'd wanted to earn my living as a writer, but my father said, 'It's too risky. Get a proper career'. My teachers weren't encouraging either, so I gave up my dream. But I carried on writing as a hobby, and showed the things I wrote to my best friend. He said he liked them, but I'd no idea if they were really any good.

Then, one Saturday thirty years later, fate stepped in. I'd spent the morning in our local library, doing research for something I was writing, and I went into a coffee-shop next door for a break. There, on the table where I was sitting, was an advertisement for a writing course in France. I didn't hesitate. I got straight on to the Internet and booked a place.

Two weeks later I was in France. The location of the course was a complex of buildings, set in a garden. For centuries it had been a place where wine was produced, and we had our lectures and workshops in the great open-sided construction where the grapes had been pressed.

Our tutors were two young writers, both successful and established novelists. On the first day we each had to say what we hoped to get out of the course. My ambition was to write children's books and short stories. Other people wanted to work on, poetry, novels and plays. We were all passionate about writing, and desperate to get into print.

The main work was done in the morning. By afternoon the temperature had soared, and local people retired to their cool houses to sleep. The shops were closed, and walking was out of the question. There was a pool in the garden, so we spent our time swimming and reading under the trees. Paradise!

At the end of the course the tutors said encouraging things about my work, and I went home with my mind and imagination buzzing. I wrote something in a month, and sent it off to an agent. Rejection. I was devastated. But then one of the tutors invited me to a party and introduced me to her publisher. This man liked my work, and I was on my way.

My wife and I have left London and live near the Mediterranean. I'd have liked to find a house near the place in France where I learnt my writer's craft, but in the end we settled in a village in southern Spain, opposite the coast of Morocco. And I write from morning to night.

Progress test 2

Reading CAE Paper 1

Part 4: Multiple matching

1 A	**5** C	**9** B	**13** B
2 D	**6** B	**10** D	**14** D
3 C	**7** A	**11** C	**15** A
4 D	**8** B	**12** B	

Use of English CAE Paper 3

Part 3: Word formation

1 regularity
2 upbringing
3 tendency
4 misbehave
5 refusal
6 unpleasant
7 Admittedly
8 justified/justifiable
9 affectionate
10 willingness

Part 4: Gapped sentences

1 time **2** front **3** look **4** fast **5** light

Vocabulary

1 C	**5** C	**9** A	**13** A
2 B	**6** D	**10** C	**14** D
3 A	**7** C	**11** A	**15** B
4 B	**8** B	**12** C	

Listening CAE Paper 4

Part 4: Multiple matching

1 D	**2** H	**3** A	**4** B	**5** E
6 B	**7** F	**8** H	**9** E	**10** C

Listening script Part 4 Multiple matching

Speaker 1

I started diving as a hobby when I was a student, and decided I wanted to do it professionally, so I trained up as a maintenance diver on oil rigs. Very dangerous. Very very good money. We're on call for break-downs, and get rushed out to the rigs any time, night or day. We dive in pairs, and there's a team on the surface supporting us. My diving buddy is vitally important to me, not just to work with me and watch out for me, but as a companion in a pretty unfriendly environment. And we both depend on the team on the surface – and have complete faith in them.

Speaker 2

You'd expect an artist to need solitude to concentrate on their work, but I can't work alone. I'm a painter and sculptor and I employ 20 people in my studio. Each person has a specific skill, whether it's computer design, metal welding, working with colours ... Everybody is part of the manufacturing effort, and I'm the co-ordinator. We all get inspiration from each other. We also fight a lot, but that's part of it, and feeds the creative process. I'm not a practical person at home – I'm hopeless with personal finances and getting things done around the house, but at work I actually like organizing people and making sure we're all working as a team.

Speaker 3

I'm not much good at hard physical exercise, but I do like walking. I go out most weekends with a friend, hiking in the mountains. We cover miles without realizing it, talking about everything under the sun. This friend was away once, so I joined up with a hiking club – I didn't fancy walking on my own in the mountains. It wasn't a good experience. Nobody talked to anyone else, and even though we were in beautiful countryside, we hardly got a chance to stop and enjoy the views. We had a leader who set a punishing pace. When I got back in the evening, I was exhausted and in a very bad temper.

Speaker 4

I'm a home-worker. I've got a young family, so I need to be at home when the children get in from school. I sit at the computer from 9 to 3.30, and the only contact with the outside world is by telephone. In fact, I don't mind really. I quite like the peace and quiet, and it's employment, after all. Anyway, life hots up at the weekend. My husband and I belong to a dance group, and we go round local towns giving exhibitions of salsa and samba. It keeps us fit and it's good fun. We joined the group 15 years ago, and we've never looked back.

Speaker 5

I have to admit, my firm does charge a lot for the work it does, and at the end our clients say, 'but you've only told us something we already knew.' I think they expected us to train them into new ways of working, or provide magical solutions to their problems. That's not our job. We're a consultancy team, and we demonstrate to companies what they are, and what they're capable of. In a way, we help them organize their thinking so they can get out of their rut and move forward. We're bringing them objectivity and a fresh approach. Whether it's worth what they pay us, that's another matter.

Progress test 3

Reading CAE Paper 1

Part 2: Gapped text

1 G 2 C 3 E 4 A 5 F 6 B

Use of English Paper 3

Part 1: Multiple-choice cloze

1 C	4 A	7 B	10 A
2 D	5 A	8 D	11 B
3 B	6 C	9 C	12 C

Part 4: Gapped sentences

1 ease 2 most 3 keep 4 past 5 cross

Part 5 Key word transformations

1 I did was (to) set
2 to being criticized in public
3 me that if the boss lost
4 is bound to pay/give
5 (that) I should have
6 from going/pressing ahead with
7 ate/were served was second to
8 to give Tim a lift

Vocabulary

1

1 E	4 I	7 B
2 G	5 C	8 F
3 D	6 A	9 H

2

1 D	4 C	7 B
2 F	5 E	8 I
3 H	6 A	9 G

Listening CAE Paper 4

Part 1: Multiple choice

1 B 2 A 3 C 4 A 5 C 6 B

Listening script Part 1

Extract One

You will hear two people on a radio programme talking about a type of diet.

Woman: What was it that made you try this particular diet in the first place?

Man: Desperation! When I turned 40, I suddenly put on quite a bit of weight. I took up running and I became fitter – but the weight just wouldn't go. Then I happened to come across an article on the Internet – about people who follow the kind of diet that Stone Age man would have eaten. The idea is, you see, that early man evolved to eat only the kind of food he could hunt or gather – and humans haven't genetically changed since then. So the foods we're supposed to eat are lean meat, fish, vegetables and nuts. You have to avoid grains, beans and dairy products. I thought I would try it out for a month.

Woman: And when the month was up – what were the results?

Man: I certainly had more energy, and I dropped four inches around my waist. I actually lost all desire for sugary foods. I missed pasta – and I still do occasionally, but I was utterly convinced that the diet worked and I was determined to keep going with it. It's been four years now.

Extract Two

You will hear part of an interview with an engineer called Angus Robson.

I: Angus, I believe the original trebuchets were designed by the ancient Chinese to throw rocks at their enemies. Why build one now?

Angus: Well, in our case, our machine threw a block of steel, not rocks. In the Guinness Book of Records it states that Angus Robson and Rocktec – that's the company that helped build it – threw a block of steel – of three and a half tons – 15 metres. As far as I know no one's thrown anything heavier any further. The original trebuchets were simple but dangerous – and I wanted to demonstrate how a few modifications could affect the physics – to show how my trebuchet would work even better. And in the end – it all went according to plan.

I: Would you say it takes a special kind of mind to invent this sort of thing?

Angus: Well – I've always been curious about things and that was to do with my upbringing. We never had a TV and we were expected to entertain ourselves. That means you have to know how to make something out of nothing – like bits of wood in the shed and stuff you find in rubbish skips. You learn to believe you can create whatever you want. I guess that's why I was so interested in physics at school – even though I didn't like the teacher very much – and why I went on to become an engineer. I think that kids today don't have the same opportunity – I mean to be resourceful and think things out for themselves. Their parents just let them sit in front of the TV and they're quite happy to listen to other people's ideas rather than come up with their own.

Extract Three

You will hear part of an interview with Andrea Harris, a campaigner for green issues.

I: Andrea, most people are already aware that air travel causes environmental damage. What do you hope to achieve with this campaign?

Andrea: Well, we'd like to increase that awareness. For example, the next time you book a flight, go to the website climatecare.org. Enter your departure point and your destination into their calculator, and it'll show you how many tons of carbon dioxide that flight will emit, per person. I think most people would actually be shocked at the amount. But look, we're not attacking the tourist industry. There are local communities all round the world that depend on tourism and therefore flights. It's doubtful that planes will ever be truly fuel-efficient, so we're asking travellers to at least think about what they could do for the environment in return.

I: Air travel isn't the major contributor to the world's carbon dioxide, though, is it?

Andrea: No – which is why some people feel it's not worth them giving up flying. They ask 'why should I feel bad'? And when you consider that power stations account for 24% of carbon dioxide, and deforestation for another 18%, the 2% that air travel contributes is sigificantly less, I admit. Still we all have a responsibility to do whatever we can.

Progress test 4

Reading CAE Paper 1

Part 1: Multiple choice

1 A **2** C **3** B **4** D **5** D **6** B

Use of English CAE Paper 3

Part 2: Open cloze

1 what
2 the
3 from
4 a
5 that/which
6 for
7 of
8 as
9 in
10 all
11 how
12 was
13 without
14 had
15 Despite

Part 3: Word formation

1 enables
2 downside
3 presumably
4 admiration
5 substantial
6 readily
7 unbearable
8 outburst(s)
9 strengthen
10 alienates

Vocabulary

1 tide
2 upbringing
3 charges
4 setback
5 suggestions
6 nightmare
7 grant
8 stretch
9 slam
10 write
11 catch
12 make
13 solidly
14 deafening
15 in-depth
16 strangely
17 constant
18 widely

Listening CAE Paper 4

Part 2: Sentence completion

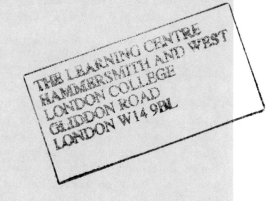

1 short story
2 crime novels/books
3 silver fox
4 research
5 eighteen/18
6 (South-East) Asia
7 style
8 experts

Listening script Part 2 Sentence completion

If you want to be a writer, there's only one way to start – just get on and do it. I used to be a teacher, but I'd always wanted to be a published writer, so I sent in a collection of poems to a magazine. It wasn't accepted, but the same magazine asked me to write a short story for them, and that was published. I wrote a few more that were well received, then decided I'd like to try something more ambitious.

I didn't have the confidence to tackle such a project without help, and I joined a writing class, run by a successful author. He taught us how to construct plots and create characters, which was very useful. He mainly wrote crime novels, and although I'm not really keen on that sort of thing, I adore travel books, so I thought I'd set a novel somewhere overseas.

Then I heard about an award called the New Writers' Trophy, which was a competition for the first 15,000 words of a novel, and the prize was a little silver fox. I really wanted it, so I wrote the beginning of a novel called 'Going Away', and won the prize.

I finished 'Going Away', and immediately started on the next novel – also about travel. People say, 'Clever you, choosing subjects that involve travelling. It must be like going on holiday.' But it isn't, of course. You have to carry out a tremendous amount of research – and that can be hard work – very time-consuming. And when I'm abroad, it always takes longer than at home because of the language and culture differences.

I wrote my first novel in 15 months – it all came tumbling out, because it took place on an island I knew well. The next one still only took just under eighteen months, because I set the story in another favourite place. After that I was on unfamiliar territory, but I felt free to explore places and ideas that were new to me. One book, called 'The Power of Light', was set in South-East Asia, and took three years to write. I spent many hours reading in libraries, and took two trips out there as well.

Anyway, here are my top tips for new authors. First, when you send in your manuscript to publishers, include an interesting letter with it. It should be serious but not pushy, but with a different sort of style, which will make you stand out. Publishers are always looking for writers that have something out of the ordinary about the way they write. If you get stuck, don't be shy to ask for help from experts, but be professional about it. Enclose details about yourself and what you're doing, together with an idea of what you want.

Good luck! And remember, what you'll need is patience and – especially – perseverance!

Progress test 5

Reading CAE Paper 1

Part 3: Multiple choice

1 B 2 A 3 C 4 D 5 D 6 A 7 C

Use of English CAE Paper 3

Part 3: Word formation

1 tasteless
2 healthily
3 exception
4 diners
5 appearance
6 mouthfuls
7 deceptive
8 promising
9 distrusted/mistrusted
10 overrated

Part 4: Gapped sentences

1 pick 2 fall 3 see 4 hard 5 work

Vocabulary

1 C	4 D	7 C	10 B	13 D
2 A	5 D	8 D	11 A	14 C
3 B	6 A	9 B	12 C	15 B

Listening CAE Paper 4

Part 3: Multiple choice

1 D 2 C 3 D 4 B 5 A 6 A

Listening script Part 3 Multiple choice

Presenter: My guest today is Carrie Beale, the producer of the popular TV crime series, 'Nice Work'. Carrie, this is about fraud and deception – crime that involves skill and intelligence and good planning. You've created a gang of criminals that are attractive and civilized, and don't go in for violence at all. Why did you decide on this formula?

Carrie: I thought it was time to get away from the usual stuff. There's a lot of violence on TV now, and programme makers are having to dream up ever more extreme ways to ring the changes on murder and bloodshed. It becomes a downward spiral, and eventually, to me, just boring and ridiculous. Actually, my formula isn't new, there've been plenty of films about brilliant frauds. I've just tried to give a modern look to what's always been a very popular subject for drama.

Presenter: Yes, but however brilliant, the criminals have always ended up in jail. So far your gang has got away with it.

Carrie: There's another series in the pipeline, and who knows what'll happen at the end of that! I know, there's a bit of a moral dilemma here. You can't help liking the criminals, and you have to admire their creativity. Also, their targets are not the innocent public, but other greedy, dishonest people. The victims are always extremely rich, and have come by their wealth through exploitation or tax evasion or cheating of some sort. Does that make the fraud acceptable? Of course it doesn't, but it makes a good story.

Presenter: I have to admit, I adore the series. And what I love is the way the deceptions are set up. There's a lot of technology involved – and a huge amount of hard work, and planning.

Carrie: Yes, first of all the gang has to find their target and persuade him or her that there's a lot of money to be made by investing in some project. When the target is hooked, the gang creates a completely false environment to play out the fraud – a virtual reality with Hollywood-type sets. Actors are employed and briefed, and each person trained in detail. The victim is drawn into this, and very quickly relieved of his money. The scenario is so convincing and the victim so focused on the million or so dollars he thinks he's going to make on his investment, that he doesn't ask questions.

Presenter: And before he knows it, the Hollywood sets and his investment have vanished into thin air. There's a lot of psychology involved, isn't there?

Carrie: Yes, especially the psychology of greed. This is the department of the gang boss, Camilla. She does research on the target, finds out his weaknesses, and plans round those. Perhaps he's desperate to join a particularly exclusive golf club with a long waiting list. Camilla persuades him she knows the people who have influence in the club, and creates a scenario where he can meet them. He so badly wants this to be true, that he allows himself to be taken in. And he's nicely softened up for the real business of taking his money off him.

Presenter: The gang plays on his vanity and his need to be accepted in the smart world. It's cruel, really.

Carrie: Yes, however much we enjoy their skill and inventiveness, and laugh at the victim for his stupidity, when it comes down to it, it's an ugly business. The people the gang steals from are nasty pieces of work, but they're quite pathetic in a way, and they don't only lose their money, they lose their dignity. Another irony is that the gang never seems to make a profit, and they don't have a particularly luxurious lifestyle. Their expenses are huge – hiring office suites, golf courses, technical equipment and so on costs a fortune. They have to pull off one crime in order to fund the next one. Perhaps they do it for the excitement and the fun rather than the money.

Presenter: And the other thing that's so clever about the series is that you manage to fool the audience as well.

Carrie: Television audiences are very sophisticated. We wouldn't keep them for long if they found the storyline predictable, so we try to keep them guessing. We don't show them all the preparations that the gang make, but tease them with glimpses of someone setting up a complicated communications system, renting a glamorous venue, or rehearsing a group of actors. Then finally, like the victim, the audience is ushered into this incredible scene where the crime is to take place, and all sorts of little tricks are played, and nobody knows whether everything's going to work out or not, right up to the last minute.

Presenter: Well, I hope the gang manage to stay out of jail long enough to make a few more series. Thank you Carrie.

Final test: Papers 1–4

Paper 1 Reading

Part 1

1 A 2 D 3 C 4 A 5 C 6 B

Part 2

7 C 8 D 9 G 10 A 11 E 12 F

Part 3

13 C 14 B 15 D 16 B 17 A 18 A 19 C

Part 4

20 A 23 B 26 D 29 D 32 B
21 B 24 A 27 B 30 D 33 C
22 D 25 C 28 C 31 A 34 A

Paper 3 Use of English

Part 1

1 A 4 D 7 C 10 A
2 B 5 C 8 D 11 B
3 A 6 B 9 B 12 C

Part 2

13 enough 18 to 23 than
14 which 19 of 24 it
15 there 20 like 25 before/until
16 the 21 in 26 their
17 is 22 though/although/but 27 compared/actually

Part 3

28 applicant 32 leadership 36 accompanied
29 preferably 33 development 37 additional
30 increasingly 34 achievable
31 motivated 35 maintenance

Part 4

38 place 39 support 40 rich 41 tight 42 wave

Part 5

43 has a film won as
44 thought to have been done
45 while to get used to driving
46 must have come as a
47 could/would have put the fire out/put out the fire
48 is/'s no use asking
49 had no intention of staying
50 would prefer it if you

Paper 4 Listening

Part 1

1 B **2** C **3** A **4** C **5** B **6** C

Listening script, Part 1

Extract 1

You will hear part of an interview with Anita Rutherford, a successful writer.

I: What do you find more difficult, – writing novels or short stories?

Anita: Well, writing a novel is very time-consuming. Just planning the structure can take forever – whereas with a short story – it could all be centred around a single scene. But short stories have their own challenges. There are few opportunities to convey a character convincingly. To present a whole person, you must very carefully select the words that they speak. And new writers sometimes make the mistake of describing physical appearance in great detail. A single gesture can say far more about a person.

I: Anita, your latest novel is about a young girl trying to fit into an alien culture. Was this based on your childhood?

Anita: Well, the girl in the book, Ofelia, – it's difficult for her to adjust and she encounters all sorts of prejudice. But it was relatively easy for me – there was no language barrier for a start. I was more inspired by a woman whose taxi I got into. We got talking and I found out that she had been a doctor before she emigrated. It got me thinking about the issues migrants face when they come to our country.

Extract Two

You will hear two people talking about the involvement of young people in crime.

Woman: So, what do you think caused you to take up a life of crime?

Man: I wasn't from a bad home, if that's what you mean. Mum and Dad always did their best for us when we were growing up. My mum thought I'd follow my older brother and get a factory job, but I couldn't be bothered. Me and my mates – we started off smashing up bus shelters and doing a bit of tagging, you know, graffiti. I actually liked the risk – you never knew if the police were already coming. Looking back, I think it all came from the fact that no one had ever said 'no' to me. I'd always done whatever I wanted.

Woman: And then you moved on to burglary and you soon ended up in prison.

Man: Yes, and I can tell you, when your cell door closes, you feel hopeless. And I was angry with myself. I swore I was never going to do anything that would put me back inside. It was a long five years – a complete waste of time – although I'm not saying I didn't deserve it. When you've got a criminal record, it's hard trying to get work but I just couldn't bear the idea of going back there. I'm lucky my family gave me a lot of support, and eventually I turned my life around.

Extract Three

You will hear part of an interview with Jeanette Macfie, a designer and owner of a fashion company in Australia.

I: Jeanette, isn't it quite unusual for someone in the fashion industry to be putting the environment first?

Jeanette: I think people believe it's impossible to change things because so much of our industry is harmful to the planet. And I did, too, until my last holiday. I'd bought this wooden deck chair for $10.99 – a ridiculously low price. And on the beach – the first time we used it, it just fell apart. And I noticed many other people had the same chair and were having the same problem. Those chairs were just going to add to the world's rubbish mountains. It made me realize we have to pay more for quality, durable products – and also consider what we could do to make the company more environmentally-friendly.

I: How easy has that been?

Jeanette: We couldn't have done it without hiring an environmental consultant. Now we only use recycled paper, energy-saving bulbs, and refillable ink cartridges. 90% of our cotton and wool now comes from within Australia – and we aim to make that 100% very soon. But actually, our first step was to stop buying cotton that had been sprayed with pesticide. We found suppliers of organic cotton instead. 25% of the world's pesticide is ...

Part 2

7 pottery
8 greenhouses
9 pillows
10 streams
11 South Africa
12 meeting place
13 (land)train
14 grass

Listening script, Part 2

Welcome to Eden. It's hard to believe that not so long ago, this beautiful place was derelict and lifeless. It had been a clay pit, supplying raw material for making pottery. For centuries it exported clay to countries all over the world. Then, when it was no longer economical, it was abandoned.

It was chosen to be the location of the Eden Project in the 1990s, and in just two years our team transformed what had been a barren moonscape into a luxuriant park. We transported 83,000 tonnes of soil to the site; then we constructed what turned out to be the world's largest greenhouses, to create micro-climates for plants from the tropics to the deserts.

It was a massive undertaking. When the plants began to arrive like moving forests, we wondered if we could make such an ambitious dream into reality. We had to create a protective environment for an enormous quantity of plants over a huge area, and as you'll see, we found an unconventional solution. Each building is covered with a dome made up of pillows, which are manufactured from a see-through material and fixed onto a network of hexagonal steel frames.

There are two domes, and there's an educational area. The tropical plants are in the bigger dome, and I advise you to start your visit there. You climb through groves of bamboo and giant palms, and see streams that tumble downwards among huge fern-covered rocks. The humidity in this dome can be exhausting and the paths are quite steep, so there's a cool rest room at the top, and seats at regular intervals on the way up.

The second dome isn't so big, and here you can experience the agriculture of the Mediterranean and the warm temperate zones of South Africa and California. This is poor, thin soil, a place for thorny desert vegetation: also olives and vines and cork trees, which look as if they've been there for centuries. Outside the temperate dome there's the educational area, where you can see tea, coffee and cocoa plants from India and South America.

There are plenty of kiosks selling snacks. And in the covered corridor linking the two domes there's a cafe, with a meeting place nearby – useful to know about if you get separated from your party. If you want to buy souvenirs, there's a shop in the visitor centre next to the car park.

It's quite a long way from the visitor centre to the main entrance, and cars or bicycles aren't allowed in the grounds. If you don't feel like going on foot, there's a land-train that'll take you down the hill. The walk to the main entrance takes ten minutes, and on your way down you can enjoy sculptures – not made of stone or wood, but created from recycled rubbish, grass and other unusual materials.

So, once again welcome. And enjoy your day.

Part 3

15 A **16** D **17** D **18** C **19** B **20** C

Listening script, Part 3

Presenter: In 1954 Roger Bannister, an amateur athlete, ran one mile in a record-breaking four minutes. Tim Campbell, a sports historian, is here in the studio to talk about this epic achievement. Tim, Bannister was 25 when he made his attempt on the 4-minute mile, which is not young for an amateur athlete.

Tim Campbell: That's right, but he expected the summer of 1954 to be his last competitive season, so he probably wasn't going to get another chance to go for the record. Also, it was going to be a big year for athletics with two major international events, and this was a perfect environment for creating new records. Everyone wanted the 4-minute barrier to be smashed, and Bannister felt he was the one to do it.

Presenter: But he knew he couldn't do it alone – he'd need a lot of help. How did he prepare for the attempt?

Tim Campbell: Up to that point he'd done all his training alone, and raced alone. I mean, normally in a big competition a runner would race as part of a team. But Bannister preferred to do everything on his own. Then, in the winter of 1953, that all changed – perhaps he'd mellowed a bit. Anyway, he spent every lunchtime training with a group of runners on a track near his work, and two other athletes, who were going to support him in his attempt on the record, joined him at weekends for longer training sessions. In December 1953 the three runners developed a new intensive course and over the next three months managed to increase their speed. By April, a month before the first race, they were making good progress, but still not reaching their target. However hard they tried they just weren't quite fast enough. They were stuck, and the training wasn't helping any more.

Presenter: So what did they do? Did they give themselves a holiday?

Tim Campbell: Yes, but they did something rather stupid, on the face of it. Bannister and one of the other runners went to Scotland for a few days' climbing. This probably did them more harm than good physically because they did hard climbs, using the wrong muscles. Then there was an accident, one of them fell, and though neither of them was hurt, they suddenly realized what risks they were taking, and thought they'd better go back. They hadn't slept much, and they'd had pretty irregular meals, but the amazing thing is, when they started training again, their times were really good, better than they could have hoped. I suppose all they needed was a change and a bit of excitement.

Presenter: After that, did they decide when to try for the 4-minute mile?

Tim Campbell: Yes, there was a major event taking place in Oxford, on the evening of 6 May. It was a race between two top amateur athletics teams, and the first opportunity of the year to go for the record. In April Bannister decided that that was when he'd make the attempt. Poor Bannister, he got into an awful state. I've read his memoirs and he says that every night in the week before the race, when he was trying to get to sleep, he saw himself at the starting line, and his whole body would start trembling. Then he'd start going over the race in his head. I can imagine what it must have been like.

Presenter: But there were other problems, weren't there?

Tim Campbell: Oh yes. The race was an outdoor event, and the weather was terrible – strong winds, rain. Bannister knew that if the wind didn't drop, the chances of success were practically nil. He says in his memoirs that he travelled to Oxford early on the day of the race, and when he went to look at the track, the wind was almost gale force, bad enough to slow him by a second a lap. It must have seemed absolutely hopeless, but he didn't give up. When his two fellow runners arrived in the afternoon, the wind didn't seem quite so bad, but then there was a shower of rain. Can you imagine how nerve-wracking all that must have been?

Presenter: The race must have been nail-biting, and I suppose Bannister couldn't make the final decision whether to go for the record or not until the last minute.

Tim Campbell: It's my opinion that Bannister had made his mind up months before. He just didn't know how much he was going to have to do. It was certain there'd be a big crowd of spectators, whatever the weather, and that was important to him. He was prepared for failure, and he believed that failure was as exciting to watch as success, so long as the effort was absolutely genuine. But I cannot imagine the sort of mental agony an athlete like Bannister must go through before he makes an effort of that sort of magnitude. Miraculously, the wind died down just before the race began; Bannister gave the signal for his final decision, and the rest is history. The plan that the three runners had made for the race went like a dream, and Bannister crossed the finishing tape in three minutes 59 seconds.

Part 4

21 C	**26** D
22 H	**27** F
23 B	**28** A
24 F	**29** C
25 G	**30** H

Listening script, Part 4

Speaker 1

I've given speeches before, at farewell parties for my employees and so on, but they were quite relaxed affairs. This was different – my daughter's wedding. I wanted everything to be done properly and I put a lot of time into working out what I would say. So when it was my turn to stand up, I didn't feel nervous – I was sure I would do a good job. I listened to the other speakers – some were embarrassed at being the centre of attention, others were emotional. There were the usual funny stories about memories and rather personal experiences. But they all said lovely things about my daughter and it was an occasion to remember.

Speaker 2

Conferences have their good points – it's great meeting a lot of people in your field of business. I have a reputation for being a good speaker, and I know my subject inside out, so I was asked to give a presentation for my company at a conference last week. I was halfway through the talk, when I suddenly felt really fed up – I just lost interest in what I was saying. It was all old stuff, however well I put it across, and I wondered what I was doing there. I finished the presentation, everyone applauded, and I went away wondering how on earth I was going to get my enthusiasm back.

Speaker 3

I lecture on health and fitness – usually to sports clubs, but recently I was asked to talk to some schoolchildren. I'm very keen on what I do, so I was enthusiastic about this opportunity. I got together some great visuals, and videos of a brilliant series they'd done on television, and spent two days going round the classes at the school. The kids were very responsive and came up with some interesting ideas and opinions. If they didn't agree with me, they let me know, and I had to work hard to bring them round to my way of thinking. It was as much a learning exercise for me as for them.

Speaker 4

This email came through – 'Could I speak at a book festival the next day? The scheduled speaker was ill'. OK, I could do it, I was free. And I knew the subject – a South-American novelist – because I was doing research on him. But he was a difficult and challenging writer and it was tough expecting me to get a talk together in one day. Anyway, I agreed to do it and went into the lecture hall feeling very anxious in case I got something wrong. The audience knew my situation and sympathized, but I didn't want to embarrass myself by saying something stupid. In the end I enjoyed it and didn't do too badly.

Speaker 5

Politicians have to enjoy speaking in public. If you're nervous, you can't do a good job. My first experience of giving speeches was when I was training for politics, and I was helping an older politician during an election campaign. I didn't like the man at first, he seemed unfriendly. But then I had a surprise. Just before a speech at an important business event I got a sore throat - I could hardly speak, and I was desperate. My colleague came round with stuff for me to take, and told me how to cope, and helped me relax. I managed the speech OK, which I couldn't have done without his help.